Germans in America

THE AMERICAN WAYS SERIES

AmericanWays

General Editor: John David Smith
Charles H. Stone Distinguished Professor of American History
University of North Carolina at Charlotte

From the long arcs of America's history, to the short timeframes that convey larger stories, American Ways provides concise, accessible topical histories informed by the latest scholarship and written by scholars who are both leading experts in their fields and polished writers.

Books in the series provide general readers and students with compelling introductions to America's social, cultural, political, and economic history, underscoring questions of class, gender, racial, and sectional diversity and inclusivity. The titles suggest the multiple ways that the past informs the present and shapes the future in often unforeseen ways.

CURRENT TITLES IN THE SERIES

GERMANS
IN AMERICA

A Concise History

Walter D. Kamphoefner

ROWMAN & LITTLEFIELD
Lanham • Boulder • New York • London

Published by Rowman & Littlefield
An imprint of The Rowman & Littlefield Publishing Group, Inc.
4501 Forbes Boulevard, Suite 200, Lanham, Maryland 20706
www.rowman.com

6 Tinworth Street, London SE11 5AL, United Kingdom

British Library Cataloguing in Publication Information Available

Library of Congress Cataloging-in-Publication Data Available

978-1-4422-6497-7 (cloth)
978-1-4422-6498-4 (electronic)

∞™ The paper used in this publication meets the minimum requirements of
American National Standard for Information Sciences—Permanence of Paper for
Printed Library Materials, ANSI/NISO Z39.48-1992.

Contents

Acknowledgments

A NUMBER OF COLLEAGUES, FORMER STUDENTS, friends, and family members—categories that heavily overlap—read and critiqued portions of the manuscript. My thanks go out to Evan Haefeli, "Chip" Dawson, Robert Resch, Bill Collopy, Tim Anderson, Craig Borchardt, Joe Porter, Bob Frizzell, Stan Nadel, Alison Efford, Paul Fessler, Steve Ehlmann, my brother Paul Kamphoefner, my wife, Anja Schwalen, and our daughter, Sandra Schwalen. Any deficiencies that remain are my own.

Fred Luebke and Kathy Conzen are deservedly enjoying their retirements and could not be imposed upon to critique this manuscript, but I have profited enormously from their scholarship, their feedback over the years, and their friendship.

I had the pleasure of working with two longtime friends on editing projects: the late Lynn Gentzler on the memoir of Missouri immigrant Gert Goebel and Walter Buenger on the reminiscences of Texas German William A. Trenckmann, both important sources for this book.

I am doubly indebted to Bill Keel, editor of the *Yearbook of German American Studies*. Serving on his editorial board has exposed me to much new scholarship in the field, and my own publications in the journal fed directly into several chapters of this work.

While on a Fulbright lectureship at the University of Bremen in 1987–1988, I enjoyed the hospitality of Dirk Hoerder and the late Christiane Harzig, who deepened my knowledge of the radical and female sides of German America.

The foundations for this book were laid with a course I taught during a Fulbright lectureship at the University of Osnabrück in 1998–1999. I am grateful to Klaus Bade, the founding director of the Institute for Migration Research and Intercultural Studies (IMIS), which hosted me, and the entire IMIS staff, in particular Jochen Oltmer. John David Smith, the series editor for American Ways, gave me the impetus to again take up a project that had lain dormant, and has been consistently helpful and encouraging, as has Jon Sisk, senior executive editor at Rowman & Little-field. More recently, a faculty development leave from Texas A&M University in fall 2016 facilitated my writing.

Admittedly, more of my examples are taken from Missouri, where I spent most of the first thirty years of my life, and Texas, where I've spent the last three decades, than the size of their German populations would warrant. The same is true of the Westphalia-Osnabrück area on the German side. However, I was merely following the recommendation of Booker T. Washington, who advised his listeners, "cast down your bucket where you are." Most of the examples taken from my two home states and my ancestral roots in Germany are reflective of larger patterns, and where they are not, I have tried to indicate why they are exceptional.

I have relied heavily on immigrant letters to bring the German-American experience to life, and it is here that I have incurred the greatest intellectual debt. Since before 1980, I have cooperated with Wolfgang Helbich in collecting, editing, and publishing German immigrant letters. Supported by the Volkswagen Foundation, the National Endowment for Humanities, and the German Historical Institute, we have published two letter anthologies in both German and American editions (the latter both translated by Susan Carter Vogel), along with an edited conference volume. During the last two decades we were joined in our efforts by Ursula Lehmkuhl, who as a professor in Erfurt, Berlin, and now Trier, extended our collection efforts to the area of the former German Democratic Republic (GDR) that was inaccessible to our collection efforts in the 1980s. The letters collected by the three of us, now numbering some 11,000, constitute the Nordamerika-Auswandererbriefsammlung (NABS) at the Forschungs-bibliothek Gotha. The majority of the correspondence quoted in this volume are either published or unpublished letters from the holdings of NABS. More importantly, I have profited immensely from the intellectual give and take and the occasional spirited debate with Wolfgang, and from the hospitality of the Helbich-Lehmkuhl household while engaged in our editing and translating work across the years

This book is dedicated to our children, Sandy and Thomas, to whom we are proud to have passed down the language of their immigrant mother and their paternal ancestors.

Introduction

FREDERICKSBURG IS THE MOST GERMAN TOWN in Texas or anywhere else in the United States. It has preserved the heritage language longer than any community in America where it was not reinforced by separatist religion. As late as 1970, a majority of the county's inhabitants claimed German as their mother tongue, and it took until the year 2000 for Spanish to surpass German in the number of people in the town and surrounding county who spoke the language at home. So it seems appropriate that in the twilight of German ethnicity, Fredericksburg's district is still represented in the Texas legislature by a local hardware merchant with the unmistakably German name of Biedermann. It translates to "upright citizen," although it's often used ironically in the Old Country.

The irony is appropriate in this case. Upon closer examination, roots and tradition apparently count for little, even in contemporary Fredericksburg, so far as politics are concerned. Although of German descent, Biedermann was born in New York state, went to college in Florida, and moved to Fredericksburg from California. In contrast to the Catholic and Lutheran affiliations of most inhabitants since the town's founding, Biedermann is an elder in a conservative Evangelical Protestant congregation. But perhaps this merely illustrates that Fredericksburg's quaint German charm has attracted so many new people and so much outside money that its old German element has been diluted to the point that its quaint German charm is endangered. The town was dubbed "the new Aspen" in a 2020 article in *Texas Monthly* on "Small Towns, Big Money."

However, the most shocking break with Fredericksburg's history and proud tradition was Biedermann's announced intention to introduce a bill in the 2021 Texas legislature giving Texans a vote on seceding from the United States. The brave Fredericksburgers who defied secessionists and gave their lives for the Union in the Civil War must be turning over in their graves. When faced with a referendum on whether to leave the Union in 1861, Fredericksburg's county voted 96 percent in favor of staying. Some Germans from the community braved hundreds of miles of brush country to reach Union territory via Mexico and joined the First Texas Cavalry, USA. Others died trying, killed or executed when the Battle of the Nueces morphed into the Nueces Massacre. They are commemorated on the "Treue der Union" monument in nearby Comfort, Texas, unique in all the territory of the would-be Confederacy.

I encountered a similar irony in the late 1980s when I took some German friends to see the historic German Evangelical Ebenezer "Stone Church" in Franklin County, Missouri, just a few miles south of the river. We were looking around the outside when a member drove up in his pickup and cordially offered to unlock it and proudly showed us the inside of the sanctuary. Although of German heritage, our host looked like the prototypical rustic Ozarker, complete with a Confederate bumper sticker on his truck. I kept my thoughts to myself, but I wondered whether he knew how local Germans had been terrorized and plundered by Confederate raiders under General Sterling Price on his October 1864 raid. In fact, they harassed the pastor's wife and ransacked their house and broke open their trunks looking for money and silverware to steal. It boggles the mind how anyone from that congregation could sport a Rebel flag, although it is unclear just what it meant to this man and probably reflected mere historical ignorance.

These anecdotes are more jarring because of the way both of these communities long stood apart from the mainstream of their respective states, in a positive sense. Although Texas, like the rest of the South, was nearly a one-party Democratic state, German Texans and particularly Fredericksburg and surrounding Gillespie County were exceptions. The county voted Republican in every twentieth-century election but two, little plagued by the racial anxieties of fellow Texans. Ebenezer Stone Church is less than five miles from the border with Gasconade County, the most German county in Missouri and the only one in a slave state to give Lincoln a majority in 1860. It has gone Republican in every presidential election since. Rather than joining the Texas and Missouri mainstream, one could argue that the mainstream joined them by rejecting the Democratic Party of the civil rights era. Be that as it may, in the twenty-first century, both are now identified with the most conservative wing of the Republican Party.

These incidents illustrate one of the most important questions explored in this book: What was the relationship of German immigrants and ethnics to the American mainstream? How long did they preserve their separate identity and cultural distinctiveness? In what ways did they stand apart, positively or negatively, or just neutrally, in matters about which reasonable people can differ? How long, and under what circumstances, did later generations preserve the heritage language? I have attempted to offer perspectives on these questions, also from vantage points that are largely lacking in current historical literature. Having grown up in something of a rural ethnic enclave of a type that often gets overlooked, I present evidence of language persistence that contradicts the three-generation model of linguistic assimilation.

The bulk of this study is concentrated on the "long nineteenth century," from the end of the Napoleonic era through the First World War, when the German influx was heaviest and German was the largest heritage language in use at most times and places, occupying a position similar to Spanish today. But the opening chapter sketches the German experience in the colonial and early national period, and a concluding chapter traces the long twilight of ethnicity over the last hundred years.

The initial chapter documents a number of German "firsts": not only the first German group settlement in British North America but also the first white protest against slavery, the first complete Bible printed in any European language, and the first newspaper to announce the signing of the Declaration of Independence. It punctures the persistent myth that German came within one vote of becoming the official language of the United States but documents the small grain of truth behind this story. Above all, it shows why there was so little continuity between the German immigrant communities of the eighteenth century and those of the nineteenth.

Drawing on evidence gained from seven full years and numerous summer visits spent in Germany, I devote a chapter to examining regional cultures and economic structures in the Old Country, and the factors that promoted or retarded emigration. Having collected and read thousands of immigrant letters and collaborated on two book-length letter editions, I let actual immigrants speak on the subject wherever possible, documenting factors that motivated them and showing that chain migration was already the norm a century before family preference visas became part of American immigration law. This chain migration plays the main role in the next chapter, which examines German settlement patterns across the United States. It demonstrates the limited role played by emigration societies, whether secular or religious, and the importance of personal social ties in structuring migration paths and choice of destination. It illustrates why "transplanted," not "uprooted," is the appropriate metaphor for the immigrant experience.

The following chapter shows that only a small minority of Germans were religious refugees, but that does not mean they were indifferent to religion. Regardless of denomination, many believed that "language saves faith," and established parochial schools soon after founding church congregations. Although often divided by religion, Germans were also quite successful in placing their language in the public school curriculum, sometimes in two-way immersion programs where half of the school day was conducted in their language. Sometimes Germans cooperated with other ethnic groups in promoting heritage language options in school laws, but in other cases they arrogantly asserted this right for themselves alone.

German schools maintained a symbiotic relationship with the German language press, the subject of the next chapter. More than one journal asserted on its masthead: "This is not a German paper but an American newspaper published in the German language." Because of the size and prosperity of the ethnic group, the German press in the mid-1880s comprised almost 80 percent of the foreign-language press and still made up over half of the total on the eve of World War I. By 1920, only one-quarter of all the immigrant press was German, but a few papers have survived until today. There were also significant German cultural contributions in theater and particularly in music but surprisingly little literature of quality authored in the German language.

As the next chapter shows, Germans were not as heavily concentrated in American agriculture as their public image would have it, but over generations they tenaciously expanded their foothold so that by the end of the twentieth century, more than one-third of U. S. farmers were of German ancestry. For example, the farm where the author grew up is a Missouri Century Farm, in the Diederich-Kamphoefner family since 1889, with my nephew representing the fifth generation on the place.

But Germans were also prominent in industry, dominating some such as brewing, and producing a number of prominent entrepreneurs, some of whose firms have survived into the present century. But a closer examination reveals that while some successes were built on German technical training, often one sees a symbiosis of the two cultures, and other cases in which the German background played little or no role in an immigrant's success.

One area of considerable cultural clash between German Americans and the host society was the role of women. Though it is often stereotyped as *Kinder, Küche, Kirche* (children, cooking, and church), German women had a broader sphere in the world of work, particularly in farming families. In artisan households as well, they no doubt participated more than is indicated by the census. German women as well as men were generally skeptical of the women's suffrage movement because it was so entwined with the Prohibition movement. But even on the suffrage issue, not all German women fit the stereotype, particularly among Forty-Eighters and socialists.

At times I find it necessary to push back and debunk the claims of ethnic enthusiasts and "professional Germans," but I do not hesitate to debunk the debunkers where their corrective has gone too far. In the chapter on the Civil War, readers will learn of St. Louis German "Wide Awakes," whose decisive action helped keep Missouri in the Union, but also of German draft riots in Wisconsin. They will learn which German Union generals were competent and which were venerated by their compatriots despite their incompetence; which German regiments were among the "fightingest" and which ones deserved the epithet "Flying Dutchmen." As this chapter shows, patriotism, or even the National Anthem, can be expressed just as well in the German language, especially when pushing back against insurrectionists speaking English.

Germans took the lead in the emancipation movement in Missouri, and often found themselves in an alliance, or a marriage of convenience, with freedmen in the Republican Party of former slave states, including Texas. The question was whether these former Unionists would continue to "vote how they shot." Whenever Republicans attacked their language or their beer-drinking tendencies, they were sure to trigger a pushback. Carl Schurz stands out as the first and only German-born U. S. senator until the very end of the nineteenth century. At the congressional level,

German immigrants were vastly overshadowed by Irishmen, but at the mayoral level, they surprisingly held their own and shaped city government in their interest.

There was a radical side to German America ever since the sometimes violent student revolutionaries took refuge here in the 1830s, followed by a much larger group of bourgeois radicals after the failed democratic Revolution of 1848. But they mellowed with age and had little in common with the militant anarchist and socialist labor radicals of the late nineteenth century. The latter were largely discredited by the Haymarket Affair of 1886, even though they were innocent of the crime for which four of them were executed. German urban socialists of the twentieth century were much more pragmatic. Twenty-first-century conservatives should be reassured by the splendid record of socialists in German Milwaukee, the last of whom left office only in 1960.

As this book shows, there is more to the ethnic experience than discrimination and persecution; in fact, there are times when it is the ethnics who are engaging in discrimination. Those who view the World War I era only through the lens of victimization will be surprised to find German Americans on both sides of some violent confrontations. But they will also see the absurdity of Theodore Roosevelt's fulminations against the hyphen, refuted by doughboys writing home from France *auf Deutsch*, and, when they paid the ultimate sacrifice, sometimes commemorated on tombstones in the German language. And on a lighter note, readers will learn just who was responsible for the absurdity of "liberty cabbage."

Along with sauerkraut, the German language survived after 1918 to a greater extent than is often realized, sometimes into the twenty-first century. Germans resisted legal attacks on their language and parochial schools all the way to the Supreme Court and won. With the rise of Nazism in Germany, its stigma rubbed off to some extent on German Americans, but the establishment of a democratic and economically thriving West Germany reflected favorably on them as well. The positive experiences of several million GIs and their families stationed in the Federal Republic also did their part. From the 1983 German-American Tricentennial on, a revived ethnic consciousness combined with heritage tourism in a last hurrah of German America. But even in Texas, a 1948-model German American such as myself seldom encounters anyone younger who grew up with the German language, unless they have an immigrant parent. At long last the sun is setting on the twilight of German ethnicity in America.

This book is an attempt to make the latest scholarly research on German Americans accessible to the educated general reader without any specialized background knowledge, particularly those interested in their ethnic heritage. It seeks to bring the experiences of everyday immigrants to life, especially through their letters. The book's chapters follow in rough chronological order but in part take a topical approach; they are designed so that they can be read independently in any order.

1

Before the Great Flood

Germans in Colonial and Revolutionary America

THE "OFFICIAL" BEGINNING OF GERMAN settlement in America, commemorated in numerous tricentennial celebrations on both sides of the Atlantic, was the arrival of a group of Mennonites from the Rhineland town of Krefeld at Philadelphia on October 6, 1683. They were certainly not the first Germans in the New World, although there is still considerable controversy over who was the first, and when and where that person arrived. In the English language, Deutsch and Dutch are easily confused, and there was no "Germany" as such, so record-keeping was unsystematic in the literally hundreds of German petty sovereignties. It appears quite likely that a few Germans were present among the first permanent settlers at Jamestown, Virginia, in 1607. All this is of greater interest to ethnic enthusiasts and antiquarians than to historians, so long as the immigration consisted only of isolated individuals who had not acquired the "critical mass" to establish ethnic institutions, and thus of necessity quickly adopted the language and customs of the English.

The makeup of the 1683 Mennonite group from Krefeld and its destination of Pennsylvania were hardly coincidental. The English Quaker William Penn had received a proprietary grant of land on the Delaware River in 1681, where he founded a colony offering religious tolerance for Quakers and other persecuted religious groups. Penn had established previous contacts with Pietists in Germany, having visited the country in 1671 and again in 1677. Two of Penn's circulars publicizing his colony

were translated and circulated in Germany in 1681 and 1682. They
attracted a group of thirteen Mennonite families from Krefeld, who traveled under the leadership of Franz Daniel Pastorius, a lawyer from Som-
merhausen near Würzberg who had been in contact with pietistic circles
downstream in Frankfurt am Main. This party of thirty-three persons
settled about five miles outside of Philadelphia, where they founded
the village of Germantown. Questions have been raised as to how German the town and its founders really were. Krefeld is barely twenty
miles from the border with Holland, and some of the settlers had Dutch
names; others had originated in Switzerland. It is clear that they were
united more by religious identity than by ethnicity. But the family op den
Graaf, for example, with one of the most Dutch sounding names, had
lived in Krefeld since 1609, so that the emigrants were all of a German-
born generation.

Already in the next year, another group of immigrants arrived from
Krefeld and Mülheim an der Ruhr, and in 1685 a group of Swiss Mennonites who had taken refuge in the Palatinate came over. Mennonites
were the most numerous among the radical Pietist groups that came
to America. They took their name from their leader Menno Simmons
(1496–1561) of West Frisia; this Anabaptist movement spread from the
Netherlands to Germany and the Swiss cantons. The Amish, a more
stringent offshoot of the Mennonites, originated in Switzerland, and a
majority of those who emigrated had been born there, although many
may have lived in Germany in the interim. The Moravians originated in
Bohemia and Moravia as an outgrowth of the Hussite movement, and
took on the name Unitas Fratrum, or in German *Mährische Brüder*. They
were known for their communalistic economic practices and their active
conversion efforts, also toward the Indians. Although these groups, particularly the Amish and Mennonites, dominate our image of colonial
Germans, their numbers were quite small. During the century after 1683,
only an estimated 1,500 to 4,200 Mennonites arrived in British America,
and, at most, 750 Moravians. The Amish and Dunkers (the latter a German Baptist group) each numbered three hundred or less, and two other
small sects, the Schwenkfelders and Waldensians even fewer. All told,
these radical Pietist groups, often known as "sect people," numbered only
5,500 at most, a mere 6 percent of the roughly one hundred thousand

Germans who arrived during the colonial era; the great bulk were Lutheran or Reformed "church people."

Even without any mass immigration before 1710, the town of Germantown proved quite successful, not the least because of the artisan skills the immigrants brought with them. Many families continued in the linen-weaving trade they had practiced in Krefeld. An English traveler wrote in 1690 that Germantown was a town "of Hollanders and Germans, who have built up a linen manufacture, weaving and producing many thousands of yards of fine linen cloth every year." The first paper mill in the colonies was founded there in 1690 by Mülheim immigrant William Rittenhouse, and a second mill was established in 1710. Later, the town became important as a site for publishing. Christopher Sauer, who had immigrated in 1724, in 1738 founded a printing establishment that became the largest in the colonies. The next year saw the appearance of his *Hoch-Deutsch Amerikanischen Calender* and also the first successful German newspaper, both of which lasted until the Revolution. Sauer is perhaps best known for his publication of the first complete Bible in any European language in the American colonies, a German edition from 1743.

Germantown had made its mark with another first in 1688: the first public protest against slavery in North America. The German Quaker assembly passed a resolution condemning slavery. First of all, it was against the Golden Rule: "There is a saying, that we should do to all men like as we will be done ourselves." Secondly, some slaveholders "commit adultery in others, separating wives from their husbands and giving them to others." Moreover, just as Christians should not steal, they "must, likewise, avoid to purchase such things as are stolen." The petition was written in English, probably by Pastorius himself, and was passed on to the monthly English Quaker meeting for discussion. Here, economic interests won out over moral principles; the English brethren were too timid to take a position. This was only one of the many roles Pastorius played in the new settlement. He founded a school in 1702, which he led for fourteen years; he was elected to the Pennsylvania assembly in 1687 and again in 1691; and he was appointed a justice of the peace in 1693.

During its first decades, German migration to colonial America consisted mainly of radical Pietist religious refugees like the Germantown founders, though the numbers were very small, perhaps three hundred.

Germantown itself still numbered only 250 inhabitants at the onset of the eighteenth century. A new phase began in 1709, when an agricultural crisis, combined with rumors of free passage and free land to be granted by British authorities, led to the first mass exodus, particularly from the Palatinate. So many would-be emigrants crowded the Dutch ports and the outskirts of London that they led to a major disaster. Many ended up being sent home or became stranded in Britain, where Daniel Defoe, among others, took up the cause of the "Poor Palatine Refugees." It was at this time that the term "Palatine" became established in the English language as a term for Germans in general. About 650 of these refugees secured passage to North Carolina, where they met many hardships but ultimately formed the nucleus of the New Bern settlement. Ten shiploads carrying several thousand immigrants were granted passage to New York, but instead of being settled on free farmland, they were sent to produce pine tar and pitch in camps along the Hudson. This enterprise soon collapsed, and many of these Germans settled west of Albany in the valley of the Mohawk and its tributary, Schoharie Creek. They maintained good relations with local Mohawk Indians because their leader Johann Conrad Weiser sent his son Conrad to live with them and learn their language. But they continued to have problems obtaining land titles, with the result that a number of Palatines relocated to Tulpehocken in Berks County, Pennsylvania, among them Conrad Weiser. Ironically, the New York town of New Paltz, although its name is derived from the dialect pronunciation of the Pfalz (the German term for the Palatinate), was not associated with these immigrants, but rather with French Huguenots who had taken temporary refuge in the Palatinate before coming to America and founding the town in 1678, predating Germantown.

From roughly 1717 on, and particularly from the 1730s all the way to the outbreak of the American Revolution, German immigration intensified, but because of the bad experiences of the Palatines, New York played only a minor role. Some three-fourths or four-fifths of colonial German immigrants arrived in Philadelphia, and most settled initially in Pennsylvania. Though primarily motivated by economics, these migrants were, for the most part, not as desperately poor as those from the Palatinate. Radical Pietist sects made up only a small, if significant, minority of this influx; instead, the majority was either Lutheran or Reformed, some of whom were also religious refugees. Lutherans expelled from the bishopric of Salzburg settled near Savannah, Georgia, in 1734, followed by Moravian settlers the next year. But many of them soon began relocating to Pennsylvania.

Although some hundred thousand Germans came to the future United States during the colonial era, British North America was not the only, or even the leading, foreign destination for Germans in the eighteenth century. At least a half million migrated to Eastern Europe, over three hundred thousand to Hungarian lands alone. Catholics in particular tended to migrate east, where they would enjoy the protection of their Habsburg coreligionists, though there were also some Protestants moving east from German states and some Catholics bound across the Atlantic. But it took until 1789 before the first German Catholic parish was established in the new nation, not surprisingly in Philadelphia.

The Protestant "church Germans" of colonial America have gotten much less scholarly attention than the "sect Germans," such as the Amish (perhaps the subject of the most studies per capita of any element of American society). Arguably, the sect Germans deserve this attention, for they have preserved their "Pennsylvania Dutch" dialect down to the present and across the continent, whereas it has nearly gone extinct among church Germans, though only in the course of the twentieth century. In any case, several recent transatlantic studies of the "church German" majority have somewhat restored the balance. One study examined emigration to "greater Pennsylvania" from the northern Kraichgau, an area roughly between Heidelberg and Heilbronn, while a similar study focused on emigration from Baden-Durlach, the area around Karlsruhe. In both instances, eighteenth-century patterns turn out to resemble those of the nineteenth century much more than was previously realized.

Both of these areas suffered much devastation during the Thirty Years' War, which ended in 1648. Baden-Durlach also suffered several French invasions under Louis XIV in the last quarter of the 1600s. By the mid-1700s, these population losses had been made up, in part through the immigration of religious refugees, and the region was once again suffering population pressure. In 1809, the average resident of the Kraichgau had to live off less than four acres of land per person. In Baden-Durlach, over one-third of the emigrants possessed resources ranging from fifty guilders downward, which officials considered as poor. Less than one-fourth of them were worth two hundred guilders or more,

regarded as a good holding; not even 5 percent were worth over five hundred guilders. More than half the emigrants were left with one hundred
guilders or less, roughly the price of an acre of cropland or one-third of an
acre of vineyards. Many emigrants had owned more land than this, but
the settlement of debts often cut into their resources quite substantially,
and local authorities took at least a 10 percent cut from anyone not totally
impoverished. To some extent, the population pressure in this region may
have resulted from partible inheritance; what partibility undoubtedly
caused was an extreme splintering of holdings. This was particularly true
of vineyards, but also of cropland; one emigrant from Baden-Durlach who
owned a scant eight acres had it scattered over thirty-four different par-
cels. Many were smaller than the legally prescribed minimum of a quarter
acre, which led to great inefficiency and numerous boundary disputes.

More than a century before 1848, economic discontents were closely
intertwined with political ones. The Markgraf of Baden-Durlach and
the numerous petty sovereigns of the Kraichgau in this era of absolut-
ism were attempting to reestablish their authority and rebuild the palaces
devastated by the wars of the seventeenth century. As a result, there were
increases both in the taxes and fees and a plethora of regulations (even of
the number of guests at weddings or godparents at baptisms) imposed
upon their subjects. Peasants were restricted in their access to firewood
from common forests, while they were prohibited from hunting and
were left without recourse when wild game (which was reserved for the
nobility) laid waste to their fields and vineyards. Emigration could be
regarded as "voting with one's feet" against these conditions—the only
kind of voting such peasants were allowed.

Perhaps it was the religious sects who provided the first example of
migrating to escape intolerable conditions. Few of the "church Germans" emigrated in formally organized groups as did most members of
Pietist sects, but only about 4 percent of those from the Kraichgau traveled as isolated individuals. Usually, one or two dozen people from the
same or neighboring villages, often bound by ties of birth, marriage, or
godparentage, came across together. Although one-quarter of the emigrants leaving Baden-Durlach were unmarried individuals, one-half of
the males and nearly all the females in this category traveled along with
single or married relatives.

While the ocean trip was not much more arduous than a sailing voyage in the early nineteenth century, the route to the port of embarkation before the advent of steamboats, railroads, and German unification required considerably more money, time, and effort than it would a century later. Gottlieb Mittelberger reported that in 1750 he had spent seven weeks shipping down the Rhine from Heilbronn to Rotterdam, held up by no less than thirty-six customs stations along the way, though this was somewhat of an anomaly. But since there were no regularly scheduled voyages, additional weeks could be lost, and more money spent, waiting at the ports for a ship. In view of this, and of the financial resources of emigrants cited above, it comes as no surprise that at least half and perhaps as many as two-thirds of eighteenth-century emigrants crossed the Atlantic as redemptioners, financing their journey with credits that had to be worked off at their destination.

The redemptioner system and other forms of indentured servitude that preceded it have enjoyed a bad reputation, evoking charges of abuse, exploitation, even "white slavery." Undoubtedly, there were individual instances that would justify all these charges; the question is how widespread or typical such problems were. First of all, according to the customs of the times, temporary bound servitude was nothing out of the ordinary; it applied to many apprentices who remained in their home villages just as it did to transatlantic voyagers. Secondly, there was an element of free choice in the redemptioner system, not only in the choice to go to America on credit in the first place but also in seeking and contracting with a master who would refund the captain for the passage and "redeem" the passenger in return for a term of servitude usually ranging from three to six years. If one had relatives or friends already in the Philadelphia area who could come up with the price of redemption, the result was often servitude in name only. Thirdly, even those who ended up in service to a stranger had legal protections that a slave did not, including the right to testify against a master in court. Finally, if the situation became intolerable, there was always the option of running away, as numerous newspaper ads attest.

Redemptioners were forbidden to marry during their period of service and, like slaves, could only leave the master's place with his permission and received little or no pay. But at the end of their term they normally received two suits of clothes, an axe, and some farming tools, and they had usually accumulated valuable training and experience in American agriculture, as well as the English language or artisan skills if the master had command of them. The boundary between indenture and apprenticeship was often indistinct. One Swedish observer noted that many Germans with sufficient money to pay their passage nonetheless entered servitude to learn the language and gather experience. One indication that redemptioners bore no permanent stigma is the fact that many of them later became landowners and indeed sometimes employed redemptioners themselves. Nor was it unheard of, once the term was served out and the redemptioner was free to marry, that the spouse turned out to be none other than a son or daughter of the master. Sometimes, too, employment would continue on a wage basis once the term of indenture was up.

One clearly unjust feature of the system is that survivors were held responsible for the expenses of any family members who died on the second half of the voyage, though with an average mortality rate below 4 percent overall, and lower for adults, this was of less impact than one might imagine. A more serious problem was that redemptioners were at the mercy of supply and demand, so a large influx of passengers could leave many of them languishing on the ships, waiting to be redeemed and facing only unattractive offers for their services. The immigration curve was subject to wild fluctuations during the eighteenth century, and those who arrived at the peak of the curve were especially faced with difficulties. There were only a few years during the eighteenth century when ten or more shiploads of Germans arrived at Philadelphia: 1732, 1738, 1741, 1764, 1773, and each of the six years between 1749 and 1754. The record year was 1749, with twenty-five ships and more than seven thousand passengers; and for the next five years the annual total ranged from fifteen to nineteen ships. By contrast, the eight years beginning in 1755 saw a total of only four arriving ships, as the Seven Years' War disrupted travel by land and sea.

One of the harshest and most frequently cited critics of the redemptioner system was Gottlieb Mittelberger, whose warnings were still reprinted by Prussian officials in 1862. However, he experienced the absolute nadir of immigration conditions during his sojourn from 1750 to 1754. His misfortune started with the ocean crossing on the ship Osgood, which was much more crowded than the average ship and took three months for the voyage when some ships made it in less than two, exposing it to an unusual degree of misery and mortality. Moreover, as a recent German study points out, Mittelberger "was not an objective chronicler characterized by personal integrity." His return to Germany was precipitated less by disillusionment with America than by the loss of his organist's position because of a sexual offense, and his traveler's account was encouraged, subsidized, and probably edited by Württemberg authorities to discourage emigrants. His American employer, Pastor Henry Muhlenberg, wrote in an unpublished chronicle that organist Mittelberger "in the night of 8–9 July [1753] allegedly conducted himself so sinfully and most outrageously toward an unmarried female in our school house that he is unworthy in the future to touch the organ in the church or to instruct the youth in the school."

Still, it should be noted that other, more neutral observers including Muhlenberg himself, were also critical of the redemptioner system. One of the responses of local ethnic communities was the founding of German Societies in various port cities, beginning with Philadelphia in 1764 and Charleston two years later, followed by Baltimore in 1783 and New York in 1784 as the end of the Revolutionary War brought a reopening of immigrant traffic. Although they fulfilled a multitude of functions, including purely social ones, these societies played an important caritative role, particularly for new arrivals and others who found themselves without a personal network of support in time of need.

Such persons, however, were in a small minority; to a great extent, personal and village ties structured the process of migration and settlement. At first glance, this would not seem to be the case: The 152 immigrants from the Kraichgau town of Ittlingen scattered across more than forty destinations all the way from Philadelphia to North Carolina; the 102 from Hoffenheim could be found in more than thirty locations across the same range of territory. But upon closer examination, one preferred location often attracted a fourth or a fifth of all immigrants from a given village. In fact, one needed look in only three townships to find the majority of immigrants from the typical Kraichgau parish, and this despite the dispersive effects of the redemptioner system and the need to settle farther west, as land near Philadelphia became more expensive. The great bulk of the immigrants from Baden-Durlach were concentrated in parts of the Pennsylvania counties of Lancaster, Berks, and Dauphin; in fact, a large majority could be found in just a dozen adjacent townships.

Through 1770, 42 percent of the children of Baden-Durlach parentage baptized there were sponsored by godparents of the same origins. The Warwick Congregation in northern Lancaster County was one of their strongholds, where they made up nearly three-fifths of the parishioners and held five of the seven seats on the church council.

Immigrants from Kraichgau and Baden-Durlach were quite typical of colonial German immigrants generally. Regardless of where they originated, they tended to settle near other Germans to the point of totally dominating some areas. A surname analysis of the 1790 census showed that German immigrants and their descendants made up nearly 9 percent of the free population, making them by far the largest element from beyond the British Isles and also the largest linguistic minority in the new nation. The leading state for Germans, not surprisingly, was Pennsylvania, where one-third or more of the population was of German stock, rivaling the English in numbers. Neighboring Maryland was next in line with 12 percent, followed by New Jersey with 9 percent. Even New York fell slightly below the American average at 8 percent German; none of the other states had a significant German presence that went beyond scattered local pockets.

Germans were also the most heavily segregated of all the ethnic groups in Pennsylvania, and their segregation level in Maryland was even higher. In the areas west of Philadelphia, a surname analysis of the white population in the 1790 census showed that over 70 percent of Lancaster and adjacent Berks and Dauphin counties was ethnically German, along with nearly two-thirds of Northampton County, over half of Montgomery County and practically half of York County. In fact, there was a heavy German presence throughout southeastern Pennsylvania. From there, Germans continued to migrate into the southern back country. German concentrations in "greater Pennsylvania" include the adjacent Maryland counties of Frederick and Carroll that were more than half German, as was Shenandoah County in Virginia. As far south as the North Carolina back country, Stoles County was over one-third and Lincoln County over one-fourth German.

Although the German presence was also relatively large in New York and New Jersey, Germans tended to be less segregated and more quickly assimilated there than in the areas mentioned above. For example, a thirteen-year-old Palatinate immigrant named John Peter Zenger, who arrived in 1710, was apprenticed to an English Quaker, learned the printing trade from him, and later established his own English-language paper. He made history in 1735 when he was prosecuted for printing "false, scandalous, malicious, and seditious" criticisms of the governor, but he was acquitted on the ground that what he published was true. But as important as Zenger was for the establishment of freedom of the press, he had in effect become part of Anglo-American (and to some extent, Dutch-American) society rather than any German ethnic community, despite his foreign birth.

The situation was quite different in Pennsylvania, where Germans had the numbers and concentration to support a thriving network of ethnic institutions. Before the Revolution, the only places beyond Pennsylvania with German printers were Baltimore and New York City, but it took until 1819 before a New York German newspaper was attempted. The next half-century saw some expansion, but of the fifty towns with German printers before the onset of mass immigration in the 1830s, thirty-one were in Pennsylvania, which was home to three-fourths of all the 288 German printers of that era. New York's first purely German Lutheran congregation was only established in 1750, although Germans, particularly of Reformed background, often joined Dutch parishes. Pennsylvania was a different story. By the outbreak of the American Revolution, there were 375 German churches in the colonies, two-thirds of them in Pennsylvania, with Maryland a distant second. Lutherans held a slight edge over Reformed congregations; a strong dynamic leader left his mark on each of these denominations.

Henry Melchior Muhlenberg (1711–1787), perhaps the most influential German religious leader of the colonial era, was sent to Pennsylvania in 1741 to counteract the Moravian inroads on Lutheranism. Often considered the father of Lutheranism in America, he organized the first Lutheran synod in America in 1748, prepared a standard liturgy for the denomination, authored its constitution, and contributed substantially to its hymnal published in 1787. He traveled widely beyond his own congregations, often being called upon to mediate disputes, and was capable of preaching in English and Dutch, as well as German.

Michael Schlatter (1716–1790), a Swiss native educated in Germany, arrived five years later than Muhlenberg in 1746, and played a similar role for the German Reformed. He initially served churches in Germantown and Philadelphia, but he also traveled widely to minister to Reformed congregations throughout Pennsylvania and neighboring states. Like Muhlenberg, he organized a synod in Philadelphia in 1747. He visited Europe in 1751 to seek support and returned the next year with six ministerial recruits and funds totaling some twenty thousand pounds, which he collected to support schooling for Germans in America. Although Schlatter devoted himself fully to these educational efforts after 1755, he encountered much resistance to the teaching of English required by his British benefactors and gave up his efforts after two years.

There was greater receptivity to English by the time leaders of the Lutheran and Reformed churches cooperated to found Franklin College at Lancaster, Pennsylvania, in 1787. This was the first bilingual college in the new nation, offering instruction in both English and German. For a brief period at the outset it was also the first coeducational institution, with women constituting almost one-third of its initial enrollment. It was named after Benjamin Franklin, who was also a generous benefactor and one of a number of its politically prominent supporters. Its first president was Henry Ernst Muhlenberg, a son of the Lutheran patriarch.

Two other Muhlenberg sons had equally distinguished careers. Frederick Augustus was not only elected to the Congress but also chosen as the first Speaker of the U. S. House of Representatives. His brother John Peter Gabriel was serving as a Lutheran minister in Woodstock, Virginia, at the outbreak of the Revolution. Seventy-five years later, his grand-nephew recorded that he preached a sermon from the text in Ecclesiastes, "To every thing there is a season," and at the verse, "a time of war, and a time of peace," stated "now is a time of war," flinging open his clerical robe to reveal a Continental officer's uniform. Though the authenticity of this incident is doubtful given that there is no earlier documentation, what is beyond dispute is that Muhlenberg was instrumental in recruiting the eighth Virginia Regiment and served as its first colonel and then as a general under Washington, all the way to Yorktown.

The American Revolution was controversial among colonial Germans, sometimes even within families. Frederick Augustus Muhlenberg initially objected to his brother Peter's military role, but Peter accused him of being a Tory sympathizer before the British bombardment of New York drove Frederick out of the city and over to the Patriot side. Michael Schlatter had earlier served as a chaplain to a British regiment and was again retained by them at the outbreak of the Revolution. But when they occupied Germantown in 1777, he resisted orders and was imprisoned, and his house was plundered by the British. General Nicholas Herkimer, the son of Palatine immigrants to New York, is known for commanding a German patriot militia and giving his life for the cause in 1777; largely forgotten is his younger brother, Loyalist Captain Johan Jost Herkimer, who found permanent refuge in Canada. But prominent Loyalists were relatively rare among the Germans. Christopher Sauer Jr. was more of a pacifist than a Loyalist but saw his press destroyed by Patriot forces in 1777 because he printed pamphlets for both sides. His sons, Christopher III and Peter, more actively supported the Loyalist cause and accompanied the British when they withdrew. More commonly, Germans split less between Patriots and Loyalists than along confessional lines between Patriots and pacifists, with many "sect people" holding fast to their pacifism, whereas "church people," such as the Muhlenbergs, were more sympathetic to the Patriot cause. Another way in which Germans, even pacifists, contributed to the Patriot cause was in undermining the morale of Hessian mercenaries and convincing them to desert or switch sides. Deserters could easily melt into German communities, and Hessian captives were held in Lancaster and several other Pennsylvania German communities, where they were often indentured out as laborers. It is much to the credit of local Germans that as many as five thousand Hessians opted to remain in America after independence was achieved.

Particularly in places like Lancaster in the rural hinterlands of Philadelphia, Germans left their mark not only on religious institutions but on the material culture as well. Even Benjamin Franklin, who otherwise expressed reservations toward Pennsylvania Germans, remarked positively upon their agricultural practices: "I am not against the Admission of Germans in general, for they have their Virtues, their industry and frugality is exemplary; They are excellent husbandmen and contribute greatly to the improvement of a Country." Another prominent Philadelphian, Dr. Benjamin Rush, was a particular admirer of the German inhabitants of his state and their agricultural practices, as he laid out in a 1789 treatise. He especially praises the intensive and productive style of agriculture these Germans practiced, the care they took of their livestock, their frugality, and the way they valued "patrimonial property," which "should be possessed by a succession of generations." According to him, German farms were "easily distinguishable from those of others, by good fences, the extent of orchards, the fertility of soil, productiveness of fields, and luxuriance of the meadows." Rush no doubt exaggerated these German virtues, and yet they have a certain ring of truth. The productivity of their farms helps explain why Pennsylvania produced a 50 percent surplus of foodstuffs on the eve of the Revolution, the greatest in all the colonies. One of Rush's observations, "A German farm may be distinguished . . . by the superior size of their barns," was still echoed two centuries later by a Missourian commenting on his German neighbors: "They take more pride in their barns than in their houses." Another characteristic that persisted through the centuries and across the continent was the determination of Germans to establish the next generation in agriculture, so that their settlements often became more homogeneous over time.

For a while, particularly in Pennsylvania, it was a question of who would assimilate to whom. Back in the 1750s, Benjamin Franklin had fulminated against the Pennsylvania Germans: "why should the Palatinate Boors be suffered to swarm into our settlements? . . . Why should Pennsylvania, founded by the English, become a colony of <u>Aliens</u>, who will shortly be so numerous as to Germanize us instead of our Anglifying them, and will never adopt our Language or Customs?" He went on to observe that "few of their children in the Country learn English," complaining that many books were imported from Germany and German printing rivaled English in Pennsylvania, where even deeds and other legal documents were often recorded in German, and many signs and ads were bilingual. One reason Germans aroused Franklin's ire was their growing political independence: "For I remember when they modestly declined intermeddling in our Elections, but now they come in droves, and carry all before them, except in one or two Counties." In earlier times, most Germans had been politically passive, but now they largely supported the proprietary party that Franklin opposed.

Franklin's fears were unwarranted; there was never a threat that German would supplant English, not even in Pennsylvania. Nonetheless, the rumor has persisted that the United States nearly adopted German as its official language and was foiled by a single vote in Congress, cast by none other than a German American, House Speaker Frederick Muhlenberg, who allegedly stepped down from his speaker's chair to cast the deciding vote to break a tie. The story has some basis in fact, albeit very slight, from an incident in 1795. What was at stake was not the official language of the United States, nor even elevating German to the status of equality with English. One glance at the country's population makeup would reveal the absurdity of such a proposition. All that was voted upon was the request by some citizens of Augusta, Virginia, to have federal laws translated and published in German at public expense. The bill was apparently rejected by one vote, cast by Muhlenberg, but its impact should not be exaggerated. German as the official language was never a possibility, but particularly at the state and local levels, and occasionally at the federal level as well, there are numerous instances where public funds were expended to meet speakers of German (and other languages) halfway. But by the onset of the nineteenth century the need for such accommodation was fast declining. By 1812, there were no longer any German newspapers being published in Philadelphia.

Although German immigration never stopped entirely, it was seriously curtailed by the American Revolution, the economic depression in its aftermath, and the disruptions of the French Revolution and the Napoleonic conflicts. German immigration to the new American nation totaled only twenty thousand for the whole period from 1783 through 1819. That many Germans arrived in 1836 alone, and for the rest of the nineteenth century there were only three years when German immigration fell below that mark. But by the time that mass immigration resumed in the 1830s, most colonial Germans, unless their ethnicity was reinforced by religious separatism as in the case of Amish or Mennonites, were well on the way to assimilation.

This transition did not always go smoothly. In 1816, one Friedrich Eberle and fifty-eight other German Americans went on trial, accused by fellow ethnics of riot and conspiracy in a vehement and sometimes violent dispute over language use in Philadelphia's (and the nation's) largest German Lutheran congregation, St. Michael's and Zion. The language controversy involved a number of prominent Philadelphians, including two sons of the Lutheran patriarch Henry Melchior Muhlenberg. The case was fraught with a number of ironies. The German Society of Pennsylvania at one point offered its building as a meeting room for members of one side of the controversy—the "English" side. At issue was not the persistence of the German language, but rather whether any English would be allowed into the congregation at all. Nevertheless, most people involved on the "German" as well as the "English" side of the dispute were bilingual in practice, and even the sole witness who required a translator advertised his cabinet-making business in English. Both sides, moreover, framed their arguments in the language of American democracy. Neither the verdict nor its long-term repercussions proved to be at all clear cut. Although unanticipated by the litigants on either side, Philadelphia in the 1820s was on the threshold of a new mass immigration from Germany that would dwarf that of the eighteenth century, reviving the use of German in the churches and in the German Society of Pennsylvania, which by the time of the trial was conducting its business in English.

The language transition proceeded more slowly in rural areas than in cities. But even among the Rhinelanders on the Yadkin in the North Carolina backcountry, where frontiersman Daniel Boone had originated, German was disappearing from the churches by the 1830s and 1840s. Symptomatic of this fading culture is the story of an old immigrant named Klein whose great-grandchildren carried on his surname under the spellings of Klein, Kline, and Cline, as well as the translated forms of Small, Little, and Short. Especially outside of "Greater Pennsylvania," where they were geographically dispersed, later generations of German descendants essentially disappeared, becoming submerged in the normal Anglo-Protestant Southern culture. A German newspaper in the nineteenth-century immigration stronghold of St. Charles, Missouri, remarked in the 1850s: "Among the earliest inhabitants we find a significant number of names that, however mangled, cannot belie their German origins. Their descendants who were still here in 1832 and were bought out by the more recent German settlers were mostly Americans in the worst sense of the word: rough, brutal, ignorant, and ashamed of their ancestry if they were still aware of it." This somehow brings to mind that most famous German American of all, at least according to some ethnic enthusiasts: Elvis! His name and ancestry can be traced back to one Johann Valentine Bressler or Pressler, a winegrower from the Palatinate who emigrated to New York in 1710 and later moved south. Some 150 years later in Alabama, a descendant serving in the Confederate army anglicized the name to Presley.

2

Sources and Causes of
Nineteenth-Century Emigration

THE STARTING GUN FOR AN UPSURGE of mass emigration from Germany was set off by a shot that was felt, if not heard, around the world. On April 11, 1815, the volcano Tambora on an island off the east coast of Java exploded, sending more than forty cubic miles of material into the atmosphere. A cloud of volcanic ash and dust spread around the entire globe, darkening the sun and lowering temperatures in the whole northern hemisphere, with the result that 1816 was called "the year without a summer." Snow fell in June in Germany; it froze during every month in North America. Much of the grain failed to ripen, and prices in France and Germany reached levels that were not exceeded in the whole next century. Tens of thousands of people, mostly from the southwest of Germany, made their way to the ports in the hopes of escaping to America. As in the case of the Palatinate emigrants a century earlier, this mass exodus overwhelmed the shipping facilities, with the result that many emigrants had no choice but to return home. But enough found ocean passage that they also overwhelmed the redemptioner system. Supply so exceeded demand that many shipowners faced ruin because they were unable to hire out the passengers they had transported. Emigration subsided again in the 1820s as agricultural prices normalized within a couple of years, but it did not stop entirely.

If the United States indeed became the default option for German emigrants by the mid-nineteenth century, it was not because it had been so all along. In the 1820s, when emigration rates began to revive after a generation-long pause imposed by the French Revolution and the Napoleonic Wars, Brazil was able to compete on a fairly equal basis with the United States. There were even "Brasilienlieder" that sang the praises of the Amazonian empire in much the same way that the "Columbuslied" of the 1830s celebrated the United States. The immigrant journalist and chronicler Nicholas Gonner recorded one Brazilian song that had become part of oral tradition in Luxemburg, dictated to him in 1885—ironically, but tellingly, by an immigrant woman in Ohio. According to one estimate, Brazil attracted some seven to eight thousand Germans during the 1820s, about the same number as recorded arrivals in U. S. ports. In fact, only about one-quarter of German emigration during the 1820s was directed to the United States, though by the 1830s it was above three-quarters, and for the rest of the century it hovered around 90 percent.

The first year that official German immigration to the United States exceeded the ten-thousand mark was in 1832. It began in the region where emigration had been heaviest in the eighteenth century, the southwest, particularly the Palatinate, Württemberg, and Baden. Something new, however, was the increased share of Catholics, who had earlier tended to move eastward to Austrian and Hungarian lands. Until 1832 emigration was restricted for the most part to these areas of southwest Germany. Only after that time did it come to be a mass movement, spreading north and east to affect all of Germany to varying degrees before the American Civil War.

Since there were no dramatic economic setbacks in Germany in 1832, political events of the years 1830 to 1832 probably played a larger role, as did the appearance of several guidebooks promoting emigration, in particular that of Gottfried Duden. The effects of economic forces are clearly evident in the 1840s. Though nothing elsewhere in the nineteenth century even approached the catastrophe of the Irish potato famine, it had a milder echo all across northern and central Europe, sending emigration rates soaring. One future emigrant wrote from Franconia in 1846, "the situation in Germany has been very distressing because all bread and other provisions are so very high. This year will be the very worst of all, for the grain harvest has turned out badly, and the potato crop will be almost a complete failure. This disease of the potato plant prevails not only in Germany, but is spreading all over Europe."

As late as the 1850s, there was at least one whole German district in the Black Forest region that experienced a surplus of deaths over births for two successive years, without even taking migration into account. Baden as a whole had a surplus of births between 1852 and 1855, but still saw its population decline by more than 3 percent in those three years because of out-migration. Emigration was so heavy in this era that there were a half dozen or more German districts where the 1852 or 1855 population was not surpassed again for at least a dozen years. In two cases it took fifteen years; in another, eighteen; in yet another, it took twenty-one years, while the Black Forest District had not yet regained its 1852 population level by 1875. There were German counties in areas of cottage industry such as Tecklenburg that saw a 6 percent decline in population in the fifteen years after 1843. Three parishes in the county had fewer inhabitants in 1871 than in 1818. One extreme case, the municipality of Lienen, took more than a century to regain its 1818 population level—Irish conditions, one might say, if on a very local basis.

The late 1840s saw a brief economic recovery, and the 1848 Revolution temporarily discouraged emigration from both a practical and an ideological standpoint. When another economic downturn set in after 1850, German-American immigration soared to the highest per-capita rates in all of German and American history. Although only a small fraction consisted of political refugees in the narrow sense of the term, economic and political grievances were closely intertwined. Much more numerous than genuine political refugees of a bourgeois background were those of the rural lower classes who were in silent sympathy with the Revolution and were now voting with their feet against a fatherland that demanded much of them and gave them very little in return. For eight years in a row between 1847 and 1854, the United States experienced the highest relative immigration rates in its entire history, an annual population influx equal to more that 1 percent of the current population, peaking out at nearly 1.8 percent in 1854. More than one-third of this influx was German.

From this point on, immigration rates underwent a long downturn from a series of three factors. The first was the anti-foreign Know Nothing movement in the United States. It reached its peak in 1854 and 1855, whether one measures it by electoral results or the number of riot casualties. In 1855, grain and potato prices reached their highest level in decades, if not in the whole nineteenth century. One German real wage

index shows 1855 as the lowest level ever reached between the volcani-
cally induced "years without summers" from 1816 to 1818 and 1913. So
the push factor, if anything, intensified in 1855 compared to previous
years. But reports from America of anti-immigrant violence kept many
potential newcomers away. As the nativist movement waned, emigration
rates recovered only slightly before the Panic of 1857 initiated several
years of economic stagnation, followed closely by the Civil War, which
drove immigration rates even lower. As prospects for a Union victory
improved, the curve turned upward once again, though it took until
1866 to surpass the one hundred thousand mark. Much of the immigration from 1865 to 1870 was a catch-up effect involving people who had
deferred their migration because of the war.

In the last third of the nineteenth century, the migration curve
largely reflected the roller coaster ride of the American business cycle.
The Panic of 1873 and the ensuing depression curbed immigration for
the next five years; in fact, German immigration in the 1870s fell well
below that of the 1850s and barely exceeded the totals for the Civil
War decade. Recovery after 1879 set off the last and, in absolute numbers, largest wave of immigration in the 1880s, bringing almost 1.5
million Germans to America. The record year was 1882, when almost
a quarter million arrived from Germany. But the volume slacked
off considerably toward the end of the decade despite the health of
the American economy. Relatively few German immigrants arrived
at Ellis Island, which opened in 1892. This was the last year their
numbers exceeded one hundred thousand, and after 1894 on down
to World War I, they never broke fifty thousand. The Panic of 1893
and the ensuing depression sent immigration plummeting for Germans and other Europeans. But in the last couple of years of the nineteenth century and continuing into the twentieth, a new trend became
evident. Despite improvements in the American economy, German
immigration (in contrast to that of other nationalities), remained quite
low. Rising real wages and a growing demand for industrial labor in
Germany had finally made it unnecessary to leave. By World War I,
manpower shortages had even led Germany to import labor—more
labor, in fact, than any other country besides the United States. The
end of German mass migration to the United States resulted primarily from German economic development, rather than the closing of

the U. S. frontier in 1890 as is often claimed. Even though the total volume was much lower, over 90 percent of German emigration in the first decade of the twentieth century was still directed to the United States rather than to frontier Canada.

Since Germany's emigration was disproportionately rural in its origins, the structures and transformations of rural society form the starting point for an understanding of migration patterns. German agricultural patterns can be roughly divided into three types. The areas east of the Elbe River, dominated by great estates, show important contrasts to the areas with a more independent peasantry in the west. These western areas, in turn, can be further subdivided between areas north of the Main River with impartible inheritance, and those with partible inheritance to the south. (Although sometimes characterized as primogenitor, the single heir in some regions was the youngest rather than the eldest son.) Despite considerable local variation, these divisions help us in recognizing commonalities in socioeconomic and particularly agrarian patterns that form the background of nineteenth-century emigration.

The predominance of southwest Germany—in terms of both its early start and the intensity of emigration—prompted contemporaries such as economist Friedrich List, as well as later scholars to attribute mass emigration to customs of partible inheritance, equal division among all children, resulting in increasingly smaller and more splintered landholdings, too small to be economically viable. Although this explanation is not entirely wrong, it is misleading. Partible inheritance was neither a necessary nor a sufficient precondition for heavy emigration. In fact, a study of Hesse Kassel, where both forms of inheritance were present, found that areas with impartible inheritance actually saw more emigration than those where partability was the local custom. There were areas of northwest Germany with systems of impartible inheritance that had emigration rates rivaling those anywhere in southwest Germany. Moreover, areas with partible inheritance had emigration rates ranging from the highest to among the lowest throughout Germany.

Statistics at the county (*Kreis*) level for the whole of the German Empire in 1895 showed that among the areas with the highest proportion of "dwarf agriculture" (holdings under five acres), three of the top

five and six of the top twenty were indeed in the southwestern state of
Württemberg. But those in first and third place, Zellerfeld in the Harz
mountains and Siegen in southern Westphalia, both traditional centers of
mining and metalworking, had rather low emigration rates. Moreover,
among the six Württemberg counties, none fell in the top quintile of net
outmigration for the period of 1813–1867, and four were at or below the
Württemberg average. Five of the six lay within a twenty-mile radius of
Stuttgart, and no doubt reflect the combination of part-time agriculture
with industrial employment, a more modern version of what ethnologist
Wilhelm Heinrich Riehl characterized back in the 1850s as *handwerkende
Bauern und verbauerte Handwerker*: roughly "artisan farmers and agrarian artisans." A Württemberg agricultural census of 1852 found that 44
percent of all artisans also engaged in agriculture, both probably of a
marginal nature.

The southwest was also heavily involved in winegrowing, a very labor-
intensive enterprise where a surprisingly small plot of land can support a
family. In the southwest, the decline of the cottage industry in the 1840s
was cushioned by bountiful wine harvests; the 1846 vintage was the most
profitable in the surrounding two decades. However, the 1850, 1851, and
1854 vintages were among the four worst years in the century, and the
two intervening years were also below average. This, combined with
high grain prices, drove Württemberg emigration rates to record heights
in the early 1850s. These patterns reflect less the mechanistic operation of
inheritance systems than the influence of specific local economic factors
on both population density and migration patterns.

In fact, all three regions of Germany show a wide range of migration
behavior independent of inheritance systems. Using a combination of
U.S. and German statistics, it is possible to estimate the number of
natives of various German states and districts living in America in 1870.
Although the German immigrant population came to only 3.66 percent
of that in the German Reich, some districts had an overseas population equal to more than 10 percent of those living at home. The district
with the heaviest emigration of all was indeed in the southwest—the
Palatinate, a Bavarian exclave west of the Rhine, bordering on France.
Neighboring areas in Baden-Württemberg and the Eifel suffered a
heavy exodus as well, but the northwestern districts of Minden and
Osnabrück, areas of impartible inheritance, were also among the top

half-dozen districts in Germany with respect to emigration intensity. East Elbian emigration only reached its peak after 1871, but by then, Mecklenburg and especially Pomerania were beginning to experience serious losses.

The districts of East Elbia also varied considerably in their migration behavior. Through 1840, all showed migration gains, which probably resulted from the positive short-term effects of the Prussian agrarian reforms. The period from 1840 to 1864 was characterized by minor gains and losses alternating across time and place. Erfurt, a district with declining cottage industry, showed greater similarity to the northwest than to other East Elbian districts in its migration patterns—in fact, it had the highest losses in the region between 1843 and 1867. Only after 1864 did East Elbian population losses exceed 1 percent annually, a level that can be equated with mass migration. One can also see the eastward spread of "migration fever" in the region, affecting first Pomerania, then the province of West Prussia, and only belatedly the East Prussia districts.

One factor that came into play was the concentration of landholdings in the hands of great estate owners (either from the nobility or the bourgeoisie). It is probably no coincidence that the heaviest emigration rates in the east were from areas such as Pomerania and Mecklenburg where property concentration was greatest. Mecklenburg had only abolished serfdom in 1822, the last German state to do so. It was not that peasant agriculture was unable to compete—the largest estates showed the heaviest levels of indebtedness per acre. Rather, the old semi-feudal elite was propped up by the state, which showed full sympathy for the complaint of one such owner: "Our estates would become a kind of hell for us if our neighbors were independent peasant proprietors." In fact, it was hell for their underlings, as a Pomeranian immigrant wrote in 1842 three years after emigrating: "you shouldn't imagine that the good farming families here are like the ones over there in Prussia, instead they have a much more decent and free way of life. . . . You can earn your daily bread better than in Germany, one doesn't live so restrictedly and in such servitude as you do under the great estate owners, you don't have to put your hat under your arm or leave it at the door when you want to have the money you've earned." The Prussian bureaucracy in the east was largely recruited from such elites, and Prussian law greatly hindered or in some cases forbade the dividing of estates. The end result was that peasant proprietors and the rural lower classes were left to compete for the small minority of remaining agricultural land.

However, one of the striking features was the range of diversity within each of the three agricultural divisions of Germany: south, north, and east. An important factor that affected population density and emigration in the northwest, and made itself felt in other regions of Germany as well, was the rise and subsequent demise of cottage textile production and other forms of rural industry. In the Minden and Osnabrück areas in the northwest, the decline of the handloom linen industry was the prime factor in precipitating the mass exodus of the 1840s and 1850s. It undoubtedly played an important role in the Black Forest region of Württemberg and other areas of southwest Germany as well. By contrast, the areas with the lowest rates of emigration throughout Germany were those where modern, mechanized industry developed (sometimes but not always on the foundations of cottage industry). By 1860, population losses slowed considerably in the Neckar district of Württemberg (including the city of Stuttgart) as modern industrialization got underway. The Ruhr industrial district showed minor population outflows only in a couple of crisis periods, and the single loss sustained by Berlin occurred in the cholera years around 1850. The transition from cottage industry to more mechanized forms of production was not without temporary setbacks in Silesia, but it was successful enough to keep population losses low, as was also the case in neighboring Saxony, the most industrialized state in Germany.

In general, most cities had low emigration rates and also had the effect of retarding emigration from their immediate hinterlands. Immigrants from the Hanseatic port cities were specifically enumerated in U.S. censuses, showing that although the docks were within walking distance, the immigration rate from Hamburg was less than half of the national average, and that it was even lower for Lubeck, which was not surprising because it faced east toward the Baltic. While the rate for Bremen was slightly above average, it appears that much of it involved temporary sojourners.

Another development that came into play was the agrarian reforms, commonly known as the *Bauernbefreiung* (peasant emancipation). One obvious way in which they promoted emigration was by helping to make land just another freely disposable commodity that could be turned into cash at any time in order to finance the journey. More important, however, were the structural changes within the rural population precipitated by these reforms, particularly by the division of common lands. In northwest Germany the division of common lands (*Gemeinheitsteilung*) was often mentioned as a factor by emigrants of the tenant cottager class, so-called *Heuerleute*. This is not to say that they clung to a precapitalistic, communal ethos. What they opposed was the manner in which the reforms were carried out. In the northwest, division practices usually followed the biblical principle: "To him that hath shall be given; to him that hath not shall be taken away even that which he hath." Use of the commons as a source of pasture, fuel, or fertilizer were customary privileges but not legal rights for *Heuerleute*, and were usually disregarded in the process of division. Contemporary descriptions echo a standard refrain: "The *Heuerleute* went away empty handed."

In contrast to the bimodal social structure in northwest Germany—relatively prosperous peasant proprietors and propertyless tenants—there was a much broader range of property holding in regions of partible inheritance in the southwest. Nevertheless, since village self-administration was dominated by the peasant elite ("horse farmers" in the local parlance, in contrast to "cow farmers," who had to rely on cattle as draft animals, and "goat farmers," who could not even support a milk cow and combined subsistence agriculture with other jobs), the division of the commons followed similar patterns as in the northwest. In fact, even in areas where the commons remained undivided, there was a tendency to restrict the access of the rural lower classes, resulting in polarization despite a surface impression of traditional continuity.

Although peasant emancipation in East Elbia required land cessions to the nobility, class differentiation within the peasantry was as important as the conflict between peasant and noble. But even for the rural lower classes in the east, the reforms had at least a short-term positive effect, making possible the founding of new households on marginal land that peasants or nobles obtained through the division of commons but could not efficiently use themselves. These groups of *Neubauer* (new farmers) were the motor of agricultural intensification and population growth in the short run. However, this process had its greatest effect before 1840 and had fully run its course by 1865. What looked like a way out to the first generation experiencing peasant emancipation turned out to be a

blind alley for the second. And it was just at this point in time that the
focus of German emigration shifted eastward and took on mass proportions east of the Elbe.

One advantage of equal inheritance was that most people owned at
least a bit of land, even if not enough to live from. But since land was
expensive (sometimes one hundred times the price for U. S. government
land in the 1840s), even a small parcel would bring enough money when
sold to finance the passage to America. But one of the major downsides
of partible inheritance was a splintering of holdings. When David Böp-
pele married shortly before leaving his Württemberg village for America
in 1860, he had only his clothes, a silver watch, and one hundred guilders
to his name; his wife brought in another two hundred guilders, so about
$120 between them. Although David's father owned eighteen parcels of
land, none of them was as large as half an acre. Another Württemberg
immigrant wrote in 1854, two years after his arrival, "I'd rather have one
American citizenship than 25 in Blaubeuren, because in America you can
amount to something, but over there it's the opposite." In his next letter,
he advised his brother not to follow him until he could afford to take his
wife and three children along: "You just have to hang on in this vale of
tears until the time of your redemption draws nigh." Their sister added a
postscript: "we wish you were here with us . . . then you would be happy
and relieved from poverty and cares, in America you have no cares about
sustenance, just a prayer to God for health, then you will always have
your livelihood, and much better to eat than in Germany, you'll see that
for yourself."

The situation driving emigration in northwest Germany was laid out
in the "parting shot" of the Catholic tenant farmer Johann Hennerich
Buhr, sent to a local official back home from the safe distance of the
North Sea coast just before he shipped out for Missouri in 1833. It lays
out the conflicts between the landowners (*Bauern*) and the tenant farmers
(*Heuerleute*) and the grievances of the latter:

> Since I embarked on my journey the 23rd of July, and couldn't see how
> I could live any longer in this locale, I find myself moved to write to
> you, and the whole configuration of the matter, how the landowners
> handle it with the tenant farmers. First of all, you have to pay him the
> heavy rent moneys for the poor ground. Secondly, you have to help
> him with so much labor that you just can't take it anymore, so that you

have to do your own work by night. Because by day you have to help the farmers, as much as they want you to. If the poor tenant farmer wants to earn some day wages: Oh no, you should help me, or else get out of my cottage right away. . . . They say from one year to the next, that things will get different. But it remains so, just like it was, and it keeps getting worse. . . . The landowners are eating up the tenant farmers.

One emigrant song circulating at the time commenced with the ambiguous line: *Hier sind wir nur Bauernsklaven*. Although this is often taken to mean that here we are only "peasant slaves," a more plausible translation is "slaves of the (landowning) peasants." The next verse confirms this, predicting that the owners' cottages will soon stand empty and be used to stable goats, while their land will grow up in brush or heath. Such tensions between landowners and tenants were widespread in northwest Germany, though one should not overgeneralize. There were *Heuerleute*, such as my Toedebusch ancestors from Melle, who were renting from four different landowners when each of their four children were born before they emigrated. However, there were also others, such as my Niendieker ancestors on the outskirts of Osnabrück, who rented from the same peasant proprietors over two generations. There are even rare instances when a propertied peasant and his tenant *Heuerleute* emigrated together.

The main motivations for emigration were certainly economic, and the rural lower classes did not have the same political consciousness as the middle-class revolutionaries of 1848, but one should not forget how closely economic hardship and political powerlessness were intertwined. This is reflected in the "Columbuslied," a song apparently written by a recent immigrant to Philadelphia or Baltimore in the early 1830s that circulated widely in the region of Osnabrück, southern Oldenburg, and northern Westphalia. It came to the attention of Prussian authorities, who noted that it was on everyone's lips and was eagerly grasped by the "rabble." It must have struck a responsive chord, because it had spread to the Rhineland by 1840, and from there to Milwaukee and back. Other versions made their way into collections of folk songs as far away as Alsace in 1884 and Baden in 1910.

Hail Columbus, praise to thee,
We laud thee high eternally
Thou has shown to us the way
Out of our hard servitude,
To save us, if we only dare
To bid our Fatherland farewell.

So the song begins, and continues through forty-eight more stanzas of spiteful and bitter doggerel. It speaks of the chains of slavery, of hunger and cares, of princes "who drive us to despair," their courts "who consume our marrow," their "brood of rats," the ministries, oppressive taxes of all kinds, and a class system of injustice.

This is contrasted with the egalitarianism of America, "where the man from every station as a true brother is honored high." Class distinctions are unknown: "The wife of the mayor sweeps right along with the wife of the broom maker." If anything, class prejudices are reversed: "Here in the Promised Land the noble is despised by all / . . . and even the haughty baron counts for no more than the farmer's son."

But American freedom also has its more practical aspects: "Here the man from every station is free to hunt and fish." Guild restrictions, too, are unknown, for "Here anyone who wants to can practice a trade if he's able." Taxes, where they exist at all, are moderate, "For we know no excise here / On salt or wine, on schnapps or beer." Military service is purely voluntary, in contrast to Europe, "Where with his twentieth year your son / Is drilled by a barbarian." Throughout the whole song, the perception is very apparent that economic hardships are closely intertwined with political injustice.

While regional patterns of emigration can be quite revealing, any explanation of the phenomenon is incomplete without an examination of which people actually left, and where they fit into the socioeconomic structure of their places of origin. How literally is one to take an officially recorded emigration motive, "Kann nicht mehr leben" (Can't live anymore)? Were emigrants responding to absolute, or only to relative, deprivation, or indeed merely to the fact that expectations were rising even more quickly than living standards? Real wages of German artisans and industrial workers were higher in the 1820s than for the whole next three decades. The harvest failures of the mid-forties and the early fifties hit especially hard.

The selectivity of emigration relative to the local social structure is also revealing. Of the author's sixteen great-great-grandparents (and a few that extend back six generations), there was only one couple from the landed peasant class, and even they could not immediately inherit until the stepfather was ready to hand over the farm. All the rest were tenant farmers (*Heuerleute*) or small-scale artisans with little or no real property. This is fairly typical for the emigrants from northwest Germany; tenants were twice as likely to emigrate as landowning farmers. Most artisans who emigrated had little in common with the proud guildmasters of legend, no craft tradition extending back over generations, no shop full of apprentices, little or no real estate. In terms of the money they took along, married artisans were no better off than *Heuerleute*, and single artisans in the same situation as farmhands. Judging by the money they took along, many immigrants had little or no cash left by the time they reached their destination.

Along with the economic push factors behind German emigration, there were social grievances at work as well. Most German states besides Prussia imposed or reimposed marriage restrictions, which had been abolished in those areas under Napoleonic occupation. The intent was to keep the poor relief rolls from being burdened as a result of "pauper weddings." But authorities were much more successful in preventing pauper weddings than pauper births, so that rates of illegitimacy steadily climbed in the early nineteenth century. Such authoritarian measures promoted emigration both directly and indirectly. In Mecklenburg, marriage permits were granted to couples with children on the condition that they would leave and waive their rights to poor relief. Some couples also married aboard ships on their way to America.

On occasion, sexual scandals of one kind or another impelled people to emigrate. One divorcing couple from Braunschweig literally never wanted to see each other again: one spouse registered for emigration to America, the other to Australia. Some did not bother to divorce. Organist and choir director Johannes Koester left for America in 1858, accompanied by a woman twenty-four years his junior who had been a member of his choir. Over the next four years he wrote some twenty-one letters back to his wife, with rather imperious directives in matters of business or childrearing, disingenuously instructing her to keep his address secret to avoid moochers. No record of divorce or remarriage has survived, but in the 1860 census of St. Louis he and "Wilhelmina Koester" were representing themselves as man and wife, a relationship that ultimately produced seven children. Koester established himself in Bloomington, Illinois, first founding his own school and then from 1871 until his death in 1893 editing a German weekly, respected enough to rate an entry in the county "mug book." Rev. August Schmieding experienced a similar form of transatlantic redemption. The charismatic pastor in the county of Herford, left as a widower with six children at age forty, began an intimate relationship with his domestic servant that resulted in her pregnancy. Resisting pressure from church authorities to marry the woman, he resigned his pastorate and immigrated to America in 1851 with his children, following his brother to St. Louis. But within months, a delegation from Quincy, Illinois, invited him there to found a congregation, which quickly grew and flourished. Schmieding's background could hardly have been a secret in a town that was the prime destination of Herford immigrants.

Frieda Brühns paid a higher price for her indiscretion, as women often do. Married by age twenty-three, she became pregnant from an affair with the overseer of her father's estate and immigrated with him to New York, where their son Freddy was born in 1885. Disowned by her family, she corresponded only with her in-laws in Germany. In 1910, she lived with her husband, son, daughter-in-law, and a grandchild in a rented tenement in Upper Manhattan, where her husband worked as a laundry man. By 1930, she was a widow, living with her son in Alameda, California, still renters.

In other cases, it is less clear whether emigration was the result of scandal. Johann and Rebecka Witten departed for America three weeks after their wedding in 1882, four months before their first child was born. But premarital pregnancy or even out-of-wedlock birth was not uncommon at that time and place, and their first destination was Rebecka's brother's home in Illinois. Economics probably played a larger role; their previous jobs as boarding farmhands were open only to the unmarried. In any case, their economic calculations paid off; the Wittens came to own more than one thousand acres of farmland in Washington State, and set up all eight of their children on commodious farms.

During the mid-nineteenth century, many of the German states (again, except for Prussia) attempted to export their social problems overseas. Unlike Britain and France, they lacked colonies of their own for dumping grounds, but the burgeoning immigration traffic presented a tempting opportunity to send their "undesirables" surreptitiously to the United States. Two categories of emigrants were given state or municipal financial assistance to pay for the passage. The smaller group consisted of persons sentenced to prison or reformatory terms for crimes or what was considered criminal behavior at the time. They were offered remission of their remaining sentences if they accepted a one-way ticket to America. The bulk of assisted emigrants had no criminal record, but the local authorities (frequently with the state government chipping in some portion) paid all or part of their passage, assuming they would be a burden on local poor relief then and in the foreseeable future, and would ultimately cost far more than the one-time payment of a ticket. No one has counted them for all of Germany, but most of the German states except for Prussia were involved in the practice. There were thousands of people in the deportee category, and tens of thousands who were subsidized.

What both groups had in common was the characteristic of being considered undesirable by the authorities. The 1840 emigration records of the Hanoverian township of Dissen include the following notation after the entry of a twenty-six-year-old day laborer who shall remain nameless: "The original good-for-nothing, the community took a collection to get rid of him." In another typical case from Württemberg, an unwed mother with two children and a third on the way applied to village authorities for forty-five guilders to subsidize their passage to America in 1857. The council agreed, since they "would shortly become public charges" anyway. But she wrote again from Le Havre claiming they needed more money for food on the voyage, or they would be forced to turn back. The village elders grudgingly decided to "sacrifice from the treasury another 25 guilders . . . for this loose creature." She, her children, and her common-law husband Daniel Klinger from the next village over, arrived together in New York on July 21, 1857. A propertyless laborer in 1860, he had accumulated $600 by 1870.

As in these cases, subsidized emigration often took place at the municipal or county level and was not always systematically recorded at higher levels of administration. But one can safely say that it reached its peak in the late 1840s and the 1850s, and while it took place to some extent all across Germany, southwest Germany was the focus of the heaviest subsidization, as it was of the heaviest emigration. Leading the way was the state of Baden, which expended 1.6 million gulden or about $650,000 to subsidize emigration between 1850 and 1855—enough to pay the way for nearly eighteen thousand emigrants, or to put it another way, a good quarter of all the state's emigrants during these years. Baden did take measures to see that its subsidized emigrants had some help getting on their feet when they arrived, providing beyond mere passage a sum of ten gulden per capita, and twenty guilders for each head of family, about $4 or $8 respectively, at a time when common laborers in America often worked for $1 per day or less.

The neighboring state of Württemberg also engaged in exporting its social problems, though not to the same extent. In some cases such as the one above, authorities merely topped off the funds of people who had some resources of their own, but not enough to pay their passage. Württemberg expended perhaps 300,000 gulden (some $120,000) on subsidization between 1854 and 1870, with the bulk falling in the first couple of years. Subsidies in 1854 amounted to 2 percent of all exported funds; in 1855 it amounted to 4 percent of a much smaller total. Subsidies may have been higher in the late forties; in 1848 they came to 10 percent or more of the total funds exported from the two most emigration prone of the four districts of the kingdom. In fact, for one county (Böblingen), subsidies equaled private funds exported in 1851 and 1852.

From an American point of view, subsidized immigrants often slipped in unnoticed and aroused little public debate, but one great exception was the "Grosszimmern Affair" of 1846. This involved some 674 emigrants from the Hesse-Darmstadt village of the same name who turned up "bitterly disappointed, sick, miserable, and hungry" in New York. They were all supplied with bills of exchange for a New York bank, but only for a sum that amounted to seventeen cents per head, so most of them ended up in the poorhouse. This aroused general resentment and indignation, not just among Americans but also from the German Society of New York against the "highly unreasonable demands" that they take care of these paupers, and from the German population generally, which saw its public image endangered. However, it took until 1875 before the United States outlawed this practice.

Although German officials were happy to be rid of some emigrants, there were others whose departure they attempted to prevent: men of military age who had not yet served or received an exemption. But this was easier said than done. The ports of Bremen and Hamburg were sovereign city-states, and they were not about to turn away profitable passenger business as a favor to the Hanoverian or Prussian draft boards. One example among many is the first person in the Kamphoefner family to emigrate, an uncle five generations back named Johann Heinrich, born in 1815. In the Osnabrück archives it is reported that he obtained a six-month furlough from the army of Hanover in order to get married. His wife requested and obtained an emigration permit on July 14, 1842, with the provision that "Husband: Kamphoefner, Johann Heinrich, is not coming along. Her husband must remain behind until he has completed his military service." But the passenger lists tell a different story, as does a joint obituary of the couple, who both died within nine days of each other in 1895. They arrived together in Baltimore on October 10, 1842, on the ship *Ann*, and after a brief sojourn in New York and Cincinnati, they settled on a farm in the village of Farmer's Retreat, Indiana, near Cincinnati, along with some former neighbors from their home village of Buer.

One of the paradoxes of the emigration movement is that apparently those who could afford the trip had no real reason to leave, whereas those suffering the most serious deprivations hardly had the resources for the journey. However, one should not overstate this point. Families that could not afford passage for everyone at once often sent the husband or a son or daughter ahead to earn passage for the rest. Such was the case with Caspar Kamphoefner, another uncle five generations back, who probably left Germany a few months before or after his wife gave birth on December 1, 1844. When the wife and their three daughters applied for an emigration permit on July 20, 1849, it was noted in the document, "The husband lives in America and has sent the passage money." They arrived in New Orleans on October 31, 1849, but even with a brother in Indiana they settled in Missouri.

Over the course of the nineteenth century, travel became cheaper and more efficient both on the continent and on the ocean. Except for the rare immigrant who landed a job as a cook's helper or shoveling coal in steerage, they could not earn money while underway to America, so faster travel meant less down time when migrants had to live off savings and spend money on accommodations. This gradually lowered the poverty threshold of who was able to afford to immigrate.

Another factor that facilitated emigration was the post-Napoleonic consolidation that greatly simplified the map of German states, which were further integrated by the *Zollverein* customs union of 1834, even before the founding of the German Reich in 1871. The thirty-six customs stations on the Rhine that Gottlieb Mittelberger had encountered in 1750 were reduced to just one at the Dutch border, or at the Hanoverian border until 1866, if one traveled by land to Bremen instead. Although not as quick as the United States with its railroad building, Germany was not far behind. The first short line was opened in Bavaria in 1835. Antwerp had a rail connection with Cologne from 1842 on. More significant, especially for emigrants, was the 165-mile line from Cologne to Minden that opened in 1847, which connected with a line from Hanover to Bremen that same year. This largely replaced steamboat travel down the Weser to Bremen, which had been organized by Bremen merchants in 1842. By 1849, Hamburg also had rail connections with both Hanover and Berlin, as well as Kiel in the north. But Bremen had sealed its advantage early on with an 1832 law that assured that passengers would not suffer hunger. It required shippers to provide ninety days' worth of food and water rather than allowing emigrants to provision themselves. This may have slightly raised prices and hurt business in the short run, but in the long run the dependable reputation of Bremen shippers paid off.

In 1834, it took Hermann Steines an entire week or more to travel the 150 miles from Solingen to Bremen by stagecoach. Two decades later in 1854, John Bauer covered nearly twice that distance from Bruchsal in Baden in three days despite a day's layover on Sunday, as he wrote home: "It was on March 11th when I boarded the steamboat in Mannheim with many other emigrants and the moon lit up the Rhine so splendidly as I said farewell." Starting before daybreak, he reached Cologne before midnight. "We had to stay until Monday the 13th because on that day an extra train went from Cologne to Bremen. We boarded the train in the morning of the 13th, . . . and at 12 o'clock at night we came to Bremen."

For Steines and other emigrants from the northwest quadrant of Germany, Bremen was the obvious port of choice. It was closest and most accessible, and offered other advantages as well. For southwest Germans like John Bauer, Bremen was only one of a number of competing ports of embarkation within similar proximity. For emigrants from two Württemberg counties south of Stuttgart over the course of the nineteenth century, Bremen was the leading port, accounting for over one-third of the total. Next in line was French Le Havre, with one-quarter, while Hamburg was a distant third with 11 percent. Some 8 percent left from Belgian Antwerp, followed by London and Liverpool with 7 and 6 percent, respectively. Only 4 percent left from the Netherlands, primarily Rotterdam. Over 95 percent of them landed in New York, with New Orleans a distant second, but this did not hold true for all Germans. For some, the Crescent City proved to be the "back door to the land of plenty."

For areas east of the Elbe, the closest port was Hamburg, which lies about eighty miles northeast of Bremen. But Bremen's good rail connections and solid reputation allowed it to compete for this traffic as well. A rail line built in the 1870s stretching eastward from Bremerhaven to Magdeburg and Berlin was dubbed the "Amerikalinie" because it was used by so many emigrants from eastern areas of Germany and farther east beyond its borders. In the course of the nineteenth century, Bremen carried more than double the emigrant traffic as Hamburg, and there were only a few years when the latter held the lead. Not all Hamburg passengers traveled directly to America; about 20 percent changed ships, usually sailing to England and crossing by rail to Liverpool where they embarked for the transatlantic leg.

The voyage to America was a new and daunting experience for immigrants, few of whom had seen the ocean before, or even traveled on a river steamer for that matter. Immigrants who had gone ahead often tried to reassure potential followers, saying that the journey was "beschwerlich, aber nicht gefährlich": arduous, but not dangerous. For those who could afford a cabin passage, like Rev. Hermann Garlichs and his bride Adelheid von Borries, their honeymoon voyage in 1835 was, except for some initial seasickness, more like a pleasure cruise with warm weather along the southern route. They dined occasionally with the captain and spent much time reading on deck. As they noted in their journal: "On December 27th arrival in N. Orleans after a voyage of 51 days all without storm or other trouble."

For steerage passengers it was much rougher. One of 118 passengers on the *Bark Constitution*, which departed Bremen on May 20, 1837, the writer Friedrich Gerstaecker noted, "The rocking of the ship now became significant, and by God was that an amusing pleasure to observe all the faces that the seasick folks were making, because I myself, along with 6 or 7 others, were so far totally spared of it, and hope it stays that way." Ten days later he remarked, "The gurgling of people throwing up is my evening serenade." Although he complained about the crowding and unpleasant smells in steerage, Gerstaecker also wrote of various amusements on board: music, dancing, even free punch on the Fourth of July, resulting, as he noted, in "general hangover!!!!!"

Shipwrecks were relatively rare occurrences even in the days of sail. River steamboats in America were certainly more dangerous. The two-month passage in the steerage of a sailing vessel was not an experience that most people would be eager to repeat, but seasickness was not fatal, even if some sufferers felt like they wanted to die. Occasionally an outbreak of cholera could decimate a ship's population. But despite the discomforts, it was not unusual for a ship to arrive in America with a net gain in passengers. For example, another immigrant crossing the Atlantic in 1837 on the way to Cape Girardeau, Missouri, noted, "Instead of decreasing we have multiplied. Frau Sperling . . . gave birth to a baby girl last night." Back around 1980, I quoted this letter at a lecture in Cape Girardeau. A gray-haired lady in the audience commented, "That baby born on the ship was my great-grandma."

Recent research based on a sampling of nearly six hundred thousand passengers listed on some 2,600 ships arriving in the U.S. between 1820 and 1860 has revised the image of the ocean passage in the days of sail. In contrast to anecdotal reports of horrendous mortality rates, overall losses came to less than 1 percent (1.5 percent including deaths soon after arrival), and even that was highly concentrated in a few ships that experienced epidemics. The length of the voyage averaged about forty-five days from Bremen to New York, probably a little less from Atlantic ports like Antwerp or Le Havre where some Germans also embarked. But New Orleans or Galveston added another week or two to the journey.

By the 1850s, when six brothers and sisters of the Klinger family came over one after another, travel had become fairly routine. After the first daughter emigrated to New York she wrote back a year or so later: "You needn't be so afraid of America, when you come to America just imagine you were moving to Stuttgart, that's how many Germans you can see here. And as far as the Americans are concerned, whites and blacks, they won't harm you, since the blacks are very happy when you don't do anything to them, the only thing is the problem with the language."

The voyage could still be unpleasant, indeed terrifying, if one encountered a storm, as some Catholic immigrants from near Luxemburg did in 1854: "We were now having such a terrible storm that we thought the ship would be torn apart. . . . We had to hold on as tight as we could to keep from falling out. Then we all started again and prayed 17 rosaries before we stopped. All those who didn't know how to pray had to learn."

If not fighting storms, immigrants still had to fight boredom. A popular German novel based on actual immigrant letters describes a voyage in 1868: "We were beginning to think that Amerika wouldn't come at all. One of them said, look here you all, this is not going right, and one of these days we're going to fall off the earth. . . . We had all sat and laid ourselves stiff, because we couldn't work anything off. Too bad that we didn't have a few cords of wood to split." He still traveled on a sailing ship, one of the few that had not been replaced by steamships by the end of the 1860s.

The British ship *Great Western* made the first crossing under steam power in 1838, but initially only wealthy merchants could afford travel on fast packet ships such as this. Steam service was introduced from Bremen in 1847 and from Hamburg in 1850, but as late as 1854 less than 2 percent of all immigrants to New York arrived by steamship. From then on, travel by steam steadily gained ground, accounting for nearly one-third of New York immigrant arrivals in 1861, four-fifths by 1867, and over nine-tenths by 1870. Hamburg saw the end of immigrant transport by sail in 1873, Bremen in 1875. The switch to steamships cut the length of the journey down to about two weeks, and greatly lowered mortality as well. Between 1864 and 1869, the death rate on steamships arriving in New York was down to 0.2 percent, two per thousand. There was still an average of about one shipwreck per year on the Atlantic in the 1870s and 1880s.

As vessels grew safer, sturdier, larger, and faster, ocean crossings became more of an adventure than an ordeal. An immigrant wrote from Pittsburgh shortly after his arrival in 1881, "The ship we took was call[ed] the *Strassburg*, had 63,180 cubic meters, was 153 paces long, 20 wide, 1750 passengers with the officers, sailors, servants 1800 persons. We were fed pretty well also had no storms except 2 times but then it rocked so that everything that wasn't tied down fell about. Also no ship goes down in a storm unless it runs into a rock" (or an iceberg, one might add).

By the end of the nineteenth century, coming to America was no longer necessarily a permanent move. Some German relatives reconnected with my Niendieker great-great grandparents in 1904, and here is what they wrote: "I also must tell about father, that he was in America ten years ago [1892], but he had a bad experience there and that came about so: . . . father let himself be persuaded by a friend to come along to America, but in Castle Garden his friend left him behind, he had to wait around there for 24 hours, and only because of a letter he happened to have with him could he go to Philadelphia, he was there 14 weeks all told. He didn't know you, otherwise he would have visited you." As will be seen, the existence of personal connections played an important role in determining just where in America German immigrants would settle.

3

German Settlement Patterns in Nineteenth-Century America

A LIGHTNING BOLT STRUCK THE CHURCH TOWER in Wehdem, Westphalia, in 1920, causing extensive damage, but this flash also illuminated an important aspect of the migration process. With Germany just emerging from the devastation of World War I, an appeal went out to its "children" in America. And former Wehdemers responded, contributing almost 120,000 Marks, a sum equivalent to about $2,000 back then, or $25,000 at present—enough not only to repair the damage, but also to repaint the whole inside of the sanctuary. More interesting than the amount, however, is the geographic source of the donations. Although responses came from half a dozen states, almost two-thirds of the money came from the vicinity of Brenham, Texas. It had been a leading destination of Wehdem's immigrants since before the Civil War, some of whom had founded a nearby settlement called New Wehdem. Something similar occurred in 1870 with Talheim, a village of just one thousand inhabitants in Württemberg. In a wave of patriotic enthusiasm, twenty-four of its former inhabitants, all living in Utica, New York, took up a collection and raised $89, which they sent back to the homeland in support of Germany's war with France. They were all listed by name and dollar amount in the newspaper at the county seat in Tuttlingen. The small industrial city of Utica attracted about one-fifth of the total immigration from Talheim across North America.

Both incidents illustrate the importance and ubiquity of chain migration. Wherever the initial migrants from a given local area happen to settle (whether brought there by chance, propaganda, recruitment, or whatever), unless they met with a complete disaster, they continued to attract others from their locality and formed a local concentration. In this enterprise, immigrant letters played an important, perhaps crucial, role.

Nineteenth-century German conservatives often painted emigration as irrational, looking for scapegoats in order to deny the genuine socioeconomic causes fueling "America fever," as they stigmatized this mass exodus. They perceived it as a rejection of their authority, and of the existing social order, and rightly so. They often blamed emigration agents and propaganda for the exodus, claiming that the common folk could not be trusted to act in their own self-interest, and needed to be "protected" by their "betters." Although there were a few group emigrations led by the clergy, German pastors often interpreted Psalm 37:3 as a command to stay at home and make the best of things. English translations usually render it as a promise with no such implications: "Trust in the Lord and do good; so shalt thou dwell in the land, and verily thou shalt be fed."

Even accounts of immigration from the American side, although they view it more positively, also tend to overestimate the influence of guidebooks, and focus undue attention on immigration societies and group migration projects. When one examines immigrants' correspondence and their patterns of settlement across America, it leaves a contrasting impression. There is little evidence of influence by top-down sources of information and motivation, such as guidebooks, emigration societies, and agents, reflected in the letters and migration behavior of actual immigrants. Instead, the writings of ordinary immigrants offered nuanced advice to potential followers among their relatives, friends, and acquaintances. The picture that emerges is of autonomous immigrants quite skeptical of any higher authority, but still not exactly the rugged individualists celebrated by American entrepreneurs. Except for the great leap of faith in crossing the ocean, German immigrants tried to minimize risk by drawing upon personal ties and community resources to cushion their entry into a new society and economy.

Apart from a brief attempt by some southwestern German states in the 1840s and 1850s to subsidize emigration and export their social problems, most German states viewed the transatlantic movement with hostility. Bavaria went so far as to forbid advertising for emigration entirely. As one emigration historian observes, "Behind this prohibition of advertising stood the opinion that there were no economic or socio-political grounds for emigration." She cites an official in Munich who contended in 1852 that "the decision to emigrate for so many is only brought about through deception." For the government, advertisers, agents, and social democrats all had the same goal, to arouse discontent in the population and to incite them to emigrate when there were really no grounds for it.

This prevailing attitude of the mid-nineteenth century is reflected clearly in the observations of the Prussian statistician Thilo Bödicker, even if he represented a dissenting minority: "Of course, it is not uncommonly asserted that most of those who migrate to America do poorly not just at the beginning, but also in the long term, that it is a case of an artificially engendered quest for an imaginary success, that immigration is thus without any real grounds." Bödicker saw things differently; if immigrants were not at least moderately successful, a migration stream would soon dry up: "This was proven not very long ago by the emigration to Hungary. Appearing suddenly on the scene, it disappeared just as quickly once one saw some of the emigrants come back again without the money they had taken along with them." Quite similar comments were made by a statistician in the not-so-grand Duchy of Oldenburg, where emigration to "other European states" had shot up to 330 in the three years from 1858 to 1860 before falling back into insignificance: "This was the trek to Hungary, which soon came to an end because of the disappointed expectations of those who emigrated." During the five years beginning in 1860, there were one hundred in-migrants to Oldenburg (probably returnees) recorded from that part of the world.

Bödicker recognized the importance of personal contacts in easing the shocks of adjustment to the new land: "By now, most of our emigrants don't need any such instruction, at least for the beginning; *the great majority seeks out friends and relatives*" [emphasis original]. Although conceding that there were occasional forgeries, this Prussian official argued for the basic trustworthiness of immigrant letters: "If the majority of these representations of the situation were made up, they would soon lose their power of attraction." Moreover, he was skeptical whether agents by themselves could have much impact on immigration: "Only where the seed finds a cultivated field, is it able to sprout and grow, and thus the enticements of the agents and subagents would be in vain if they did not find a well-prepared terrain."

Although Bödicker through his statistical work had gained a rather realistic assessment of the forces driving German emigration, it is apparent that he was fighting an uphill battle within the Prussian bureaucracy. Perhaps as a concession to his superiors, the statistical compilation that Bödicker edited included selections reprinted from Gottlieb Mittelberger's pessimistic account, which was dubious even when it first appeared and more than a century out of date by its republication in 1874.

If there was a time when emigration guidebooks and propaganda did have an appreciable influence on emigration, it was at the outset of the movement. The first time that emigration from Germany surpassed the ten-thousand mark was 1832. Since food prices were stable at that time and real wages were rising slightly, one should perhaps look beyond the economic realm for an explanation. How much credit is due to Gottfried Duden's famous 1829 guidebook in stimulating emigration or attracting Germans remains open to question. One immigrant wrote from St. Charles, Missouri, near Duden's site in 1833, "The other families . . . who made the journey with us, traveled another 30 miles further near Duden, they like it very well there too." The casual way Duden is mentioned in immigrant letters such as this suggests that he was a household name among the folks back home. As late as 1850, Missouri was home to more Germans than any state besides New York, Pennsylvania, and Ohio, probably thanks to Duden. But a decade later, Illinois had attracted nearly 50 percent more Germans than Missouri without any Duden to plug for it, and Wisconsin had also pulled ahead.

The Duden book was especially influential in areas such as northwest Germany that did not yet have an established migration tradition in 1830. His influence can be seen in many of the first Germans in Missouri, such as the letter writer cited above and others from the same village like my Groenemann ancestors who followed the next year, taking the much more arduous, month-long Duden route from the east coast harbor of Baltimore across the Appalachians on the National Road down to the Ohio River. If they had sailed to New Orleans, they could have taken a steamboat directly up the Mississippi to their destination in just over a week. Duden was not without his critics; some denounced him as a *Lügenhund* (lying dog). But the pioneers who followed his advice were apparently satisfied enough with what they found; at least they kept bringing more of their compatriots after them.

When reports from America were negative, the reaction could be very different. The year 1855 recorded the highest grain and potato prices and the lowest real wages of the nineteenth century in Germany. And yet, as the Mecklenburg writer and social critic Fritz Reuter alertly noted in July of that year, there was a decline in immigration. The number of Germans arriving in New York in April 1855 was not even one-fifth the number of the previous year. It could not, he thought, be explained by the outbreak of the Crimean War or by European government measures to discourage emigration. "That the Know-Nothings alone or just partially are responsible for this sudden decline doesn't seem possible, since their existence is still much too recent for them to have been sufficiently known in Germany at the time of embarkation or before." However, Reuter failed to come up with a better explanation, and finally concluded, "there's no doubt that the Know Nothings and the temperance bill will scare off many prospective immigrants, especially now when they read how in Louisville the Know Nothings en masse attacked the most quiet and harmless Germans and mistreated them, without the least bit of provocation." In fact, the incident just described was merely a warm-up for the big Louisville riot of August 1855, which resulted in more than twenty deaths. In its wake, many recent emigrants no doubt warned off potential followers, as did Christian Lenz, who had been an eyewitness of "how they ran through the streets like the screaming seven to see human blood." Although his nephews had been considering emigration, Lenz, like many other immigrants at the time, now discouraged them in the most dramatic terms: "Now, dear brother should anyone else move to America, no—stay where you were born . . . even if there is nothing besides bread and potatoes and salt that is still better than meat three times a day in a foreign country."

The influence of guidebooks and propaganda, on the other hand, has often been exaggerated, both by contemporaries and by subsequent historians. References to guidebooks are quite rare in the thousands of surviving immigrant letters. Emigration societies were seldom mentioned except by their actual participants, and their appeal seems to have been largely restricted to the educated bourgeoisie. Moreover, the few references in immigrant letters to colonization societies and guidebooks bespeak anything but confidence. Writing back to his brother-in-law in 1839, Dr. Bernhard Bruns, one of the early settlers of Westphalia,

Missouri, shows nothing but contempt for two of these publications, authored by Nicholas Hesse and Heinrich von Martels, the latter a member of the so-called Berlin Society: "Which of the two authors knows best how to lie . . . the interested reader may determine for himself—both stray too often from the path of truth, neither gained any experience as a farmer . . . . Mr. v. Martels is a shameless braggart, Mr. Hesse a miserable complainer, but at bootlicking they give one another quite a run for the money." Hesse had returned to Germany disillusioned after a rather brief sojourn in Missouri.

Dr. Bruns was of a higher educational and social level than the typical immigrant, but there is evidence that his opinion of Mr. Hesse was shared also by the rank and file of his countrymen. German authorities in the Osnabrück District had purchased one hundred copies of the Hesse book to be distributed among potential emigrants in hopes of dissuading them, but the high level of emigration from the area continued unabated. Nearby Westphalian peasants applying for emigration permits after 1840 were routinely asked whether they had read Hesse's rather pessimistic account. They just as routinely replied that they had, but would not change their minds on that account. However, the uniform wording of question and answer for case after case suggests that this was a mere formality on the part of both official and applicant. Perhaps most of the emigrants did know the book at least from hearsay, but this was not what they relied upon in making their decisions.

Emigration societies have gotten more than their share of attention, both by contemporaries and in the historical literature. They often made headlines, and their well-educated, articulate leaders left behind more firsthand accounts than ordinary immigrants. But most Germans traveled to America alone or in small groups of family or friends, without a common treasury or any formal organization. Nevertheless, there are several secular or religious group migration projects during the first half of the nineteenth century that deserve mention.

Gottfried Duden's writings attracted two different societies in 1834 to attempt colonization in the area of eastern Missouri that he had publicized in his book, the Giessen and the Solingen emigration societies (three, if one counts the so-called Berlin Society, which numbered only fourteen members). The Giessen Emigration Society was formed by two friends and members of the radical democratic student movement,

Friedrich Muench and Paul Follenius. After the failed Revolution of 1830, they wanted to found a model republic in the American west. Two shiploads totaling about five hundred persons sailed for America in 1834. From the outset, however, they were plagued by sickness and dissention, so that their organization hardly survived the ocean crossing. Their common treasury was divided up and their plan of a homogeneous settlement abandoned, although the two leaders and perhaps a dozen other families did settle in the same neighborhood in eastern Missouri made famous by Gottfried Duden's writings. The Solingen and Berlin societies were even smaller and similarly short-lived.

From eastern Germany there was also the Thuringian Emigration Society led by the brothers John und Karl Roebling, who in 1831 led a party of forty-four to establish the colony of Saxonburg about twenty-five miles from Pittsburgh. It was no more successful than other such group endeavors. The most prominent member of the group of followers that was recruited the next year was a former member of a Prussian provincial assembly named Carl Angelrodt. He was dissatisfied with the site, denounced Roebling as a swindler, demanded his money back, and effectively discredited the colony back home. The site of Saxonburg was in fact not exactly propitious; despite its proximity to Pittsburgh it has yet to surpass 1,500 inhabitants. But its fate was rather typical of such organized migration efforts. The two opponents went on to happier fates than Saxonburg itself: Angelrodt became a merchant and German Consul in St. Louis; John Roebling and his son Washington went on to fame as builders of suspension bridges, above all the Brooklyn Bridge.

The largest colonization project, and according to one German historian the biggest catastrophe, was the Society for the Protection of German Immigrants in Texas, often dubbed the *Adelsverein* (Society of Nobles). These nobles, headed by Prince Carl von Solms-Braunfels, started their colonization attempt while the Texas Republic was trying somewhat desperately to attract settlers. Over seven thousand persons were transported from Germany between 1843 and 1846, before the society went bankrupt in 1847. Promises of free land went largely unfulfilled, and few preparations were made for the arriving newcomers, so many of them died from the hardships of the trails leading inland from the ports of Galveston and Indianola. From that point on, immigration societies were regarded with deserved skepticism. Writing in 1845, a university-educated, politically liberal immigrant made no bones about his disdain for colonization schemes in general and the "protective subordination" of the *Adelsverein* in particular: "Prince Solms, the director of this company, seems to have made himself totally laughable and hated through his ignorance of democratic conditions. On my tour I met a knowledgeable man from Texas. He said, 'We will cowhide him when he comes again.' That is to say, give him a most disgraceful thrashing with a whip made of cowhide."

The mistrust exhibited by ordinary immigrants toward such emigration societies was perhaps even greater than that shown by the more educated. Nor did religious societies fare much better than secular ones in this respect. Religious minorities in general had a stronger propensity for emigration than the rest of society. This was particularly true for Jews (who made up about twice the share of the emigration as they did of the population, though still only a tiny percentage), but Mennonites in Bavaria also had a stronger propensity to emigrate than their neighbors. In terms of size, the most important religious-group migration was that of the so-called Old Lutherans in the 1830s and 1840s. Resisting the forced merger of the Lutheran and Reformed denominations, some Germans sought refuge in Australia, but three main groups looked to America for religious freedom. One group from Pomerania and Silesia, led by Pastor William Grabau, settled in Buffalo and Milwaukee, while a second from Bavarian Franconia settled in Michigan. A group from Saxony, often called Stephanites after their bishop Martin Stephan, settled in southeast Missouri.

One should not overemphasize the significance of any of these projects. Even in the peak year of 1843, no more than 1,600 Old Lutherans emigrated to America, thus comprising only a tenth of the total German immigration volume for that year. However, they did make up a rather large proportion of emigrants from east of the Elbe during that era. Despite the low levels of immigration in the early years, the organized migrants from Giessen and Solingen made up only 3 percent of all the Germans arriving in 1834. Even the largest of these projects, the *Adelsverein*, transported only 6 percent of all immigrants coming over between 1843 and 1846, although it did account for a large share of those going to Texas.

Another indication of the relatively small impact of such organized migrants is the regional composition of the German population in the states where the colonies were located. Despite the settlement of the Giessen Society from Hesse and Old Lutherans from Saxony, Hessians and Saxons made up a lower proportion of Germans in Missouri than in the nation as a whole. Despite the homogeneous Lutheran settlement of Bavarian Franconians in the Frankenmuth area of Michigan, the state as a whole attracted less than its share of Bavarians. Wisconsin did attract a large settlement from eastern Germany, but this was just as true of Mecklenburgers, who did not suffer any religious grievances, as of Pomeranians, who did. The Badger State also had a large population of Catholics from Rhineland Prussia who came over without any group organization, forming homogeneous communities in what came to be called the "Holyland" because of all the villages named after saints.

The state where organized immigration had the most visible impact on the makeup of its German population as a whole was Texas. This was reflected particularly in the large number of settlers from Nassau, home of *Adelsverein* leader Prince Solms-Braunfels. But here, too, persons actually transported by the society were less important than the relatives and friends who came after them. Although the *Adelsverein* met its demise by 1848, the number of Germans living in Texas more than doubled between 1850 and 1860, and even of the Germans present in 1850, not all had been recruited or transported by the *Verein*. The Rhine Prussian village of Hambach provides a good illustration of the *Verein's* influence and also its limits. Ten people left in 1844 and eight more in 1846 bound for Texas, a total of eighteen presumably recruited and transported by the *Verein*. But in 1851 a larger group of twenty-seven immigrants followed on their own, while only three other emigrants from this village went anywhere else but Texas.

The Germans have a saying: "Lies have short legs," which certainly applies to immigration propaganda. If the advertisements were not accurate, they only worked for a season; thereafter, potential migrants would be warned off by letters from relatives and friends. For example, in 1847 there was a major recruitment campaign for South Africa in the Osnabrück region, which attracted nearly two hundred immigrants, including thirty-six from nearby Westerkappeln. But upon arrival in the Cape Colony, they encountered unfulfilled promises and great privation. As a result, they were apparently the only Westerkappelners in the entire nineteenth century who emigrated to South Africa. The average

European peasant was not nearly as credulous as has often been claimed. On-site reports from personal acquaintances at the potential destination exercised a constant control over the trustworthiness of immigration propaganda and agents.

Agents appear somewhat more frequently in immigrant letters than guidebooks or emigration societies, but primarily as facilitators, not as promoters of emigration. Potential followers were often advised as to the dependability of a particular agent or how they could get the best deal. One Württemberg immigrant wrote back in 1854 advising potential followers of the name and address of a ship's agent in Bremen who could give him an exact quote "and save 30 to 40 guilders which the subagent would stick in his sack." But another from Baden wrote that at Bremen in that peak year "the crowd of emigrants was so large that the price of passage rose to 105–108 guilders for a poor berth & 120 guilders for a better one, but since I already had a ticket I could go for 96 guilders."

Negative experiences were just as readily reported as positive ones. In 1854, an immigrant from eastern Westphalia described the hardships of his ocean passage on an English sailing vessel and warned, "Don't anyone let himself be misled into booking with Korte, the safest is with Buddl in Bremen and his agent is Witte in Herford." According to him, of 465 passengers on the ship, 110 died on the voyage, although the U. S. passenger list only records sixty-four dead. According to the writer, the passengers filed a complaint through the German Society of New Orleans, and the captain and crew were arrested, and the ship seized. Newspaper reports indicate that twenty-one German passengers did indeed sue for $500 each, but the defendants claimed the deaths were the result of cholera that some passengers had brought on board, and the judge ruled in favor of the ship's captain. In any case, this kind of mortality was an exception. Despite this harrowing experience and the fact that his sister had died on the voyage, even this writer did not see his emigration as being totally negative: "Here nobody has such worries about sustenance as over there; I wouldn't advise anyone against it, nor for it, going to America."

This formulation, not advising for or against, shows up repeatedly in German immigrant letters across time and place. A settler in Wisconsin wrote back to the Prussian Rhineland in 1841: "Still, I won't advise anyone for or against, to come over. Because one likes it, the other doesn't. . . . Still, we're quite contented, and have no desire to go back." It comes up in a letter written back to Oldenburg from near Oldenburg, Indiana, in 1867: "Also, Arnold Mucker wrote that they probably want to come to America. I would be glad if they would come to me, because I myself think that they would do better coming to me than staying in Germany. Otherwise I don't push anybody toward it or hold them off, because everyone has to know for themselves." An illiterate Saarlander mining gold in California was also quite noncommittal in an 1858 letter he apparently dictated: "About my brothers I can't say anything at all, they are of age and have to know themselves what's best for them, some like it in American and some don't. Of course it's a foreign country foreign customs foreign people foreign customs [sic] and so forth." A similar attitude is reflected in an 1875 letter that an immigrant in New Melle, Missouri, wrote back to the heirs of a peasant farm in Melle, Hanover: "Dear Brother and Sister, do write us whether you might also want to come over here or not, because it's my opinion that land is expensive over there that you could get so much for it that you could get a good one over here for it. Do write me how much you would get for it over there, because if you both want to come over, then come right on over, but if you don't want to, then stay there."

In the latter two cases above, they stayed home. Someone who enticed relatives or friends to follow them to America with overly optimistic reports not only had to provide support and accommodations at the outset, but also had to put up with their reproaches. This was clearly the calculation of John Bauer, whose half-brother had followed him to America in 1868, but, as John put it, "got so terribly homesick & left America in such a hurry" that he did not even visit John in Missouri. In the next letter, Bauer reflected further over his brother's "very strange" behavior:

> I am very sorry that he did not like my letter, but I can't do anything about it. As far as I know, I wrote him a friendly letter; that I didn't advise him firmly one way or the other is also true; but . . . if I didn't exactly say he should come here, it's because I thought that if he comes here and he doesn't like it, he could blame me and say, You should not have written. I dealt much the same way with Georg [another brother who had followed him west].

As a result of calculations like this on the part of letter writers, most emigrants had a rather realistic and differentiated picture of America before they set out there. One aspect of this differentiation is that often in the same letter one relative or friend would be encouraged to come to America while another for whom conditions were less promising would be warned off. For example, the Westphalian peasant's son Wilhelm Stille wrote in his first letter from Ohio in 1834: "I'm not in the position to tell any of my relatives to come here except Rudolph, if he were here, he'd do all right. He could learn cabinetmaking and earn 1/2 dollar from the first day on." But Wilhelm goes on to mention that eighty families had settled in the vicinity, "and almost all of them have a hard time keeping themselves clothed and having enough to live on, that's why it's best if Heinrich doesn't come here." He was just as noncommittal in his advice to some stagecoach drivers who had helped him to his port of embarkation: "Even if they were my own brothers then I couldn't tell them they should come here or stay there, some like it here and some don't." One sees a similar differentiation in an 1840 letter: "I was supposed to write whether it would be good for Ernst to come here or not, I and Wilmena and Krumme [his sister and brother-in-law] think he should come here, if he can't get work right off then he can come to me, I'll give him work for one year or 2 years." In the very next paragraph, however, he had much different advice for another family member: "The rumor is out that my sister Eliesabeth is uncertain if she should come here or not, but we strongly advise <u>stay there stay there</u> [underline in original]. They know what they have and don't know what they can get again."

Another member of the same extended family wrote a very enlightening letter, describing his arrival at New Orleans in 1846: "we landed after a safe trip and went right into town and met a few friends: . . . The first thing one of them said was: what on earth are you doing here, why didn't you stay with the Stilles [i.e., in Germany]. This was not a pleasant thing to hear but it didn't scare me because I already knew about that in Germany." So even bad times in America were sometimes judged as better than conditions back home, which is not surprising given that this was in the midst of the "hungry forties" when Germany was experiencing a milder version of the Irish potato famine. But it demonstrates that potential immigrants were generally well informed, whatever they ultimately decided.

Another example of differentiated migration advice is presented by the impoverished Klinger family from Württemberg, which during the decade after 1848 sent six siblings one after another to New York. The first sister to emigrate carefully strategized whom to bring over next, who was most immediately employable and who would be advised to wait. But eventually all but two of the eight siblings became established in America. The last brother to emigrate was sent the cost of passage, which he could use either to emigrate or to purchase the tools of his trade if he remained, another indication that relatives were not unduly pressured to follow.

Even during the Civil War, when immigration dropped precipitously, the advice on migration varied from one letter writer to the next. One cautioned against immigrating as a contract laborer, but another discounted warnings against emigration issued by the Bishop of Paderborn, calling them "secessionist stories" and pointing out that those who were not naturalized ran no danger of being drafted.

The influence of immigrant letters could extend even to those who were illiterate, as an amusing Pomeranian example from 1855 shows. A Prussian official investigating the cause of an upsurge of emigration from a village in the county or *Kreis* of Arnswalde learned that "widow Volkmann from Reetz brought a letter, which her son had written from America and cook Krebs read it to us, he has also read several letters to us, which he received from Ziegenhagen and Butow. Also the shepherd servant W. Page, whenever he came to see us in the kitchen, told us a lot about America." When Page was questioned by the official, he replied, "I already made the decision to emigrate to North America two years ago, this decision has been determined by several reports that I got orally or in a written form from Germans who have already settled there." These letters and others like them led to a huge concentration of Pomeranians from Arnswalde in the state of Wisconsin, over 450 individuals, 267 of them in Green Lake County alone.

The sprouting up of such informal colonies in various locales in America is one clear indication that immigrant letters were inducing such chain migration on a broad scale, even if only a tiny fraction of it can be documented by letters such as those cited above. The splintering of Germany into a number of small and even tiny sovereignties makes it easier to reconstruct settlement patterns of emigrants from a restricted locale. Of some ten thousand natives of Oldenburg in the 1870 census, more than one-fourth lived in Hamilton County, Ohio, and along with those across the river in Kenton County, Kentucky, one-third of the Oldenburgers nationwide could be found in the greater Cincinnati area. As a contemporary reported, "among the North Germans it has almost become proverbial, 'he comes from Damme [in Oldenburg] where they all come from, and before long the old church tower will probably follow them.'" Of some eighteen thousand with origins in Schleswig-Holstein, more than half were found in Iowa and over one-third in Davenport and elsewhere in Scott County, which together with adjacent Clinton County accounted for 44 percent of the nationwide total. Without having been steered by any organized colonization efforts, one-twelfth of all natives of Braunschweig in the whole United States in 1860 lived in Cape Girardeau County, Missouri, where they even outnumbered Prussians, making up a quarter of the local German population, compared to 0.3 percent nationally.

Lippe Detmold, another tiny principality barely thirty miles wide at its greatest extent, provides a similar example. Fewer than two thousand natives of Lippe were identified in the 1860 census, with almost three-quarters of them living in just three U. S. states. Missouri was the leading destination for this group, attracting more than one-third of the total. In fact, two adjacent counties, Gasconade and Warren, alone accounted for more than one-fourth of the nationwide total. Second in line was the state of Illinois, with over one-fifth of the total, nearly all of them concentrated around the towns of Freeport and Quincy. Third in line was Wisconsin, with 19 percent; again, one county, Sheboygan, accounted for the bulk, tallying 14 percent of the U. S. total. The best explanation for such concentrations is chain migration instigated, or at least mediated, through immigrant letters.

Immigrant letters contain a multitude of evidence of chain migration and local concentrations of immigrants. There was a regular transatlantic exchange of gossip, greetings, and advice on immigration, which bears witness to settlers surrounded, sometimes literally, by friends and acquaintances from the Old Country. For example, Johann Andreas wrote to his brother from Newburg, Wisconsin, in 1861: "my neighbors around me here not more than an hour's walk away from me are almost all originally from Roth from Achenbach from Eisenhausen Breitenbach Hommertshausen and what all the places are called 17 families." Despite some misspellings, all could be located on a map of Germany, none of them ten miles from one another or from the writer's home town of Wei-delbach in the tiny Duchy of Nassau. Ten miles away from this cluster lies another village, Wunderthausen, with a completely different migra-tion history, but an equally strong chain migration. It can claim practi-cally a daughter village in Wheatland, Iowa. This settlement traces its roots to two Riedesel brothers who set out on foot from Ohio in 1851. Their favorable reports were confirmed by the Schneider family who fol-lowed the next year, and soon other acquaintances, whether from Ohio or directly from the old home town, were heading for eastern Iowa. By 1857, sixteen adult men combined to found a church. Common origins made for a consensus, as a parish history records: "Since most of the members had emigrated from Wunderthausen, Germany, and thus were Reformed from back home," they had learned to cherish the Heidelberg Catechism and called their first pastor on the condition that he would use it and the Reformed hymnbook. These "island communities," which maintained their self-sufficiency until the very end of the nineteenth cen-tury, were not merely ethnic islands; their internal cohesion was often reinforced by local, personal ties of family and acquaintance reaching back across the Atlantic.

As the previous example shows, migration chains sometimes acquired additional links within the United States, regardless of the denomina-tion involved. The adjacent Missouri counties of St. Charles and War-ren were home to a large immigration from the county of Tecklenburg, Westphalia, over four hundred people by 1850, including more than two hundred from the village of Westerkappeln alone. They were distrib-uted across several settlements, with the heaviest concentration in the Evangelical parish of Femme Osage. As land in eastern Missouri became scarce, they got word from one of their compatriots who had settled in Lafayette County near the western border of the state that land was still available at good prices there. Between 1875 and 1880 no less than thirty-four Femme Osage families moved west. When new Evangelical con-gregations were founded in the neighboring villages of Napoleon and Levasy, people from Femme Osage made up 70 percent of the members, as well as one-quarter of those in nearby Wellington. In a similar case, the Lutheran settlement in Block, Kansas, drew heavily from the Hanove-rian settlement at Cole Camp, Missouri, one hundred miles to the east. In yet another instance, so many German Catholics from the St. Elizabeth area in central Missouri settled in two daughter communities, Okeene and Okarche northwest of Oklahoma City, that the Jefferson City *Volks-freund* mentioned these settlements several dozen times and even published news columns in 1919 and 1920 with the dateline Okeene, the only out-of-state location where the paper had a subscription agent.

The map of the Midwest is dotted with towns such as New Minden, Illinois, New Melle, Missouri, and New Holstein, Wisconsin, that took their names directly from German origins. However, place names are not always a reliable clue to the origins of settlers. With Hanover, one is never sure whether the German province or the British royal house is being commemorated. With Minden, the Illinois town denotes origins, but several other towns with the same name commemorate a British victory in the Seven Years' War. Westphalia involves no such ambiguity, but Rhinelanders came to outnumber Westphalians in settlements of that name in both Michigan and Missouri. The county seat of Rhinelander, Wisconsin, denotes not its settlers but F. W. Rhinelander, president of the railroad on which it is located. Another German town name and heavily Lutheran community, Freistatt in southwest Missouri presents yet another variety. It took its name from a town not in Germany but in Wisconsin, and was founded in 1874 largely by secondary migrants from Minnesota and Wisconsin who were tired of the snow. But despite the name origins, more of its settlers came from Illinois.

The Flusche brothers, Anton, August, and Emil, were immigrant land promoters and speculators who founded towns for their fellow Catholics: Westphalia in western Iowa (1874), named after their home province, and Olpe in eastern Kansas (1879), named after their home town. They also established a Westphalia, Kansas (1881). None of these colonies grew beyond a couple of hundred inhabitants, though each had a flourishing Catholic parish. But the Flusches' greatest success was a Texas town sixty miles north of Ft. Worth that they founded in 1889 and named Muenster for the provincial capital, since the state already had a Westphalia established a decade earlier. Shortly thereafter, they also founded nearby Lindsay, and then Pilot Point in the adjacent county. Muenster, a town of some 1,500, is still 90 percent German and Catholic, and has continued to grow in recent decades.

However, none of the Flusche colonies could match the record of Stearns County, Minnesota, where German Catholics comprised half of the county population, probably a nationwide record. There were a dozen German Catholic parishes in Stearns County by the Civil War, and no less than thirty in 1880, as well as one-third of all the "Saint" place names in the whole state. In a block of eighteen townships (over six hundred square miles), 80 percent of the population was German—or even more: in eleven of them, Germans topped 90 percent; in six, they ranged from 98 percent upward. And this was achieved without any group land purchases. All it took was an 1854 letter from Father Franz Xavier Pierz, published in the Cincinnati Catholic *Wahrheitsfreund*, calling upon "thrifty Catholics" in "overpopulated cities" to "make an earthly paradise of this Minnesota" on land ceded by the Winnebago Indians. German Catholics across the Midwest responded, and often recruited kinsmen from abroad as well.

Secular colonization societies within America also founded several towns. The Missouri River town of Hermann was a project of the German Settlement Society of Philadelphia, which in 1837 sent two agents to purchase 11,300 acres of land that it then sold to settlers. Several dozen families with children born in Pennsylvania bear witness to this secondary migration. Like Philadelphians, many of the settlers were of southwest German origins, and they soon established a thriving wine industry in and around the town.

New Ulm, Minnesota, started out in 1854 as a project of Chicago Germans, but it limped along until two years later when the socialist Turner Society bailed it out and recruited hundreds of Germans from various eastern cities. In resistance to encroachments on their land, natives attacked New Ulm during the Sioux War of 1862 and burned much of the town, but the survivors rebuilt and persevered. Although originally settled by freethinkers who named streets after Benjamin Franklin, Thomas Jefferson, and Thomas Paine, New Ulm later attracted a heavy settlement of German Catholics from Bohemia and in 1957 became the seat of a diocese. It is also the site of a German Lutheran college founded in 1884. But the secular tradition of New Ulm's founders has persisted as well; its Turner Hall dating from 1873 is the oldest of its kind in the nation in continuous use for its original mission.

Notwithstanding such organized settlement projects, whether from the German side or the American side, most German communities were the result of a multitude of bottom-up decisions. Private sources of information, above all immigrant letters, were much more influential than any public sources, be they guidebooks, colonization projects, or state immigration agencies, in determining immigrants' destinations. And this ongoing feedback effect of communications and chain migration prevented most immigrant writers from giving an overly optimistic assessment of their own situation or of immigrant conditions generally. One immigrant related the conversations before he left for America: "Wilh. Fink, he's doing well, he has a tavern." But he contrasts that with what he found on site: "when I arrived in Philadelphia I looked all around to find his tavern. I finally found Mr. Fink, who even cheated me out of 7 dollars, & it turned out that he had rented a boarding house together with a wretched bar." (Most prone to exaggerating their circumstances were writers whose recipients were not potential followers—for example, the wife of a Civil War soldier who "promoted" her husband all the way from private to colonel.)

One potential distortion that is of little concern with German immigrants is the ability to read and write. By the founding of the German Reich in 1871, male illiteracy, at least in Prussia, was down below the 4 percent level, and many of the unschooled were in fact ethnic Poles. Earlier in the century, and also to some extent in other German states with poorer educational systems, rates were somewhat higher. But even at the outset of mass emigration around 1830, at least 90 percent of German men, and only a slightly lower proportion of women, possessed rudimentary skills of reading and writing (though spelling is another matter, even in the late nineteenth century, as a perusal of their letters makes clear). So the great majority of German immigrants were in a position to write home if they chose, and even some of the illiterates managed to dictate letters that others wrote for them.

Of course, others chose for whatever reason not to write, as is apparent from some transatlantic gossip transmitted in an 1856 letter: "You can reassure Johannes Durst's family and tell them that I myself put their letter in their son's hands, & every time I visited him I entreated him to write to his parents. If he hasn't done it yet it's not my fault." Probably the greatest distorting factor with immigrant correspondence was that of silence: Immigrants sometimes refrained from writing when they were doing poorly. This was not the case with Durst, judging by the 1860 census. But another immigrant, who could stand in for several dozen correspondents in German letter collections, writes excusing ten years of silence: "If I had stayed poor I would have been lost to you forever, and I couldn't write what was untrue, and I was ashamed of being poor." But even here, any false impressions created by the reticence of impoverished peasants were to some extent counteracted by letters of bourgeois prodigal sons begging for funds—and forgiveness.

As in such cases, immigrant letters dealt not only with material circumstances in the New World, but also involved emotional ties to those left behind. In fact, the emotional world and the material circumstances, and their representations in letters, were often inextricably bound up with one other. Although separation was long distance, often it was not long term, at least not from all the readers of a given letter. Letters were exchanged as much from community to community as from individual to individual. An answer to an 1846 letter from America describes the sensation it aroused in an Upper Franconian village: "Then we went to Christopher Schöbel's Tavern at Redwiz for a beer and there many people assembled and each one wished to hear what my brother-in-law had written. We would read nothing, however, and went to the schoolmaster at Wölsau to have him make a copy, so that we could send the original letter to cousin Hagen . . . and up to this time there have been some 20-odd copies made of your letter." An extreme example, perhaps, but not entirely atypical.

Much more decisive for the migration process than agents, guidebooks, or emigration societies were families or lone individuals, sometimes accompanied by relatives, friends, or neighbors, but without a common treasury or any formal organizational framework. The risks involved in such an undertaking were greatly reduced through chain migration, the choice of an initial destination where one already had personal contacts, family, and friends who could provide temporary lodgings, arrange a job, and generally ease the shock of confronting a new society, culture, and economy. When American immigration authorities in the early twentieth century began to pose the question whether arriving immigrants were coming to join relatives or friends, only 6 percent of all newcomers said no. Friends provided the initial point of contact for some 15 percent, but nearly four-fifths were awaited by relatives. Germans were quite near the overall average in this respect, except that slightly more were joining friends rather than family. In fact, over one-third of all Germans during this era traveled on ship's passages that had been prepaid by someone in America. From all the evidence presented above, it is apparent that patterns of German immigration in the mid-nineteenth century were quite similar.

The regional distribution of Germans in America also changed little during the nineteenth century except for the general trend of westward migration. The heaviest concentrations were in northeastern cities between New York and Baltimore, and above all in the urban and rural Midwest. If one calculates the proportion of German immigrants and their children in relation to total population and total foreign stock in 1900, there were nine states where German Americans exceed the national average of both 10.5 percent of the population and 30.5 percent of all foreign stock. Among them were two East Coast states, New Jersey and Maryland, with a largely urban immigrant population. The other seven states form a compact bloc, a "German belt" stretching from Ohio in the east to Nebraska in the west, from Missouri in the south to Wisconsin in the north, with large immigrant concentrations in both cities and rural areas. North of the German belt from New York to the Dakotas lies a band of states where Germans made up more than 10.5 percent of the general population, but fell below 30.5 percent of the large immigrant population of these states. California also belongs to this category. South and southwest of the German Belt in the states of South Carolina, West Virginia, Kentucky, Arkansas, Kansas, Oklahoma, and Texas, Germans made up more than 30.5 percent of their small ethnic populations, but less than 10.5 percent of all inhabitants. Despite the heavy German settlement of Pennsylvania during the colonial era, it fell slightly below average on both indicators, but only because the census counted the third and subsequent generations as native born.

The question of ethnic heritage beyond the second generation was finally posed by the 1980 census, which confirmed the importance of the German element in populating America, and its geographic stability in the midwestern areas of initial settlement. The forty-nine million Americans of German heritage are second only to the fifty million claiming English heritage; in fact, if the Welsh and Scots are considered as separate nationalities, Germans would take first place. Next in line come the Irish with forty million. The English hold the lead in twenty-three states, dominating the South and West and sharing the Northeast with the Irish. Germans form the largest element in eighteen states, a solid block stretching from Pennsylvania and Maryland throughout the entire east and west north central regions and beyond, from Ohio to the Canadian border and as far west as the tier of states from Colorado to Montana. They also lead in Alaska. If one looks at absolute numbers rather than percentages, however, California leads in the number of persons of German heritage, showing that they, too, have participated heavily in the twentieth-century migration to the West Coast. In Wisconsin and Nebraska, Germans held the lead in every single county in the year 2000. The same was true in Iowa, except for in two counties where the Dutch outnumbered them, and in all Kansas counties except four in the extreme southwest that have seen a recent Hispanic influx.

The area of the midwestern German belt offered the newcomer a climate and vegetation that was rather familiar from the homeland. Like Germany, it was largely forested in its natural state, although it did include some prairie land as well. Its northern and southern borders corresponded rather closely with the isothermal lines of fifteen and thirty-five degrees Fahrenheit average winter temperature; on the west, there was little German settlement beyond the line where annual rainfall dropped below twenty-five inches. Also within states on the borders of these lines, Germans were concentrated in the more temperate parts: southeastern Minnesota and Wisconsin, and eastern Nebraska. Still, one should not exaggerate the similarities with the homeland. Despite nearly identical annual average temperatures, the continental climate of the United States presented more of both extremes than that of continental Europe, which is moderated by the warm ocean currents of the Gulf Stream. This was true despite the fact that even Munich in extreme southern Germany lies farther north than Montreal, while New Orleans lies roughly on the latitude of Cairo, Egypt.

Since the census made the first full enumeration of immigrants in 1850, Wisconsin has for more than a century remained the state with the heaviest German concentration. In 1900, more than one-third of its population was of German birth or parentage. In second and third place were Minnesota and Illinois, the only other states whose inhabitants were over 20 percent German stock. Following in close succession were Nebraska, Iowa, New York, and Ohio. Germans were ubiquitous in the United States—at least a few made their way to practically every part of the country. In 1910, when the number of persons of German stock reached its peak, there were only seventy-six counties among some three thousand in the U. S. without a single resident of German birth or parentage. Except for five counties in west Texas and two in the South Dakota Indian country, all of these lay east of the Mississippi and south of the Mason-Dixon Line.

To a striking extent, Germans avoided the South, except for Texas, and were very lightly represented in New England as well. The 1910 census shows only five southeastern counties with as much as 5 percent German stock in its rural population, and all of those were urban fringes. Nor were there any rural counties in Maine, Vermont, or Massachusetts reaching this 5 percent figure, and only two urban centers in New England that were as much as 10 percent German. Similarly, the desert Southwest of Arizona, New Mexico, Nevada, and Utah was largely devoid of Germans.

Among the cities, New York always had far and above the largest number of Germans. At the turn of the twentieth century, its German immigrants alone would have constituted a city equal to the eighth largest in the Fatherland. If one includes the second generation, the eight hundred thousand New Yorkers of German stock would take second place only to Berlin, and their nearly four hundred thousand compatriots in Chicago would take eighth place among German cities. Like Chicago, the cities with the highest percentages of Germans all lay in the Midwest. In relative terms, Milwaukee continued to hold the lead. According to the 1850 census, Germans actually outnumbered the native born. Over half of all heads of households and more than one-third of the inhabitants were still German in 1860, but by then the native born had surpassed them in numbers because the census counted the children of immigrants as natives. Cincinnati and St. Louis were the only other cities that were over 30 percent German on the eve of the Civil War. By 1910, the picture had changed somewhat, influenced by changes in transportation technology and economic development. Milwaukee still held the lead, but the river cities of St. Louis and Cincinnati now showed lower German proportions than the faster growing centers of heavy industry on the Great Lakes such as Buffalo, Detroit, and Chicago.

On the neighborhood level, the German dominance was often much heavier than citywide figures would suggest. One often sees such characterizations in the local press, and in nicknames such as New York's "Kleindeutschland," Chicago's "Nordseite," or Cincinnati's "Over the Rhine," so named because it lay beyond the Miami and Erie Canal from downtown. An 1865 German visitor described it thus: "one really believes that one has been transported into a German city as soon as one crosses the 'Rhine.' One hears hardly anything but German spoken, the shops are adorned with German signs, and . . . every third house is a beer or wine pub." Of course, the impression of a "purely German neighborhood" could arise despite a considerable minority of natives and other immigrants in the population. The four wards of New York's Kleindeutschland in 1855 were less than 30 percent German, or below 40 percent of the adult male voting population, disregarding the second generation. As a rule, Germans were somewhat more segregated than British or Irish immigrants, but not to the same degree as later arrivals from southern or eastern Europe, and much less so than Blacks or Asians in the late twentieth century. But segregation rates were higher in the faster growing cities of the interior than on the East Coast. Over one-third of all St. Louis Germans lived in the two wards of the south side, where they constituted more than three-fourths of the voting population on the eve of the Civil War. Less than 10 percent of the adults were native born, and only another 10 percent were Irish or other English-speaking immigrants.

The *Buffalo Commercial Advertiser* complained in 1857 that Buffalo could no longer be considered an American city. In its eyes, the four German wards on the east side were "as little American as the duchy of Hesse Cassel; their population speaks a foreign language, reads foreign newspapers, isolates itself from the American element, and steeped in ignorance of American politics, it clings to the bald name of Democracy, and claims the right to subject the sons of the soil to the despotism of the force of brute numbers." Perhaps it had a point: in one of the wards, "only" three-fifths of the voters were foreign born, but in the other three, Germans alone made up three-fourths of the voting population. Citywide, one-third of Buffalo voters were German. The 1858 city census showed St. Louis voters to be 60 percent foreign born, with Germans alone constituting 37 percent of the electorate. Milwaukee was even more extreme, especially in the northwestern quadrant, where over three-quarters of all heads of households were German in 1860. Although such heavy concentrations tended to dissipate with time, as late as 1890 there were two wards in Cincinnati's "Over the Rhine," where Germans (including the second generation) still dominated to the tune of 71 and 80 percent.

One of the paradoxes of German-American migration is this group's high rate of urbanization in the New World. Despite the fact that emigrants were recruited most heavily from the rural elements of society, Germans in America throughout the nineteenth century were much more urbanized than either the compatriots they left behind or the American population as a whole. The 1871 census of the newly founded German Reich revealed that only 12.6 percent of its inhabitants resided in cities with populations over twenty thousand. By contrast, over 39 percent of German immigrants resided in the fifty largest U. S. cities, which ranged upward in population from twenty-five thousand in 1870 and thirty-five thousand in 1880. In fact, there was a larger share of Germans living in U. S. towns of more than twenty-five thousand inhabitants than of people residing in towns of two thousand and larger among the folks back home. During the entire second half of the nineteenth century, eight large metropolitan centers alone were home to between 20 and 30 percent of all German immigrants. Moreover, they were less concentrated in the farm population than most other "Old Immigration" groups except the Irish and the British, even among those who arrived later and should have had more difficulty gaining access to land. As late as 1920, the Dutch, Swiss, Norwegians, Danes, and even Czechs were more concentrated in the farming population than the national average, while Germans (and to a lesser extent Swedes) remained slightly underrepresented.

German Americans were nevertheless quite visible in farming because they were such a large group; in raw numbers they surpassed any other immigrant nationality in agriculture. But much the same could be said for their presence in American cities. During the whole second half of the nineteenth century, Germans were the leading ethnic element in American cities. Since the runner-up was the English-speaking Irish, Germans were by far the largest foreign language group. As late as 1920, a quarter-century after mass immigration from Germany had subsided, only Italians outnumbered Germans in America's urban population, and the largely Jewish immigrants from Russia were the only other nationality group that even came close.

Germans in cities stood out from other immigrant groups in their regional concentrations. Very few settled in urban New England, where the Irish predominated, and Germans came in a close second to the Irish in the Mid-Atlantic region. But in nearly every city west of the Appalachians, Germans were the largest immigrant nationality and by far the largest foreign language group. This held true not only for such leading and well-known German centers such as Milwaukee, Cincinnati, and St. Louis but also for Buffalo, Chicago, Detroit, Indianapolis, and the Ohio cities of Cleveland, Columbus, Dayton, and Toledo. This gave Germans major advantages as they attempted to preserve their native culture and language.

One might suspect that the urbanization rate of the German state of origin influenced the propensity of its natives to settle in American cities, but this played a negligible role. Even from maritime Hamburg, a city-state with over three hundred thousand inhabitants in 1871, only a bare majority of its immigrants were found in cities of more than twenty-five thousand in 1870—enough, however, to give it the lead. Among the larger German states, Saxony was in a class by itself in respect to urbanization and industrialization, but Saxons in America hardly stood out from natives of Hesse, Württemberg, or Baden. In fact, Bavarians led the way despite relatively low urbanization rates at home.

This raises the question of whether such urbanization was voluntary, or if it resulted from lack of funds to travel inland. Southern and particularly southwest Germans (40 percent of the Bavarians were in fact Palatinates) were the most urbanized and most concentrated in the eastern states, but it appears unlikely they were stranded in port cities because of poverty. Despite being the poorest immigrants arriving in the 1850s, Mecklenburgers were the least urbanized of all. It could hardly be the reluctance of Catholics to settle beyond the reach of the church and its ministrations, for Hessians and Württembergers, both more than two-thirds Protestant, were just as heavily concentrated in the east as immigrants from Baden, who were two-thirds Catholic, or Bavarians, the most Catholic of all.

Southwest German urbanization reflects specific local and regional migration traditions, some going back to the eighteenth century, rather than general urban preferences. The German population of each East Coast city was dominated by a different group: Württembergers were

overrepresented in Philadelphia by a factor of three, Hessians in Baltimore and Badensians in Boston by more than double. Meanwhile, Bavarians took a consistent, if less spectacular, lead in New York City. These
concentrations probably resulted from migration traditions going back
to the colonial era, when immigration was largely restricted to southwest
Germany.

For example, William Frick, who emigrated from the Bavarian Palatinate in 1839, first went to Pennsylvania and stayed for a year with relatives
who had arrived before the American Revolution, although he eventually
settled in Missouri. Another immigrant of the same origins, Katharina
Risser, reported in her first letter home in 1832 that she was hospitably
received upon her arrival by a cousin and other relatives, people who had
settled in Lancaster County a full sixty years earlier. Obviously, many of
these contacts persisted beyond the first generation. Johannes Blickensdörfer, who emigrated from the Palatinate in 1833, proceeded directly to
Canal Dover in northeastern Ohio, where he found employment with the
grandson of another Blickensdörfer who had left the same town eighty
years earlier. Such connections were more numerous in states on the East
Coast, but where they existed farther inland, they also attracted concentrations of southwestern Germans. The pioneers of a Württemberger
settlement in Ann Arbor, Michigan, arrived in 1825, with the result that
even a half-century later, more than three-fourths of the German population in the town and surrounding county was of those origins.

Northwest Germans first started immigrating heavily in the 1830s,
before there were many good rail connections, so most traveled inland
by steamboat. As a result, natives of Hanover, Oldenburg, and Westphalia were heavily concentrated along the Ohio, Missouri, and upper Mississippi rivers, especially in Cincinnati and St. Louis but also in smaller
cities like Quincy, Illinois. By the time immigration from East Elbian
areas such as Mecklenburg took off in the 1850s, there were good rail
connections from New York to Chicago, supplemented by steamers on
the Great Lakes. As a result, Milwaukee could be called the Mecklen-
burger capital of the United States, but large concentrations were also
found in Michigan, Iowa, Chicago, and elsewhere in northern Illinois.
Since the census seldom records Prussian provinces, the destinations of
their immigrants are more difficult to trace. But those from east of the
Elbe share many commonalities with Mecklenburgers. For example, the

Pomeranian presence in Wisconsin goes back to the Old Lutherans of the 1830s, and its Low German dialect has survived into the twenty-first century in places such as Marathon and Lincoln counties in the northern part of the state.

Especially with artisans, the choice between city and country was strongly influenced by life-cycle stage. Among a group that was traced from the Duchy of Braunschweig, more than two-thirds of the journeymen, who were usually single, settled in cities, compared to scarcely one-third of the masters, who were usually heads of families. Already in 1838, an immigrant guidebook advised, "The unmarried cabinetmaker finds his living better in the larger cities; the father of a family, by contrast, does better in smaller towns or in the country, especially if he has grown sons and is inclined to agriculture, which he can practice on the side and thereby provide food and shelter more easily than in the expensive cities." Similar recommendations were given for carpenters, blacksmiths, wagonmakers, tailors, shoemakers, and saddlers, practically all the important artisan trades. The tradeoff between higher wages and higher living costs in the city was different for single men who could live as boarders than for families with children. Married women seldom worked outside the home for wages, but in a rural setting they contributed to family subsistence with gardening, and often to family income as well, with "butter and egg money." A Westphalian who spent the first winter after his arrival in St. Louis before moving on to Burlington, Iowa, wrote in 1853, "Already in the first days my wife liked it better here because she could occupy herself with the garden which I had rented here; the daily inactivity in St. Louis often tormented her, and was the reason why she sometimes wished she was back in Germany."

Many Germans followed similar paths. Although the Turnerian idea of the agricultural frontier as a safety valve for discontented urban workers has largely been refuted, it held true for some immigrants. All of them landed at port cities, and nearly all traveled through urban transfer points on their way to the interior. Many stopped off for a season or several years to earn cash for land purchases. In Washington County, Illinois, forty miles southeast of St. Louis, more than 10 percent of German families living there in 1860 had stopped in the city or another Missouri location long enough for at least one child to be born. One sees a similar pattern with Mecklenburgers in Chicago, whose numbers declined by nearly 1,500 during the 1870s, almost exactly the gain shown in rural Illinois during the decade. Oldenburgers in Cincinnati also saw a decline of about 1,100 over the 1870s as many moved on to locations such as St. Marys, Ohio; Oldenburg, Indiana; and Teutopolis, Illinois. Such temporary sojourning in cities probably gave Germans in the hinterlands more contacts and firsthand information from cities than was the case with the Anglo-American neighbors, and promoted trade in both directions.

Seven years after arriving in America and settling in the country sixty miles west of St. Louis, Wilhelm Brüggemann continued to correspond with a friend in the city, gossiping about acquaintances from their home town of Lotte and exchanging tips about the livestock market. His initial arrival in the city had set off a round of celebration: "That's where life started again. They all said, 'Brüggemann has arrived!' I went to see all the people from Lotte. The visiting lasted the whole night through." He goes on to mention the names of eight different people or families from the home village whom he met there, and reported seeing many others, and many from the neighboring town of Westerkappeln. "It was as if the prodigal son had returned to his father, that's how we celebrated." He continued on to the rural hinterlands of the Gateway City, where he was again surrounded by dozens of former acquaintances, among them his brother and sister-in-law. Immigrants like Brüggemann were anything but uprooted; they were transplanted.

4

Religion, Education,
and Interethnic Relations

GERMAN EVANGELICAL THEOLOGIAN H. Richard Niebuhr wrote, "Perhaps religion is as often responsible for ethnic character as the latter is responsible for the faith." While this holds true for homogeneous groups, religious diversity was often an obstacle to German ethnic identity and solidarity. The founders of Germantown in 1683 can be regarded as religious refugees, but this was not true of most German immigrants even in the colonial era. The great majority of them were Lutheran or Reformed Protestants who had enjoyed religious toleration since the Peace of Westphalia in 1648. The situation in the nineteenth century was similar. There were some small Protestant group migrations before the Civil War, and some Catholic clergy and religious orders took refuge from Bismarck's Kulturkampf in the 1870s. Nevertheless, for most German immigrants, the primary motive was economic. However, this does not mean that they were religiously indifferent, although there was a significant rationalist "freethinker" element, especially in the higher ranks of the ethnic group.

The two-generation break in mass immigration after 1775 meant that the colonial German Protestant churches that newcomers encountered after 1830 were well on their way toward linguistic and theological assimilation. The Ohio Synod was formed in 1818 as a more conservative offshoot of the Conference of the Pennsylvania Ministerium, whose origins went back to Muhlenberg, but it was still more liberal than most Lutheran bodies founded later in the century. So Lutherans with colonial roots and those arriving in the nineteenth century usually went their

separate ways, with little institutional continuity between eighteenth-
and nineteenth-century German Protestantism.

The German religious landscape on both sides of the Atlantic was further complicated by a development in 1817, the three-hundredth anniversary of the Protestant Reformation. Prussian king Frederick William
III, dismayed that he could not attend communion with his Lutheran
wife because of his Reformed faith, issued a decree combining the two
denominations into a new Evangelical state church, also known as the
Prussian Union. In some parts of his realm this was accepted, but there
was also resistance from some "Old Lutherans," and to a lesser degree
from some "Old Reformed" Protestants. Besides these separatist movements, there was also a Protestant *Erweckungsbewegung* (Awakening
Movement), a pietistic undercurrent within the established church in
areas such as Württemberg, Franconia, Wuppertal, or eastern Westphalia and Lippe, often centered on a charismatic pastor.

There are several interesting parallels among the early Lutherans,
Evangelicals, and Catholics. All were supported by German institutions
specially set up to prepare clergy for overseas missions, if not exclusively
for America. In all three confessions, clergy initially sent to minister to
the Indians turned to their compatriots instead, whom they saw as "sheep
without a shepherd." For example, the Slovenian priest Franz Pierz,
originally a missionary to Michigan Indians, became the main promotor of German Catholic immigration to Minnesota. Mission societies founded by Pietists in Basel, Switzerland (1815) and Barmen in the
Wuppertal (1818), were originally intended to serve Africa and Asia, as
was the Lutheran training institution in Hermannsburg, Hanover (1847).
Only the Barmen offshoot in nearby Langenberg (1837) was specifically
tasked to serve North America. But all of them came to be important
sources of Evangelical and Lutheran clergy. Similarly, on the Catholic side, the Leopoldine Foundation was established in Vienna in 1827
and the Ludwig-Missionsverein by the Bavarian king in 1838 to support
American missions. During the 1860s there was a seminary in Westphalia devoted specifically to training priests for America. Not surprisingly,
the two dioceses that sent the most priests to the United States were both
Westphalian: Muenster and Paderborn. Down to the end of the century, most German-speaking priests were immigrants, but an increasing

minority of them had immigrated as children and received their training in America or arrived freshly ordained.

Catholics, and particularly their clergy, received an additional impetus for emigration from Prussia with Chancellor Bismarck's "Kulturkampf," an attempt to exercise tighter state control over Catholics with new legislation in 1873. It prescribed the course of study for clergy and required them to be examined by state inspections before appointment to any church position. Seminaries that refused to comply were closed. Some two hundred priests, five bishops, and even a Polish archbishop were deposed, for repression was most severe in Prussian Poland. Many went into exile in America, helping to relieve the shortage of priests and fill the ranks with especially dedicated clergy. But Bismarck succeeded only in mobilizing political Catholicism and before the end of the decade had backed down.

Decades earlier, dissenters from the Prussian Union, often dubbed "Old Lutherans," came over in several organized groups in the late 1830s and early 1840s. One group from Pomerania and Silesia, led by Pastor William Grabau, settled in Buffalo and Milwaukee. Five shiploads from Saxony, (one of which was lost at sea), traveled with their leader Martin Stephan and founded a "Zion on the Mississippi" on an isolated site of several thousand acres purchased in southeast Missouri. But the unbending zealotry of these dissenters led to three different Lutheran bodies, the Buffalo, Wisconsin, and Missouri synods. Lutherans were not the only ones to emigrate in protest of church policies—in the 1840s, several shiploads of Reformed Protestants emigrated from Lippe Detmold at least partly because they had been denied use of the Heidelberg Catechism.

The names of Lutheran synods were usually geographical, but they extended beyond the place that gave them their names, and usually had important doctrinal components to their identity as well. The oldest and until recently the largest of them, the "German Evangelical Lutheran Synod of Missouri, Ohio, and Other States" (commonly known as the Missouri Synod), was formed in Chicago in 1847 by a dozen ministers representing fourteen congregations. The Iowa Synod broke off from this conservative group in 1854, incorporated the Texas Synod in 1896, merged with other groups in 1930 to form the American Lutheran Church, and in 1988, together with some Scandinavian elements and Missouri Synod dissenters, formed the Evangelical Lutheran Church in America (ELCA). It is now the largest Lutheran body, though not as heavily German as the Missouri Synod.

That Synod's key leader and its first president, C. F. W. Walther, and many of his parishioners were from the Saxon Stephanite settlement in Missouri. Walther had rallied the group when its bishop, Martin Stephan, was ousted for financial and sexual improprieties and summarily rowed across the Mississippi River. However, the Synod's founding congregations had little in common besides doctrine; several had split off from the Ohio Synod. They hailed from six states: two each from Missouri, Ohio, and Illinois, and four from Indiana. One from Frankenmuth, Michigan, was the result of a group migration from Franconia, and another from Buffalo, New York, split off from Pomeranian Old Lutherans there. But not all founders were religious refugees or group migrants. One of the charter congregations in New Melle, Missouri, had its roots in Hanover where Unionism was not an issue, as did Friedrich Wyneken, organizer of several of the Indiana congregations and the Synod's second president.

Only a minority of Lutheran immigrants of this era were religious refugees. Many had come from Hanover, where the Lutheran and Reformed churches remained independent of each other, or from Mecklenburg, which was overwhelmingly Lutheran with virtually no Reformed or Evangelical presence. Nor did all immigrants from Prussia object to the Evangelical Union; many, especially from the Rhineland and Westphalia, appeared perfectly happy with this arrangement. In 1840, they founded an American church body much like it, originally called the *Kirchenverein des Westens*, later known as the German Evangelical Synod (a very different type of Evangelical Protestant from those that have recently attracted the attention of political pollsters). Five of the seven founding ministers represented congregations in Missouri, the other two in Illinois. From the outset, its ethos was more ecumenical than that of Lutherans. The designation "German" was dropped in 1925, and the denomination merged with German Reformed elements in 1934 to form the Evangelical and Reformed body, at which time it counted over 280,000 members in twenty-one states and Canada.

However, the lines between German Lutherans and Evangelicals were not so stringently drawn in the early years. At times they even shared church buildings, though at some point they usually went their separate ways. One of the founding pastors of the *Kirchenverein*, Rev. Hermann

Garlichs, served for a decade at Femme Osage, Missouri, the first German parish west of the Mississippi, but then, returning from a visit to Germany, was called to a Lutheran congregation in Brooklyn where he served the rest of his life. More than one of my ancestral families had some children baptized in each of the two denominations (some of them by Garlichs), or were married in one and had children baptized in the other.

Both denominations soon developed their own educational and social service institutions, forming parallel societies much like Catholics did, although that of the Evangelicals was not as extensive or long lasting given their ecumenical tendencies. Beginning in a log cabin in Altenburg, Missouri, in 1839, the Lutheran seminary moved to St. Louis a decade later where it developed into the Synod's Concordia Seminary. For more than three decades starting in 1850, the Evangelical *Kirchenverein* maintained a seminary in rural Missouri near the Femme Osage congregation that Garlichs had founded, the forerunner of Eden Seminary in the St. Louis suburb of Webster Groves. Both denominations also established teachers' colleges in Illinois: the Evangelicals at Elmhurst dating from 1871, the Lutherans at Addison in 1864, later relocated to the Chicago suburb of River Forest. Lutherans also founded nearly a dozen preparatory schools across the country modeled on the German Gymnasium. As late as the 1960s, the high school and junior college in Concordia, Missouri, still designated its classes by traditional Latin names in the German tradition, starting with *Prima* for the highest class and working its way down to the *Sexta* for beginners, the opposite order as with American grades.

Not everyone remained in transplanted denominations. German immigrants became members of Anglo-Protestant churches by two rather different paths. It was not unusual for them to join local English-language congregations on an individual basis, particularly if they were of Protestant background, had intermarried, or lived in an area where there were insufficient Germans to constitute a critical mass for their own congregation. All three of these characteristics held true for Methodist convert John Bauer. Barely one hundred Germans lived in his home county of Missouri, less than 1 percent of the population, and in his home township, never more than sixteen.

But early on in the nineteenth century, several Anglo-Protestant denominations developed German-language auxiliaries. By far the largest and most important was the German Methodist movement, which owes much to the efforts of one man, William Nast. An immigrant from Württemberg with theological training and a background in Swabian Pietism, Nast converted to Methodism in America and was appointed an immigrant missionary in Cincinnati. The denomination that developed numbered up to twenty thousand members, nearly 140 congregations and 165 ministers, many of whom served as circuit riders. German Methodists even founded several of their own colleges, in locations such as Warrenton, Missouri, and Brenham, Texas, the latter of which trained nearly one hundred preachers. One interesting characteristic of German Methodism is its transatlantic element. Many of its converts, like Nast himself, came from a background of Pietism and Protestant revivalism in Germany. Immigrants from areas where this movement was strong, such as Württemberg and Lippe Detmold, made up a disproportionate share of converts to Methodism and students at their seminaries.

Two of the most influential U. S. theologians of the twentieth century both have roots in German Pietism. An immigrant pastor who had grown up in the Pietist hotbed of Wuppertal converted to the Baptists on the Missouri frontier in the 1850s and in 1858 became the founder of the German division of Rochester Theological Seminary. His name was August Rauschenbusch, and his son Walter, who also taught there, is considered a cofounder of the Social Gospel movement. Reinhold Niebuhr was equally indebted to German Pietism. His immigrant father Gustav had originally tended toward rationalism, but underwent a religious conversion among his immigrant relatives and found his calling as a pastor of the German Evangelical Church—the same denomination that nurtured and trained Reinhold (and his brother Richard) during the early decades of their lives.

While the language transition took place more quickly than in purely German denominations, it was not until the mid-1920s that the German conferences of Methodism were disbanded and their congregations integrated into the normal, geographically based church districts. There were also other Anglo-Protestant denominations with German branches, for example Presbyterians and Baptists, but they were of much less significance. The Lutheran Missouri Synod early on had some English-language congregations, but tellingly kept them segregated in a separate, non-geographical district, partly for reasons of communication, but primarily because English speakers for a long time remained culturally and doctrinally suspect.

The bulk of the immigrants were concentrated in transplanted confessions, especially the Catholic, Lutheran, and Evangelical. For example, in St. Louis, with a German population of about fifty thousand on the eve of the Civil War, there were only three German Methodist churches, with a combined membership of about seven hundred, and struggling flocks of German Baptists and Presbyterians that together barely totaled one hundred. Eleven German Lutheran and Evangelical parishes (not clearly distinguished from one another in the city directory), numbered about three thousand members, and the four German Catholic parishes probably doubled that figure. Thus, at best 10 percent of St. Louis Germans belonged to Anglo-Protestant denominations. This appears fairly typical for other cities at the time. Only about one-tenth of Buffalo's Germans belonged to denominations of Anglo-Protestant origins; most were Catholics or Lutherans. Cincinnati was the home base of German-American Methodists, yet they claimed barely 1 percent of that city's German church members. It is true that in older states such as Ohio and Pennsylvania there was more carryover of colonial Lutheran and Reformed traditions than was the case farther west in Missouri, Illinois, or Wisconsin.

In the early nineteenth century, arriving Catholics found even fewer resources in the German language than Protestants. Their numbers were very sparse among the Germans in colonial America. They did not feel particularly welcome in the Protestant British colonies, and they often had more attractive options in the Habsburg lands of eastern Europe. Several hundred did settle in eighteenth-century French Louisiana, but they apparently never had a German priest and assimilated rather quickly to the Francophone society. There was a small Catholic minority among the Germans who settled in Greater Pennsylvania, perhaps numbering one thousand adults by the American Revolution.

German masses were usually available in Philadelphia after 1741, but not until 1787 was the first German congregation established. Baltimore Germans formed their own congregation in 1799, while New Yorkers shared parish life with Irish Catholics until 1833. Midwestern cities were not far behind in establishing German-language parishes. Cincinnati's first dates from 1834; that was the year the first German sermon was preached to St. Louis Catholics, though it did not lead to an ethnic parish until 1844. In other river cities on the main migration routes, Louisville's first German Catholic congregation was established in 1837, Pittsburgh's in 1839. Lake cities were slower; Chicago got its first German parish in 1846, Detroit and Milwaukee in the following year.

Already in 1855, the lay societies and social service organization in German parishes nationwide united to form a federation called the *Centralverein*, headquartered in St. Louis. The Midwestern concentration of Germans held true for Catholics as well as Protestants. At the end of the nineteenth century, three-quarters of all German parishes were located in the archdioceses of Cincinnati, St. Louis, Chicago, Milwaukee, and St. Paul.

Although constituting a minority of nineteenth-century German immigrants, Catholics were the largest single denomination, comprising perhaps two-fifths of the total before the Civil War and declining to about one-third by the end of the century as the focus of emigration shifted to the heavily Protestant areas in northern and eastern Germany. Catholics experienced a tension between religion and ethnic consciousness that their Protestant compatriots did not, often seeing themselves as Catholics first and Germans second. But the Irish dominance of the Catholic church and hierarchy, by virtue of their numbers, early arrival, and facility in English, aroused considerable German resentment. The first Irish bishop in the United States was appointed in 1810; the country's first cardinal appointed in 1875 was an Irish American.

Meanwhile, Germans secured only a toehold in the hierarchy. Hanoverian Frederick Rése became the first German-born prelate when he was appointed bishop of the new Detroit diocese in 1833, but his influence was limited when he became incapacitated and was recalled to Rome in 1840. Swiss-German John Martin Henni, who was recruited by Rése, cut a much wider swath, founding and editing the first German Catholic newspaper in Cincinnati before he was named bishop of the new see of Milwaukee in 1844. When it was raised to an archdiocese in 1875 he became the first German archbishop. Meanwhile in 1845 he initiated what grew into the first German Catholic seminary in the country. Bohemian-born John Neumann was the third German-speaking bishop, presiding over the see of Philadelphia from 1852 to 1860. Next in line was the Lorraine native Henry Damien Juncker, who served as bishop of Alton, Illinois, from when the diocese was founded in 1857 until his death in 1868. The year 1857 also saw the naming of the fifth German bishop, Westphalian John Henry Luers, with the establishment of the new see of Fort Wayne, Indiana. With only two of the first five bishops native to the future German Reich, language rather than nationality was the telling criterion, confirming the oft repeated assertion of Bishop Henni: "Language saves faith." What four of the five do have in common is that each was appointed to a newly created diocese, where they did not have to compete with an existing religious establishment. Even such heavily German cities as Cincinnati, St. Louis, and Chicago had no German bishops, immigrant or otherwise, during the nineteenth century; Buffalo has never had one. In 1900, nearly half of the 210 U. S. bishops were of Irish stock, as were all but four of the seventeen cardinals. Only twenty bishops were German speaking, half of whom were Austrian or Swiss, far behind even the French with thirty-five. Often it was lay initiative that overcame the indifference or hostility of Irish and French prelates in the founding of ethnic parishes.

At Germantown, Illinois, parishioners cut logs and sawed planks and had their church building practically finished by Easter 1840, so they would not need to travel to St. Louis to fulfill their obligations. But when they gathered for Easter service, they were told by their priest that there would be no service until the deed was signed over to St. Louis Bishop Rosati. "Father Fortmann was inexorable in this demand." So the deed was made over, and Mass was celebrated in Germantown, but a week late.

Such trusteeship controversies between Germans with a tradition of lay control of property and a dominating hierarchy of other ethnic backgrounds erupted in several other locations. In 1848, John B. Stallo represented Cincinnati's first German Catholic parish, Holy Trinity, in a lawsuit with Irish Archbishop Purcell over the issue of trusteeship. Buffalo, New York, was the scene of a particularly bitter controversy from 1843 to 1855, pitting an Irish bishop against German and Alsatian laity who wanted to retain title to the church property of St. Louis parish, which was twice placed under the interdict.

Tensions between German and Irish Catholics intensified during the 1880s beyond the local level. When Milwaukee Archbishop Henni attempted to appoint a German coadjutor who would succeed him, he encountered resistance from "Americanizing" prelates such as the aptly named archbishop of St. Paul, Minnesota, John Ireland, who claimed

Henni was "Germanizing" the diocese. Conversely, eighty-two mostly German priests in national parishes of the St. Louis archdiocese protested to the Vatican in 1884 over their second-class status, subordinated to the authority of territorial parishes. Two years later, Father Peter Abbelen was sent by the archdiocese of Milwaukee to present a "Memorial" to the Vatican, asserting "The only means by which Catholic Germans . . . shall be able to preserve their Catholic faith and morals is that they shall have their own priests, who shall instruct them in the language and in the traditions of their fatherland," which their (Irish) bishops had often refused them.

The peak of the confrontation came with the "Cahensly controversy," which drew its name from a prosperous German philanthropist and parliamentarian who made the cause of overseas Catholics his own. He organized chapters of the St. Raphael's society, named after the patron saint of travelers, across Europe, and from 1883 on also in America. At the society's convention in Switzerland in 1890, they issued the Lucerne Memorial, which was submitted to the Vatican, calling for a reorganization of American Catholicism along lines of nationality up to the rank of bishop, and demanding that nationalities be proportionately represented in the hierarchy. The Vatican made no formal intervention to lessen the dominance of the Irish, but did appoint two more German-speaking bishops in Wisconsin, and in 1899 issued a condemnation of the "Americanism" heresy for being too accommodating to Protestantism. The German struggles for ethnic rights against an Irish hierarchy set the pattern for other more recently arrived groups, although Germans were not always supportive of other groups such as Poles when they asserted their language rights.

In the long run, faith did not save language, nor was the front on these issues drawn purely along ethnic lines. There were Irish clerics such as New York Archbishop Michael Corrigan and Rochester Bishop Bernard McQuaid who were quite sympathetic to the German (and French-Canadian) cause. By contrast, Chicago Cardinal George Mundelein, whose grandparents emigrated from Paderborn, announced shortly after assuming his position in 1916, "I have no separate message for any particular nationality. I shall not speak to the Germans as Germans." One of his first measures was an "English only" order requiring all parochial schools to use English as a medium of instruction in all courses except catechism and reading, which evoked more resistance from Poles than Germans. Another third-generation German prelate attacked a more insidious form of ethnocentrism. Despite the large German element in St. Louis, it took until 1946 before one of their own headed the archdiocese, future Cardinal Joseph Ritter. Although culturally conservative where movies and colleges were concerned, he was a strong supporter of racial integration, desegregating Catholic schools as one of his first acts in office, as he had done previously as bishop of Indianapolis. But by then, Germans had largely merged with other Catholics into the "Triple Melting Pot." The 1906 Census of Religious Bodies counted 1,881 German-language Catholic parishes (ignoring those using multiple foreign languages); however, more than two-thirds used English along with German, which fewer than six hundred parishes used exclusively. By 1916, a year before the declaration of war with Germany, the number of parishes using German was up slightly to 1,890 but only 206 of them used it exclusively.

Of course, not all German immigrants were Christian, or religious at all. A decade after arriving in Missouri as part of a Catholic group migration, one immigrant wrote back home in 1843: "The old women in Velmede would cross themselves [in horror], if they knew that I never go to church, that during Lent I eat meat three times a day, that my children are not baptized, and yet, in the end, will enter the same heaven as all those who follow the ministers scrupulously. . . . But enough of this, I am in a free country, you my friend are in an unfree country." Freethinkers like him constituted a significant element, especially among the better educated classes of Germans, but the population's size is difficult to gauge since an organizational presence was largely lacking, although not entirely. North St. Louis had a "Freie Gemeinde" of freethinkers since 1850, and there was another in south St. Louis that combined with it in 1894. It maintained its own building until 1961 and did not disband entirely until 1972. Even earlier in the 1840s, some fifty Germans in three counties of rural Missouri, led by Friedrich Muench and other political activists, organized a similar group, though they disagreed on whether to call themselves an Association of Rationalist Christians or to leave out the "Christians" entirely.

There were five so-called Latin Settlements scattered across Texas, established by educated political refugees of the 1840s, many of whom continued their activism in America: Millheim in Austin County, Latium in Washington County, Sisterdale and Tusculum in Kendall County, and Bettina in Llano County. Two of these names go back to the Roman Republic; Tusculum was renamed in honor of German-Jewish literati Ludwig Boerne. A third name honors the liberal romantic Bettina von Arnim, but its attempted communal society broke up within a year. In Sisterdale, a Freethinkers' Society met regularly during the 1850s. Tellingly, none of the five communities had a church through the end of the nineteenth century.

Wisconsin had probably the largest organized freethinking movement, and doubtless the longest lived. A Free Congregation was founded in Milwaukee in 1851, and after some struggles brought in Eduard Schröter from New York as their speaker the same year. He also published the first of two freethinking journals in the city, but resigned two years later because of splits in the rationalist movement. He found a better reception in Sauk City, where he served until his death in 1888. There were thirty such rural free congregations in the state, eight of which had their own speakers, although most of them had gone under by the late 1850s. Not so Sauk City, which had more than eighty members in the 1870s and built an imposing hall in 1884. The Free Congregation in Sauk City switched to English in 1937 and in 1955 joined the Unitarians. It still hosts a Unitarian-Universalist assembly twice monthly as of this writing.

Jews comprised somewhat more than 1 percent of the German population, and at least twice that proportion of the emigration, and perhaps as much as 5 percent. Whatever the exact figure, they played a role disproportionate to their numbers. Like German Protestants, they came from a religious and social background that was itself in flux. Jewish emancipation, the attainment of normal civil and political rights, had been advancing intermittently in Germany since the Enlightenment, though civil equality was not attained everywhere until the founding of the German Reich in 1871, or the 1867 constitution in Austria. And German Judaism itself was undergoing a modernizing, assimilative influence known as Reform Judaism, which was transplanted to America and developed further there.

In some respects, the identity of immigrant Jews in mid-nineteenth-century America was similar to the triangular situation experienced by German Catholics, in a tension between Jewish, German, and American. Chicago Rabbi Bernhard Felsenthal explained these multiple identities in 1901; "Racially, I am a Jew, for I have been born among the Jewish nation. . . . Politically I am an American as patriotic, as enthusiastic, as devoted an American citizen as it is possible to be. . . . Spiritually I am a German, for my inner life has been profoundly influenced by Schiller, by Goethe, by Kant, and by other intellectual giants of Germany." As this quote indicates, the German identity was reinforced by the Jewish respect for *Bildung*, education in the broadest sense. The American identity was reinforced by the constitutional separation of church and state, so that migration itself was an act of emancipation. But there was no need to sacrifice a Jewish identity to gain full access to most American and German-American institutions. One historian characterized the nineteenth-century situation thus: "the German-American and German-Jewish communities were overlapping and inextricable entities."

The contrast between Germany and America is exemplified by the saga of the Lorelei statue, commissioned by the Empress of Austria and intended as a tribute to poet Heinrich Heine as a gift to his native city of Duesseldorf. However, rising antisemitism led to its rejection there and in other German cities. But thanks to a fundraising effort by the Arion Society of New York and Germans across the religious spectrum, in 1899 it was erected instead at a park in the Bronx, its unveiling celebrated by hundreds of Germans from Carl Schurz on down and a broad spectrum of Vereins.

Jews probably adopted English more quickly than other Germans. Milwaukee editor Emil Rothe remarked in 1886, "It seems that German Jews make the most effort to divest themselves of the German language and customs, but one cannot rightfully expect from them any special attachment to the German Step-Fatherland." This would certainly be true of those engaged in peddling, especially in the South where they were practically the only Germans in many communities, irrespective of religion. But that was not the case everywhere; in the Northeast and Midwest most synagogues continued to use German for sermons and records until quite late in the century. There were anthologies of rabbis' sermons published in the German language into the 1890s, and Reform Judaism's 1897 hymnal lifted the tune for #95 from "Deutschland über alles." Even Cincinnati Rabbi Isaac Wise, the father of the Reform movement who promoted the use of English, preached just as often in German. His weekly *American Israelite*, although published in English, for decades after its founding in 1854 included untranslated poems and advertisements in German and reviews of German theater locally and in New York. Its female counterpart, *Die Deborah*, was published entirely in German from 1855 to 1902.

What took place from the 1880s on was less an alienation of German Jews from other Germans than simply a shift in priorities, namely concern for fellow Jews from Eastern Europe. German Jews were sometimes embarrassed by their "poor cousins" from the Russian Empire, fearing that an "army of Jewish paupers" would precipitate a rise in antisemitism, as *The American Hebrew* put it in 1882. But instead of distancing themselves from their coreligionists, they organized an array of social service institutions to help newcomers become established. Even after the turn of the century, one sees German Jews such as immigrant lobbyist Simon Wolf cooperating with other Germans such as Missouri Congressman Richard Bartholdt to thwart a literacy test for immigrants—aided by the German language press. When the bill finally passed in 1913, President William Howard Taft vetoed it upon recommendation of his cabinet secretary Charles Nagel, a Texas German refugee from the Confederacy who was the brother-in-law of Louis Brandeis.

Religion played an important role in German-American education. Until the Prussian Kulturkampf of the 1870s, elementary schooling was under the supervision of the church in most German states, albeit an established church supported by public revenue. In locations with mixed populations, Protestants and Catholics usually attended separate schools. So it is not surprising that congregations attempted to carry on this role in America despite the financial sacrifice involved. Catholics and Lutherans both believed that "language saves faith," and quickly set up their own German-language schools for both religious and cultural reasons. Where public schools were available at the start of mass immigration, they were often anti-Catholic or at least imbued with strong Anglo-Protestant overtones. Despite the Constitutional clause forbidding the establishment of religion, most public schools at the time required reading from the Protestant King James Version of the Bible and engaged in other religious activities. Catholics saw this as religious discrimination and resented having their children subjected to what they considered Protestant indoctrination. A German Catholic weekly in Louisville editorialized in 1870: "If the Protestant Bible in the free schools is declared as constitutional, then the free schools are <u>religious</u> schools, . . . but then the demands of Catholics for state support can no longer be denied." Though hardly sympathetic to Catholics, German Lutherans who had emigrated in protest against a forced denominational merger in Prussia were thus bitterly opposed to ecumenical Protestantism and were similarly determined to establish parochial schools along with their churches. Within the Catholic Church, Germans were caught in a struggle with the dominant Irish for recognition of their language and culture. As soon as a parish or congregation had been established, therefore, Germans on both sides of the Reformation divide strove to establish their own schools as quickly as possible, with impressive results. Some two-thirds of German Catholic parishes in the Midwest established parochial schools within their first two years, but barely a quarter of their Irish counterparts did the same.

By 1869, the roughly seven hundred German Catholic parishes had more than 130,000 pupils enrolled in their parochial schools. By 1881, over one thousand German parishes provided schooling for 160,000 Catholic children. In 1910, over 95 percent of German parishes had parochial schools where their heritage language was taught or used as the means of instruction. In 1915, although immigration had slowed to a trickle, Germans in Cleveland had six thousand pupils enrolled in Catholic schools with their language, second in number only to the city's Poles. A nationwide survey of Catholic schools in 1935 showed that German instruction had almost died out by then, though the German dedication to parochial education had not. Of the 237 German-nationality parishes remaining in 1940, almost 90 percent maintained parochial schools, the highest of any nationality.

The largest Lutheran body, the Missouri Synod, also developed an extensive network of parochial schools. It was instructing over ten thousand children in its schools in 1861. The number of pupils surpassed thirty thousand in 1872 and grew to over fifty thousand by 1881. Enrollment peaked around the turn of the century, with almost one hundred thousand pupils enrolled in more than 2,100 Lutheran schools, operating largely or sometimes exclusively in the German language. A third German-American denomination, the Evangelicals, also maintained schools of their own, but given their ecumenical origins, this was never such a high priority. Their enrollment numbers never exceeded twenty thousand.

A comparison of the number of infants baptized in German Catholic or Lutheran churches in a given year with the number of parochial pupils enrolled reveals that there were at least two pupils for every baptism, and sometimes nearly three. Assuming an average of six years of schooling, this would indicate that only one-third, or at most one-half, of all Lutheran and Catholic children attended parochial schools in the late nineteenth century. Among Evangelicals, the enrollment never exceeded the number of baptisms, suggesting that most of their children received only a year of parochial schooling in preparation for confirmation.

The extra cost of parochial schools was certainly one factor limiting enrollment. The Louisville paper editorialized that the state could only do justice to Catholics if it gave them a share of the public school fund, "so that we Catholics would also have a <u>free school</u> and don't have to pay school tax for the state schools and for our private schools." Thus, one might expect that German Catholics would oppose German language instruction in public schools, which would only further increase public costs and divert children from parochial schools. But that was not always the case; Catholics were not immune to ethnic pride. Later that year, the same paper editorialized that it was "gratifying that German language instruction has already been introduced into the public schools in most of the bigger cities of the Union." It also attracted children of non-German backgrounds and improved the ethnic image: "We hear no educated American throwing around the term 'Dutch' any more. . . . He speaks quite politely of 'our German element.'"

German elements that did not have a stake in parochial education, such as freethinkers and German Jews, were strongly supportive of public schools in general, and of those offering heritage language instruction in particular. Beginning with Pennsylvania and Ohio before 1840, various states and cities, primarily in the Midwest, provided for instruction in German or other languages in the public schools upon request from parents or school boards. Ethnic politics undoubtedly played a role in these initiatives. As a Milwaukee observer cynically remarked, the German program there was indebted to "shrewd politicians who cared neither for the educational value of German nor for the beauty of its literature, but who recognized the . . . strength of the so-called German vote." The timing of when German was introduced was hardly coincidental; there was a surge in the wake of the Civil War when the German vote was up for grabs. Republican St. Louis introduced the program in 1864, Chicago in 1865, Buffalo in 1866, Milwaukee in 1867, and Cleveland and Indianapolis in 1869. There, as in many cities, it was the culmination of a long campaign; a leading Indianapolis promotor was the freethinking grandfather of novelist Kurt Vonnegut.

A commission looking into the question in Cleveland in 1906 concluded that "the reason for the teaching of German in the primary and grammar grades . . . is not educational, but chiefly national and sentimental." However, testimony of school officials and others showed that employment considerations also played a major role; bilinguals had an edge in the labor market. This was obviously the case when non-German children took part in such programs. It was probably the reason twenty-six Indianapolis Blacks petitioned in 1870 for German instruction in their schools. Even at the San Antonio German-English school, a private institution that charged tuition averaging $3 per month, more than one-sixth of the pupils were from non-German households, most of them Anglo, but also including a few Hispanics. Religiously neutral by its charter, the school also attracted a fair number of German Jews. Half of the entire Cincinnati school population participated in its two-way immersion program when only two-fifths of the city was of German stock. In Cleveland after 1899, only three-eighths of the participants came from German-speaking homes, another three-eighths from English-speaking homes, and the remaining quarter from households where other immigrant languages prevailed. Some pupils did claim they were enrolled in German inadvertently, because parents automatically signed any documents they brought home from school. But while Cleveland investigators disparaged the effectiveness of the program, their report showed that 90 percent of children from German-speaking homes could read the language themselves.

Some programs merely taught German as a subject one hour daily, as was the case in St. Louis, Chicago, and New York City. But Cincinnati, Indianapolis, and Cleveland offered genuinely bilingual programs, "two-way immersion" in current parlance. They divided the school day equally between German and English, using both as a means of instruction, as was the case in San Antonio. Usually two teachers were paired, one teaching all the English subjects and the other all the German in two classes, trading off at midday. There was a similar program in the public schools of New Ulm, Minnesota. A longitudinal study compared students in this program with German pupils in another similar town with an "English only" program. It concluded: "Clearly, bilingual education did not retard the social and occupational mobility of New Ulm Germans."

This may seem surprising given the reduced amount of English content students were exposed to. In Cleveland, the school week was equally divided between languages, with eleven hours of English content and eleven of German. Arithmetic was taught only in English, singing only in German, all other subjects in both. Pupils in the German track got 275 minutes of English reading, grammar, and spelling, compared to 475 minutes in the monolingual track. But Cleveland pupils obviously suffered no ill effects. On the high school entrance exams in grammar and mathematics conducted entirely in English, students from the bilingual track scored 17 percent higher than "English only" students. An Anglo principal from Cincinnati reported similar results, and students who went on to high school were equipped to handle works of Goethe and Schiller that were taught at that level.

There were other German contributions to schooling besides their language; the ubiquity of the *Gesangverein* and *Turnverein* in German communities made itself felt in the schools, public and private. It was not coincidental that singing was included in the German track in bilingual programs. It had a regular place in the curriculum of the San Antonio school, as did physical education and swimming—subjects that most American schools only adopted around the turn of the century, often prompted by German lobbying. Chicago Turners, for example, were influential in that respect.

One reason authorities were willing to meet immigrants halfway with bilingual education in the public schools was that heritage languages were even more prevalent in parochial grade schools. In St. Louis, only one-fifth of German children attended public schools in 1860 before German instruction was instituted; by 1880, over four-fifths of them were attending public schools. The figure in Cleveland was not as high, but nearly three-fifths of children from German families attended public rather than parochial schools. They were regarded as the main agent of Americanization, and even half a day of English instruction in the bilingual programs was more than pupils would have received in many parochial schools. Lesson plans for German Evangelical schools in the 1890s provided for one hour of English instruction daily at most, and German Lutherans and Catholics were, if anything, more tenacious in their language preservation. Wisconsin's governor was appalled to discover in 1888 that there were 129 Lutheran schools in his state that taught no English whatsoever: un-American, in his eyes.

But as with the ethnic press, the content—even if expressed in a language other than English—was clearly American. In fact, Indianapolis published its own German translations of American geography and history books because those imported from the Old Country were too imbued with German nationalism. Starting in 1881, St. Louis public school teachers put out a series of pedagogically advanced German primers that the Witter press published in multiple editions up through 1915. Thereafter, these books took on a life of their own. Mennonite groups put out reprints from the 1920s at least to 1978, and a Hutterite press put out an edition in the year 2000.

For all its initial success, German instruction in St. Louis public schools succumbed much earlier. Begun as an experiment in five schools in 1864, the German program met with heavy demand and quickly spread throughout the city's system. Within ten years, nearly half of all pupils were taking part. By 1880, all but five of the city's fifty-seven public schools offered the program. Nearly one-quarter of the pupils taking language instruction were not of German origins. Although such programs in other cities often persisted until World War I, the one in St. Louis was abolished in 1887, in some respects a victim of its own success. It added an estimated $100,000 annually to the school budget (with a similar figure quoted for Cleveland around 1900). In 1878, an Irish school-board member proposed dropping German, but a meeting of Germans organized to save the program. Within a month, presented with forty thousand signatures (equal to 73 percent of all German-born men, women, and children in the 1880 census) favoring retention, the school board relented. But in 1887, "a clear case of gerrymandering" of school-board districts sealed the fate of German instruction in St. Louis.

In rural Missouri, however, instruction continued in areas where Germans dominated, regardless of official sanction. Friedrich Muench reported in 1872, "In completely German school districts (like mine) we can use only German teachers, who begin with German instruction and afterward combine English with it." The state superintendent of education complained in his 1888 report: "In a large number of districts . . . the German element . . . greatly preponderates and as a consequence the schools are mainly taught in the German language and sometimes entirely so. Hence, if an American family lives in such a district the children must either be deprived of school privileges or else be taught in the German language. . . . Some of the teachers are scarcely able to speak the English language." Despite his indignation, the legislature steered clear of any intervention. In heavily German Gasconade County, half the public grade schools were taught partly in German, in some instances continuing until 1917. As if that were not enough, some public schools in the state were not only German but de facto Catholic as well. As a diocesan history relates, in heavily Catholic Osage County, where parish members dominated a district board, the school was held on church property, but salaries were paid by the public. "The school, though not parochial, is practically Catholic." The county's public/parochial schools continued to operate bilingually on through the 1920s, and retained their Catholic content as late as the 1950s, beginning the day with mass and allowing the few Protestant pupils to start forty-five minutes later, as a former pupil related to me.

In some parts of the country, a formal arrangement for public cost sharing with Catholic schools was developed, known as the Poughkeepsie Plan for the New York town where it was instituted in 1873. But it originated in the town's Irish parish and may not have even included the smaller German congregation. Half a dozen other upstate towns that adopted the plan were home to few German Catholics, as was the case in New Haven, Connecticut, and three Georgia cities that had similar arrangements.

More common during the second half of the nineteenth century were informal provisions for public financing of religious schools, which extended to Lutheran as well as Catholic communities. A study of Wisconsin found that the separation of church and state was much more stringent in theory than in practice. Public funds were expended for Lutheran as well as Catholic schools in some localities, and the German language was more prevalent than legally allowed. Irrespective of state laws requiring English as the medium of instruction but allowing an hour of foreign language instruction, the school day or year was often divided up between English and German. A former pupil recalled his school days at Cedarburg in the 1870s, where "the Irish families represented by children in school all understood German and their children could talk German. German was the language of the playground." At one district in Sauk County, the public school was taught exclusively in German for several years in the 1850s, but from 1861 to 1885 it offered two months of German and three to five of English instruction every year, (though the board minutes were kept in German through 1887). In Lutheran Freistadt, the same building housed what was officially a parochial German school in the morning and a public English school in the afternoon. The German language proved to be less resilient in the secular freethinker center of Sauk City than in Catholic or particularly Lutheran communities. But even with the latter, if children attended exclusively German schools, it was usually only for part of the year, or for two years of confirmation instruction after having attended years of English or bilingual public school.

An 1890 U. S. Census report confirmed the ambiguity of the public versus parochial classification, but for reasons of confidentiality, it did not identify locations where, for example, "3 Lutheran schools . . . are parochial in the forenoon and public in the afternoon," or "our school is a public school taught by Franciscan sisters." This publication does present state-level statistics for various church bodies, which is of little help with multiethnic Catholics. But they show that Evangelical Lutheran schools (mostly German, but including some Scandinavians), enrolled nearly ten times the pupils as German Evangelicals. In both cases, their concentration in the Midwestern (North Central) states was apparent, encompassing 87 percent of the Lutherans and 90 percent of the Evangelicals.

At the beginning of the twentieth century, an unofficial and incomplete survey conducted by the German-American Teachers Association revealed that over half a million children were being taught German in elementary schools. Of those, a plurality of 42 percent attended public schools, followed by Catholic schools with more than one-third. Lutherans accounted for 16 percent, while the remaining 7 percent were divided among Evangelical and secular private schools. Coverage was quite high in some areas; over 90 percent in homogeneous communities such as New Braunfels, Texas; Hermann, Missouri; and New Ulm, Minnesota. Chicago experienced a peak enrollment of some forty-four thousand, and a total of sixty-eight thousand pupils were learning German in New York and New Jersey. Ohio held the lead with some one hundred thousand students of the language. A survey in 1908 found over sixty-six thousand in Ohio public schools alone, at a time when there were about ninety thousand school-age children of German stock. Measured another way, they comprised nearly 8 percent of all students in a state whose population was almost 14 percent of German stock counting the second generation. So about half of the German children in Ohio received instruction in their heritage language, though some pupils in these programs were not of German background.

Just as today, not all languages were equal in the public support they received—German was clearly in a favored position. This was not only the result of ethnic lobbying (though it obviously played a role), for also in an area where public funding was minimal, German publications comprised over two-thirds of the foreign-language press as late as 1892. Of primary importance was the fact that Germans were more likely than other groups to assemble the "critical mass" to make bilingual programs feasible, especially in many Midwestern enclaves where they were the only foreign-language group of any size.

World War I was not the first time that German instruction in schools came under attack. One German linguist (and chauvinist) argues that German Americans were the vanguard of a linguistic pluralism in the American school system. This held true in some instances, but it was not always the case. The most dramatic instance of ethnic cooperation was in resistance to the Bennett and Edwards laws in Wisconsin and Illinois in 1889, when the state mandated that parochial as well as public schools teach all major subjects in English.

These laws united German Lutherans and Catholics against a common enemy and mobilized their Slavic ethnic allies, sweeping Republicans from power in both states. Pamphlets attacking the Bennett Law were published in German, Polish, and Bohemian. Slavic immigrants made themselves felt in the 1890 city election in Milwaukee, where the Democratic ticket featured a Polish candidate for controller, and the city council ended up with five Polish aldermen, equal with the Americans, and only one behind the Irish, although the Germans had an absolute majority on the board. At the state level, Democrats took a two-thirds majority in the Wisconsin legislature, and elected a Czech immigrant as

lieutenant governor in 1892. Illinois saw the election of its first Democratic governor since the Civil War, and the first immigrant and first
Chicagoan ever: German John Peter Altgeld, who carried nineteen of the
twenty Chicago wards with immigrant majorities among the voters. His
election was celebrated in the Polish press, and opposition to the Edwards
Law was one of the few issues it singled out. Needless to say, the school
laws were quickly rescinded in both states.

German Catholics were also subjected to assimilative pressure in Minnesota, but here it was the aptly named immigrant Archbishop John Ireland who attempted (with little success) to undermine German Catholic schools by obtaining public funding for English-language Catholic
schools. Poles undoubtedly saw Germans as their allies there as well,
and both were further alienated by Ireland's support for the anti-alcohol
crusade.

Besides protecting their parochial schools, German and Slavic immigrants sometimes cooperated in efforts to introduce heritage languages
into the public school curriculum. Although laws in some states speci-
fied German, most of them provided for instruction in any language
requested by the school board or a specific number of parents. Nevertheless, Germans were the main beneficiaries because they were the ones
most likely to have the critical mass in a community to sustain such a
program. But there were instances in which they supported the language
aspirations of other groups. German had early on obtained a place in
the Milwaukee public schools, but Polish was added in 1907 and Italian
shortly thereafter in a city dominated by Germans. In Nebraska in 1913,
Germans joined forces with Bohemians and Scandinavians to pass an
ethnically neutral law providing for the instruction of any modern European language in any school where the parents of fifty pupils petitioned
it, and besides Germans, eight Czech communities took advantage of
it. In Texas, one could see a similar German-Czech coalition supporting their native languages in public schools. When an 1871 law required
teachers to be certified for competency in English, Fayette County officials petitioned for one longtime teacher to be examined in one of the two
languages in which he was fluent, Czech or German, because he feared
his command of English was insufficient. After a year's grace period, he
managed to pass the English exam, and continued to instruct in all three
languages in the public schools. Not until 1905 did Texas law require

English as a medium of instruction. Despite the nationalistic wave of World War I and the English-only crusading of the Ku Klux Klan, German was reintroduced into a couple of communities, and seven districts taught Czech in 1932—schools that were sometimes de facto parochial schools, even taught by nuns.

Milwaukee Germans were relatively supportive of Polish aspirations, but in other industrial cities, German-Slavic relations were a different story. The 1906 Cleveland Education Survey reported that in the city, "about half [of the Bohemians] are Catholic and the rest are free-thinkers . . . the common Slavic feeling manifests itself most strongly in antipathy to the German language." A 1907 petition to eliminate German instruction signed by over thirteen thousand supporters was presented to the school board by a group calling itself the "Taxpayers' Educational League," but drafted by four men with unmistakably Polish names. In the discussion of the issue after 1914, a Polish immigrant expressed his resentment that the German language was forced on Poles back in Europe, but Jews from these areas tended to favor the German language. Among an eight-member delegation protesting the reduction of German instruction in Cleveland were two Austrian-Jewish members. Similarly, in St. Louis, a committee formed in 1878 to defend German instruction in the city's elementary schools was headed up by Reform Rabbi Solomon Sonnenschein.

Chicago shows a gradual deterioration of German-Slavic relations by the end of the nineteenth century. During the 1870s and 1880s, Germans and Bohemians had often been allied in the labor movement. It was police violence against Bohemian and German strikers that triggered the protest meeting that led to the Haymarket Affair, and when the Haymarket Martyrs Monument was dedicated in 1893, speeches were held in English, German, Bohemian, and Polish. But increasingly, issues of language came between them. Chicago Germans proved to be anything but proponents of linguistic pluralism. They had succeeded in placing their language in the public school curriculum, but demands for equal treatment, especially from Bohemians, were rebuffed by arguments that the German language was special compared to other "less important" tongues. This arrogance is apparent in an 1893 protest against curtailment of German instruction: "how is it possible that the study of German, a world language, can be considered useless and treated accordingly in a cosmopolitan city like Chicago?" But as the *Staatszeitung* reported in 1900, "The Bohemians insist that they have as good a right to their demands as has the German element of this city." When World War I broke out, Bohemians and Poles were determined to eliminate German from the public school curriculum, even if their own languages suffered collateral damage.

One sees a similar double standard among some German Catholics in church language policies. In 1900, when the Chicago *Zgoda* was crusading for Polish language rights within the Catholic Church, it criticized not only two Irish archbishops, John Ireland of Minnesota and John Joseph Keane of Dubuque, Iowa, but also Michigan Bishop Frederick Eis, a German native who was trained in the United States. The following year, *Zgoda* admonished, "Why doesn't Bishop Eis or Bishop Messner name a Polish priest for promotion?" The latter was the Swiss-German Bishop Sebastian Messner of Green Bay, the future Archbishop of Milwaukee. Eis had issued a directive requiring English to be preached in at least one of the weekly masses throughout his diocese, a directive quickly echoed by Messner.

This stood in striking contrast to German-Slavic relations in Texas and much of the rural Midwest. A prominent feature of Czechs' settlement is the degree to which they located in proximity to Germans, and given the sequence of migration, it is apparent that the Czechs did so voluntarily. As an early Czech immigration historian remarked in 1920, the march of the Czech pathfinders "in the footsteps of the Germans had not been fortuitous, but a matter of careful premeditation." This proximity implies affinity, but there is more concrete evidence as well.

The 1906 U. S. Census of Religious Bodies documented the frequency with which Catholic parishes shared German with one of the Slavic languages: Polish or particularly "Bohemian," as Czechs were called in this source. Although there were seven times as many French-speaking as Bohemian Catholics, Bohemians were almost as likely as the French to share parishes with Germans. The contrast with Italians was even starker. So with the possible exception of the Irish, who were subsumed under the English speakers, Germans and Slavic groups were the most likely to share Catholic nationality parishes. There is other evidence of German-Slavic cooperation down to the parish level, some of it written in stone. The cornerstone of a Catholic church near Schwertner, Texas, basically reads "Holy Trinity" in German, Czech, and Latin. Where is the English, one might ask? Presumably on the side mortared into the foundation. Another trilingual location was Spillville, Iowa, where Antonin Dvorak composed his New World Symphony among fellow Czechs. Its Catholic school provided instruction in all three of the languages spoken by the pupils: Czech, German, and English.

An unofficial 1892 directory of German-speaking Catholics in the United States provides further insights. Where there was just a small scattering of Slavic Catholics in a Germanophone parish, they may have had to communicate with their priest in whatever German they could muster. But in most locations where a parish had a Slavic majority, these churches were served by priests whose origins indicate that they were probably bilingual. Ironically, Berlin, Wisconsin, was served by a priest with the Polish name of Czarnowski, whereas Pulaski, Wisconsin, was served by the Reverend Schneider. But despite the latter's German name, both were likely bilingual, given their origins in Posen (Poznan).

There is similar evidence of cooperation on the Protestant side. Lee County, Texas, ranks second only to Fredericksburg in German-language preservation, a great historical irony in view of its population makeup. It is home to a heavy concentration of Sorbs (or what the Germans call Wends), from a Slavic-language island in eastern Germany that has hung on until the present. A shipload of some five hundred people came to Texas in 1854 in part to guard their Lutheran faith that was threatened by the Prussian Union Church. But the Sorbs came also to escape the increasing pressures of Germanization. However, they never had a critical mass to maintain their own religious institutions beyond the congregational level, and they allied themselves with the German Missouri Synod, sending their theological candidates to Concordia Seminary in St. Louis. Thus, these Sorbs became so Germanized in Texas that into the twenty-first century the "mother church" in Serbin still offered German-language services once a month. However, one really can't fault the Sorbs; they were just assimilating to the dominant culture in their area and their denomination.

This was not the only Slavic group that allied itself with German Protestants. Slovak Lutherans hardly had the numbers to sustain their own denomination or train their own clergy, so as early as the 1880s some Slovak students were admitted to a German Lutheran seminary, and in 1910 they joined a synod that otherwise consisted largely of German Lutherans. There was also a small Czech Protestant body with the Latin name of Unitas Fratrum, often simply called "Brethren" in Texas. With only a dozen or two congregations, it had similar problems of critical mass, so the Brethren solved their problem in much the same way as the Sorbs and the Slovaks did, sending their theological students off to a German-language seminary in St. Louis. But given their Calvinistic leanings, the Brethren chose not the Lutheran seminary but the Evangelical Eden Seminary.

Beyond schools and churches, secular German societies in Texas provide evidence of cordial ethnic relations not bound by narrow ethnic chauvinism. Austin County was home to nearly nine hundred Czechs, as well as the oldest German settlement in the state and the state's oldest agricultural society at Cat Spring. Its German-language minutes in the two decades before World War I show that its festivities were not bilingual but often trilingual, with "Bohemian" speakers invited to give addresses alongside German and English orators. Even after World War I, there were Czech as well as German names among the musicians hired for various dances and festivities. There were even some Texas Germans in the area who learned Czech.

It was quite typical for smaller European immigrant groups to ally themselves with Germans, especially at the outset when they did not have the critical mass to sustain their own institutions. This was particularly true of German-speaking groups; in 1900, there were half as many people born in America with one German and one Luxembourger parent as with two parents from the Grand Duchy, and three-fourths as many people with one German and one Swiss parent as with both parents from Switzerland. This even held true for groups of other linguistic backgrounds, as was apparent in the statutes that the German Society of Chicago announced in 1871, defining who qualified for their assistance: "By the term 'German Immigrants' also Hollanders, Bohemians, Poles, and Hungarians shall be understood, because these people have no representation of their nationality in Chicago." There was a particular affinity with Scandinavians, who shared a Protestant faith with the majority of Germans. Norwegian Lutherans had begun studies at Concordia Seminary in St. Louis in 1858, although they soon came into conflict when the

German clergy refused to take a stand against slavery. But it took until 1876 before Norwegians were able to support their own seminary.

Scandinavians apparently got along better with secular Germans. The 82nd Illinois Infantry, named after and commanded by Forty-Eighter Friedrich Hecker and outfitted with a similarly rationalist "chaplain," had one Scandinavian company in its ranks. This gave rise to little or no antagonism, except for a brief objection to the appointment of a German as one of its lieutenants.

The regiment also included one German-Jewish company raised in Chicago, but reactions to this company were varied. The *Staats-Zeitung* reported extensively and enthusiastically on its formation, and prominent Lutheran and Catholic politicians spoke at the "war meetings" that rallied support for the Jewish company. But the private letters of one lieutenant manifest a strong antipathy toward Lieutenant Colonel Edward Salomon, calling him the "Creole from Jerusalem." However, this may be an anomaly or merely a personal rivalry. Henry Greenebaum, a leading promoter of the Jewish company and the regiment generally, finished in second place at the 1876 Old Settlers picnic, which voted to name the most popular German "old settler." The winner, who was awarded an armchair, received 612 votes; Greenebaum, 325; the third-place finisher, 268; other contestants ranged from thirty-one votes on down. Five years earlier in 1871, Greenebaum had led the huge parade celebrating German victory over France and the country's unification.

Besides their support for and participation in German instruction in public schools, Jewish immigrants were active in other ethnic institutions as well. They took part in singing societies and the Turner movement to a greater extent than in the Old Country, and were active in the German language press. Most prominent was Joseph Pulitzer, who began his career with the St. Louis *Westliche Post*, but two of the editors of the nation's leading German paper, the *New Yorker Staats-Zeitung*, were also Jewish.

Secular and Forty-Eighter elements in the German press were most sympathetic to Jewish causes, but even the Louisville Catholic *Glaubensbote* in its first few years, although not without traces of antisemitism, spoke out against the oppression of Eastern European Jews. An 1866 article on Jewish persecution in Rumania characterized it as a staged rabble-rousing, as vandalistic and despicable as any experienced in the century, followed later that year by a report on the "outrageous" repression of Jews in Poland. This Democratic paper decried President Ulysses S. Grant as an "obdurate hater of Catholics and Jews." Even then, there was frequent emphasis on Jewish wealth and power. But the alleged "ingratitude" of Rome's Jews toward the beleaguered Papacy in 1870 brought the latent antipathies toward Jews out into the open, and soon the *Glaubensbote* was running headlines like "The Jews Rule the World." Attitudes like these were probably widespread among Christian Germans, but they seldom found expression in the immigrant press.

There was little interaction of Germans with Italians because their migrations were concentrated in different regions and time periods. They rarely shared Catholic parishes. But many Germans probably harbored similar prejudices, as one Lutheran farmer in the Northwest wrote, "California is a beautiful place, the climate is particularly nice. . . . But I don't like the people. It is partly made up of descendants of Spaniards, Italians, and Greeks."

With Mexicans, the evidence is mixed. Future Texas Congressman Henry Gonzalez was inspired to greatness by being thrown out of the public swimming pool in New Braunfels in the 1930s. But one of the town's immigrants, William Gebhardt, developed dried chili powder and in 1908 published a cookbook that helped introduce Mexican food to the American public. San Antonio miller Hilmar Guenther not only employed Hispanics but also marketed tortilla flour on both sides of the border in sacks labeled in Spanish. The German English School that his children attended also offered courses in Spanish, albeit taught by Germans, and enrolled pupils from a couple of purely Hispanic families, plus two other families that were from marriages between Germans and Hispanics. There were instances of marriage to Latinas by German merchant Carl Blumner in Santa Fe in the 1850s and by Union veteran Joseph Schmerber from Castroville, who settled on the Rio Grande; in both cases, their children were essentially Hispanicized. But the Mexican bride of another Unionist refugee, Juanita Sanchez Kleck, returned with him to Fredericksburg and became thoroughly Germanized there. Still, such relationships were rare; only 201 Texans claimed a German father and a Mexican mother in 1900, plus seventy-four with the opposite parentage. However, by the 1930s, German-Latino intermarriage was becoming more common in places like San Antonio.

The ethnic group most at odds with Germans was the Irish. Cartoonist Thomas Nast was notorious for his vicious portrayals of Irish Catholics. Much of this was due to their overwhelmingly Democratic affiliation; unreconstructed Rebels fared little better under Nast's pen. He even skewered fellow Germans along with Irish who were agitating for Chinese exclusion, calling them 1870 Know Nothings who wanted to "throw down the ladder by which they rose." Nast came to the defense of the Chinese in a number of cartoons, but his record is offset by immigrant Jacob Weisbach, who as mayor of Portland led a mob that expelled the Chinese in 1885, and by other anti-Chinese agitation by German labor. Nast does include a fairly benign image of an Irish couple in his 1869 multiracial and multiethnic portrait of "Uncle Sam's Thanksgiving Dinner," but he seldom missed an opportunity to portray the Colored Orphans Asylum in flames set by Irish draft rioters in 1863 New York. It was against this background that radical Forty-Eighter Adolph Douai characterized the Irish as "loafers, cutthroats, thieves, sharpers, and political stooges." Most Protestant and Republican Germans probably shared the views of Nast and Douai. Although both ethnic groups were targeted by nativists, German editors routinely portrayed the Irish as drunken, brawling rowdies. Even with Catholics, religion did not always trump ethnicity. The priest who compiled an unofficial directory of German Catholics in 1869 advised, "In marital ties hold to Catholic Germans, for the character of the Irish, no matter how firm and fervent their Catholic faith may be, is just too different from that of the Germans, for a bond as intimate as that of marriage to flourish." Father Abbelen claimed in his 1886 Vatican Memorial supporting German Catholic autonomy, "scarcely ever will you find German and Irish united in matrimony."

German Americans even had serious reservations about Anglo-Americans. Both Northerners and Southerners fell short in German eyes. Southerners in particular were spurned because of their association with slavery and secession and their propensity to violence. But Northerners, too, had their downsides: sharp trading, hypocrisy, and, above all, religious fanaticism, especially when expressed in a crusade against alcohol and for a Puritan Sunday. Whenever an Independence Day celebration was postponed until July 5 because the Fourth fell on a Sunday, it was an opportunity for the German press to rail against the Americans. Germans often expressed more admiration for "the true American spirit, the spirit of its free institutions," than for the American people themselves. They sometimes intimated that as Americans by choice, they understood the ideals of this country better than those who were born here: "Whoever conducts himself . . . according to the republican Constitution of our new fatherland, which by no means excludes reforms, is an American in the sense in which it is honorable to be called an American, and not all native born are necessarily through chance of birth Americans in this sense." German Americans are often characterized as rapid assimilators; had it not been for this "superiority complex," they would have been much quicker to submerge themselves in the melting pot.

5

The German-Language Press
and German Culture in America

THE HISTORY OF THE GERMAN-LANGUAGE PRESS predates
the establishment of the United States, reaching far back into the colonial era. The first complete Bible printed in the colonies in any European
language was Christopher Sauer's 1743 German edition. In 1739, Sauer
established the *Hoch-Deutsch Pensylvanischen Geschicht-Schreiber*, the
first successful venture of its kind, though Benjamin Franklin had made
a short-lived attempt at a German newspaper in 1732. By the outbreak
of the American Revolution there were already three German papers in
Pennsylvania. One of them, the *Pennsylvanischer Staatsbote*, was the first
paper in any language to announce on July 5, 1776, the adoption of the
Declaration of Independence. The paper published it in full translation
only four days later. It was mere coincidence that the *Staatsbote* broke the
news of independence on July 5; all newspapers in the city were weeklies,
and this paper just happened to be the first to appear after the vote. But
the July 9 translation of the Declaration was anything but coincidence.

The German language press, like the immigrant press everywhere,
played an ambivalent, Janus-faced role. On the one hand, it looked backward, serving to preserve the mother tongue and promote ethnic consciousness and the defense of ethnic interests. But in order to effectively
carry out this defensive function, it had to educate immigrants in American ways, particularly in the American political process, as the *Staatsbote* did in translating the Declaration. And in doing so, the immigrant
press sowed seeds of its own destruction. The *Staatsbote* lasted only from
1768 to 1779, and even during that time was suspended eleven months,

probably because of wartime disruption. The last of a number of short-lived German newspapers in Philadelphia before the mass immigration of the nineteenth century, the *Amerikanischer Beobachter* (Observer), went under in 1811.

There were exceptions. At least one Pennsylvania German newspaper, the *Readinger Adler* (Eagle), actually survived from the eighteenth century into the twentieth, as did a German almanac from Hagerstown, Maryland. Two other papers in the towns of Lancaster and Allentown, Pennsylvania, were in existence by the War of 1812 and lasted for more than a century. For the most part, however, the genesis of the ethnic press dates from the onset of mass immigration in the 1830s. Philadelphia regained a German newspaper in 1825, but the first one to gain a firm footing was the *Alte und Neue Welt*, established in 1834. The *New Yorker Staats-Zeitung*, founded in 1834, the St. Louis *Anzeiger des Westens*, dating from 1835, and the *Cincinnati Volksblatt*, going back to 1836, were the first viable German papers in their respective cities. Until 1843, Cincinnati claimed the only German-American daily. The political refugees of 1848 injected a massive dose of talent and energy into ethnic press. The seventy German-American papers existing in 1848 had nearly been doubled by 1852. By 1860 there were at least sixteen cities with German dailies, and often two or more competitors in large metropolitan areas. Except for Brooklynites, who were well-supplied from the New York side, the largest group of urban Germans without their own daily newspaper were the nine thousand in Cleveland.

The immigrant was astoundingly well supplied with reading material, even in comparison with back home. With four German dailies, New York in 1850 was ahead of the Prussian capital of Berlin and the publishing center of Leipzig. Already before the Civil War, the press run of German dailies in New York was sufficient to supply every fifth immigrant with a copy. By 1872, the *New Yorker Staats-Zeitung* with its circulation of fifty-five thousand claimed the title of the world's largest German newspaper. The centennial of American independence in 1876 was celebrated by seventy-four German-language dailies, printing one copy for every fifth German American. Counting weeklies, there was more than one paper printed in German for every two immigrants, or for every fifth ethnic if one counts the second generation. With the exception of Maine,

Mississippi, and New Mexico, every one of the "lower forty-eight" states was, at some point in its history, home to a German-language newspaper. A German population of between one thousand and two thousand in a county constituted a "critical mass" sufficient to support a weekly newspaper, as is clear from Iowa census data in 1885. At the height of the last great wave of immigration, there were even two Iowa counties that could claim a German weekly despite an immigrant population below one thousand. The *Ottumwa Journal* persisted from 1871 to 1912, though the 1885 census showed only 569 Germans in Wapello County. Of the sixteen counties with more than two thousand Germans, only Iowa County, whose immigrants were mostly separatist Amana colonists, failed to produce a paper in the mother tongue. In the twenty-one counties with between one thousand and two thousand Germans, nine were supporting German weeklies in 1885, eight had never attempted one, and the other four had seen previous attempts fail. Only in the Mississippi River counties with their heavily immigrant populations did the offering extend beyond a single weekly. Dubuque and Clinton counties, each with a potential clientele surpassing six thousand, were the smallest that could support two competing weeklies, although Burlington was supporting a daily despite a county German population numbering below five thousand. But Davenport, with over ten thousand Germans, was the only Iowa location offering the choice of two German newspapers more than once a week. The *Demokrat* with its proud Forty-Eighter heritage came out in daily, triweekly, and weekly versions, while the *Iowa Reform* offered competition on a triweekly and weekly basis. Because there was no big city like St. Louis, Chicago, Detroit, or Milwaukee dominating the state, with a German daily sending out its weekly edition into its rural hinterlands, Iowa provided an optimal environment in which county weeklies could thrive, or at least survive.

Such publications were often small, shaky, one- or two-man operations, as Friedrich Gerstaecker observed on an 1867 visit to Hermann, Missouri: "I found the editor busy with the typesetting of his paper. Good God, the condition of the small German newspapers in America is not so rosy, and it is no rare occurrence that an editor not only has to write his paper alone, set it and print it, but afterwards even has to hawk it himself if he intends to earn his living at it." Newspapers like these were often unmistakably stamped with the character and personality—and the idiosyncrasies—of their editors. For example, Ferdinand Lindheimer was the soul of the *Neu Braunfelser Zeitung*, which he edited for the first two decades of its existence, imbuing it with Confederate sympathies that were not necessarily reflective of the majority in his town. The same might be said of the freethinking, anticlerical views of editor Hermann Mühl and his *Hermanner Wochenblatt*, although in this case the majority of his Missouri readers did share his antislavery principles and made his county the only one in a slave state to return a majority for President Abraham Lincoln in 1860. William Trenckmann so closely identified with the paper he published for over four decades in Belleville and then Austin, Texas, that he often referred to himself, and was dubbed by others, as simply "Der Wochenblattmann." Similarly, the founder of the *Arkansas Echo* was referred to as "Echo-mann" and died in its offices at age eighty in 1930; his son only managed to keep the paper afloat for another two years.

Although they served many of the same functions, foreign-language newspapers played a broader role in their communities than did their English-language counterparts. For example, a Missouri county-seat weekly, the *St. Charles Demokrat*, laid out its program in a prospectus in the initial number on January 1, 1852. Because of the new rights and new duties incumbent upon adoptive Americans, the editor promised translations of important federal and state laws. He would also offer advice on crops, gardens, wine, and fruit, all the more necessary since soil and climate were different in America than in the homeland. A strong believer in the necessity of education, he promised information on local school laws. Another focus of the *Demokrat*'s attention would be the upcoming campaign of 1852. The front page of the first number carried articles explaining naturalization laws, voting rights, election procedures, and tax laws, as well as an account of the Missouri Democratic convention.

Firmly grounded in the American tradition of boosterism, an article on page two dealt with a railroad project from St. Louis to St. Charles. But the attention devoted to the Hungarian Forty-Eighter Louis Kossuth on pages two and three reflected a political horizon that extended beyond the United States, even for this small-town weekly. The back page again took up American politics, but the opposition to the proslavery Jackson Resolutions set this immigrant editor apart from many of his native counterparts in Missouri.

Founded in the same year as the *Demokrat*, the first German newspaper to thrive in Texas, the *Neu Braunfelser Zeitung*, took on very similar roles. With immigrants pouring in at the time, it published the passenger list of the *Bark Diana* that had arrived two weeks earlier in Indianola, providing complete names and German origins of all heads of families. Within the next month, it published similar lists from five other ships arriving from Germany in Galveston or Indianola, crucial information for relatives of immigrants awaiting their arrival. This *Zeitung* immediately started boosting its hometown. Its very first issue in 1852 presented a fictional dialogue with a resident of nearby Hortontown on the advantages of being annexed to the county with New Braunfels as its seat instead of having to run a dozen miles to Seguin, the seat of a neighboring county. Among other advantages it touted, was the possibility to deal with inheritance or guardianship matters in the German language at the New Braunfels courthouse. Even so, there was one Anglo business that advertised in this first issue: Ferguson & Brother, dealers in general merchandise, but its ad had sixteen lines of German text and only three in English.

Editor Lindheimer laid out a nominally independent political philosophy: "I am too proud to offer myself as the factional bellwether of a party. . . . It is enough to say that we are democrats, but we do not associate this word with any historical party concept of an American faction; rather we value the original concept that is familiar to us Germans, known by everyone and worthy of our national character." Nonetheless, he soon conceded that the party that agreed most with the principles and interests of his readers was presently the Democratic Party.

The *St. Charles Demokrat* took this role even further. Within its first month it presented a political textbook in the question-and-answer, catechism form many of its readers knew from their religious instruction. During February and March, Louis Kossuth's American tour claimed considerable copy, including a full page devoted to his speech at a congressional banquet. A March issue reported on the county Democratic convention at which the editor and one of the owners of the *Demokrat* both fared prominently and saw themselves elected as part of the delegation to the state party convention. In the same issue, the editor sang what would come to be a familiar refrain in this and other ethnic newspapers, praising a candidate for county sheriff who was born in Germany, came to America as a boy, and spoke both languages fluently. The next issue complained of the meager representation of Germans in city government and their political passivity.

"Become Citizens!" the *Demokrat* urged in one of its April numbers, announcing the upcoming court dates for this purpose in St. Charles and two neighboring counties. In fact, editor Arnold Krekel often appeared as a witness for the naturalization proceedings of German immigrants in this era. His preaching did not fall on deaf ears; in the fall elections the *Demokrat* claimed that the German vote went nine-tenths Democratic, quite plausible in view of the fact that editor Krekel won a seat in the state legislature. This too reflects a general tendency of the ethnic press, which was often a product of individual entrepreneurship and usually had a clear political affiliation. In 1854 the *Hermanner Wochenblatt* in a nearby Missouri county made a similar offer: "in our shop someone is always ready to help those who don't speak English with their registration." That was no longer an option after 1906, when knowledge of English and basic civics was added to the requirements for citizenship. But before World War I, the St. Louis *Westliche Post* still published and sold a small booklet (in German) providing information on naturalization procedures.

When the Ku Klux Klan was crusading against Texas Germans in May 1921, William Trenckmann's *Wochenblatt* in Austin provided instructions on how to become a U. S. citizen, complete with sample questions for the citizenship exam. This is not surprising; long before he moved his paper to the state capital, Trenckmann expressed broad ambitions for his county-seat weekly: "I had not planned to found a local paper . . . I always tried to extend my fields to the happenings which were important to the Germans of the entire state. I have as far as possible in an eight-page paper, reported all outstanding achievements of Germans in our country as well as matters of importance in regard to national and state laws, politics and the most important world news, so that even those who have access to no other newspaper might be fairly well informed on current events."

Like most American newspapers of the nineteenth century, the German press was often firmly associated with one party or another. There were thirty-three papers with *Republikaner* in their name, and no less than 130 with *Demokrat*. They should not be equated with a partisan breakdown; the Republican Party was much younger than the Democratic, and in the Civil War era a number of "Demokrats," including those in Davenport, Iowa, and St. Charles, Missouri, switched their affiliation to the GOP without changing their names. Competing journals were often political rivals. It was unusual to see cross-town papers support the same party, as was the case with the two ardently Republican St. Louis German dailies on the eve of the Civil War (and even that did not last long). Much more typical was the decades-long bitter feud between the Republican *Clevelander Anzeiger* and its Democratic rival, the *Wächter am Erie*, until waning demand led to their consolidation in 1893. Little Rock's only two German papers, the *Arkansas Staatszeitung* and the upstart *Arkansas Echo*, were diametrical opposites: the former Republican and Protestant in its sympathies, the latter Democratic and ardently Catholic. The *Echo* was vandalized before its first issue appeared, and its first year saw a veritable "newspaper war," involving lawsuits, threats of violence, and even a fistfight between rival editors.

Papers were often supported, directly or indirectly, by political patronage. One sure way of gaining immigrant subscriptions was the privilege of publishing the "official letter list" of arriving mail, especially before home postal delivery began in 1863 in the big cities. Another important commission, which paid dividends in circulation even if it was not directly remunerated, was the printing of public notices.

Immigrants could spend their lives largely in a German-speaking world if they chose to. Up until World War I, most cities required their public notices to be published not only in English but also in German and other languages widely spoken among their population. Even state governments sometimes went to surprising lengths to meet immigrants halfway. In 1844 and continuing for more than a decade, the Commonwealth of Pennsylvania maintained two state printers, one to do the English printing and one to do the German printing. The Keystone State required the printing of certain annual reports in German down to 1876. Indiana in 1853 and Colorado in 1877 ordered German translations of editions of state laws running into the hundreds of pages, and several other states, including Wisconsin and Missouri, provided annual or biennial translations of new legislation. Before the Civil War, Wisconsin, Minnesota, and Iowa all published draft constitutions in German translation (and also in other heritage languages), as did Illinois and Texas in the 1870s. The 1883 report of the Missouri Bureau of Labor Statistics was published in German translation. According to the foreword, five thousand copies were printed in English and two thousand in German, or 28 percent of the copies when Germans made up only 18 percent of all industrial workers in the state. Even after World War I, the Minnesota Secretary of State published voter instructions in German and seven other languages besides English.

In some respects, it appears that German Americans lived in a parallel society, linguistically speaking. County history "mug books" were ubiquitous in the late nineteenth-century Midwest, but at least one of them was published in German for Sheboygan County, Wisconsin, in 1898. A similar work covered Carroll County, Iowa, but in that case it was issued by the *Carroll Demokrat* in celebration of its twenty-fifth anniversary in 1899. With the help of a professional writer, the Ninth Ohio Infantry published its Civil War regimental history *auf Deutsch* in 1897, and Cleveland editor Wilhelm Kaufmann penned a book-length celebration of the German role in the Civil War that appeared in 1911.

Well into the twentieth century, there were Americans of German ancestry who attained prominence in the Anglophone world despite growing up with German as their primary language. Theologian Reinhold Niebuhr (b. 1892) was obviously bilingual, but he probably had German as his first language and still showed evidence of some German interference in his English during his graduate work at Yale Divinity School. Another prime example is Admiral Chester Nimitz (b. 1885), commander of the U. S. Pacific Fleet during World War II, who was brought up largely by his immigrant grandparents in the most German of Texas towns, Fredericksburg. Of equally bilingual upbringing, but seldom recognized as being of Germanic, much less Germanophone, heritage, was Leon Jaworski (b. 1905) of Watergate prosecution fame, whose immigrant father preached in German at Evangelical churches in Texas. Leon did not actually need a translator when prosecuting Nazi war criminals as a judge advocate, but chose to use one just to ensure his objectivity. Equally fluent was another assistant prosecutor at Nuremberg, Drexel Sprecher, who grew up bilingual in Wisconsin, a fourth-generation descendant of German and Swiss immigrants. To take yet another Texas example, the San Antonio German English School enrolled the cream of that city's ethnic community. Among the students who absolved its two-way immersion program was the entire second generation of the Guenther family, whose descendants still own Pioneer Flour Company after more than 150 years. The written German of the Guenther children was actually better than that of their immigrant mother, whose educational opportunities were limited in frontier Fredericksburg. Among other of the Guenthers' schoolmates who later achieved prominence was Harry Wurzbach, who became a six-term Congressman, the only Republican in the Texas delegation.

Yankee baseball greats Babe Ruth (b. 1895) and Lou Gehrig (b. 1903) both knew and spoke German. In Gehrig's case this is unsurprising; he spent his early years in the German neighborhood of Yorktown. His immigrant parents remained more comfortable in German than in English their whole life and did not become naturalized until 1941. Even in the late 1920s, Lou conversed with his mother almost entirely in German, and his wife explained his fondness for Wagnerian opera with the fact that he could actually follow the lyrics. Ruth's case is more remarkable because he was of the third and fourth generations in America. He and both his parents were born in a German neighborhood of Baltimore.

Another indication of the ubiquity and prestige of the German language was the number of prominent Americans who were exposed to it. On his way to the White House, Abraham Lincoln stopped in New York and visited one of the state's Republican electors, Jewish Forty-Eighter Sigismund Kaufmann, who was delightedly amused that the president-elect knew his surname meant "merchant," and also knew that Schneider meant "tailor." In his early years in Springfield, Lincoln and a couple of friends had hired an immigrant to give them German lessons. Lincoln reportedly distracted the class with his jokes and storytelling so that they made little progress, but obviously a few things stuck.

In April 1864, shortly before launching his Wilderness Campaign, General Ulysses S. Grant wrote a relative in the St. Louis area who was minding their children while his wife Julia was away. Missing his family, the indulgent father requested, "I wish you would urge [the children] all to join in letters to me every week. . . . How do Buck and Nellie progress in their German? I hope they will place me in their debt, the fine gold watches I promised when they learned to speak the language." The children in question were aged nine and eleven. Apparently his entreaties were heeded; just before launching his campaign against Lee, he wrote to Julia on May 2, "I received a letter from Buck this evening. It was very well written. He says he can speak German a little." On June 4, the day after the notoriously bloody, futile Union assault at Cold Harbor, Grant again broached the subject to "My Dear little Nelly . . . I expect by the end of the year you and Buck will be able to speak German and then I will have to buy you those nice gold watches I promised." It was not recorded whether the children ever collected their watches. But more significant is the fact that a man of Grant's prominence, with a lot of other pressing matters on his mind, thought it valuable for his children to learn German.

Half a century later, when former President William Howard Taft wrote Cincinnati-born journalist Gus Karger in opposition to the Supreme Court nomination of Louis D. Brandeis, he threw in the phrase, "*es ist zum Lachen*" ("it's laughable"), as if both of them were fully bilingual. This seems plausible given that his brother Charles P. Taft was vice president of the *Cincinnati Volksblatt* company. (The Queen City had dual language public schools in his era, but it is unclear whether either Taft attended them.)

In the world of German-American publishing, besides the usual daily or weekly news organs such as the *Volksblatt* (People's Page) for general readers, there were other, more specialized German journals, many appearing only on a monthly basis. After a spectacularly varied career as a Lutheran minister, Chicago banker, and Illinois lieutenant governor, Francis A. Hoffmann retired to a Wisconsin farm and from 1875 to his death in 1903 edited the *Haus- und Bauernfreund*, an agricultural supplement to the Milwaukee *Germania* and two other German papers in Chicago and Buffalo, reaching well over one hundred thousand readers by the turn of the century. Hoffmann wrote under the pen name Hans Buschbauer, while the "Haus" aspects of the paper were ostensibly written by his wife "Greta," but in fact Francis wrote much of that content as well. Another Milwaukee women's paper, *Die Deutsche Hausfrau*, established in 1904, reached a subscription of 132,000 in 1907 and still surpassed forty thousand in the 1920s, persisting for nearly fifty years.

Other German-language papers served even smaller niche markets. Not surprisingly, there was both a *Bierbrauer Zeitung* and a *Wein Zeitung*, but also German journals for pharmacists, bakers, coopers, tailors, and even chicken growers. In the 1850s there was a weekly *Deutsche Bank*

Noten Reporter designed to warn immigrants about forgeries and other pitfalls of paper currency. New York even attempted an *Automobile-Welt* (World) in 1916, though it did not last beyond the U. S. declaration of war.

The names of German papers themselves provide interesting and sometimes amusing insights. The two leading newspapers in St. Louis before the Civil War were the *Anzeiger des Westens* and the *Westliche Post*, indicative of how elastic the concept of "West" was. Friedrich Muench, a frequent contributor to these and other German papers, wrote from his farm not forty miles from the banks of the Mississippi under the English pen name "Far West." On the Illinois side, a Belleville paper dubbed itself *Stern des Westens* (Star of the West). That not enough, Columbus, Ohio, was home to a *Westbote* (Western Messenger), which was dubious even at its founding in 1843 and totally inappropriate long before its demise in 1918. But the *Adler des Westens* (Eagle of the West), did it one better, flying from Pittsburgh in the 1830s. Some titles were downright poetic—for example the *Nordstern* (North Star) in St. Cloud, Minnesota. One Cleveland paper dubbed itself the *Wächter am Erie* (Watchman on the Erie), another the *Erie Leuchtthurm* (Lighthouse), while its Milwaukee counterpart was named the *Seebote* (Lake Messenger). New Jersey was home to the *Egg Harbor Pilot*.

Other journals were much less imaginative in their naming. Dozens of weeklies could come up with nothing better than *Das Wochenblatt*, usually combined with the name of their home town. Among the states that could claim a *Staatszeitung* were Pennsylvania, New York, New Jersey, Ohio, Illinois, Indiana, Michigan, Minnesota, Kansas, California, Oregon, Washington, Virginia, Tennessee, and even Arkansas. Friendships were proclaimed far and wide across the landscape. New Jersey had a *Volksfreund,* Ohio a *Vaterlandsfreund*, while freedom-loving Pittsburgh was home for a half-century to the *Freiheits-Freund*. Among the occupations which found friends in the German-language press were both laborers (*Arbeiter-Freund*) and farmers (*Bauern-Freund*). The nation's first German Catholic paper, established in 1837 in Cincinnati, boldly proclaimed itself to be the *Wahrheitsfreund* (Friend of Truth). Unimpressed, a child of the European Enlightenment countered it with his rationalistic *Licht-Freund* in 1840, but moved with his paper to Hermann, Missouri, three years later. A like-minded St. Louis paper paradoxically claimed to be *Gottes Freund, der Pfaffen Feind!*—friendly toward God but fiendish toward preachers. This freethinking journal was relatively short-lived, but the Milwaukee *Freidenker* survived for seven full decades (1872–1942).

Nonetheless, the German religious press could hold its own against its irreligious counterparts. Most church bodies had their own periodicals, and often published books and pamphlets as well. In the city of St. Louis alone, the three leading German confessions each published journals that reached a venerable age. The *St. Louis Amerika* provided daily news with a Catholic slant from 1872 until after World War I. In the cradle of the Missouri Synod, *Der Lutheraner* imparted doctrine to the laity on a monthly basis for more than a century from 1844 to 1954, though it was supplemented since 1911 and ultimately succeeded by the English-language *Lutheran Witness*. Though theologically more liberal, the German Evangelical Synod was linguistically just as conservative; its *Friedensbote* (Messenger of Peace, 1850–1955) actually outlived the *Lutheraner* by one year.

There was little German-language outreach among Anglo-Protestant denominations, the main exception being Methodists, and here an immigrant convert, William Nast, played the leading role. There were more than one hundred German Presbyterian ministers, and their journal, *Der Presbyterianer*, carried on for more than eighty years until 1947, but its circulation never surpassed two thousand, only one-tenth that of the German Methodist *Christliche Apologete*, which persisted for a full century until 1939. Even minor American sects disseminated their beliefs *auf Deutsch* in America, as was apparent from some books passed down from my late uncle. His mother had a bilingual volume by Christian Scientist founder Mary Baker Eddy, and a weighty German tome by Mrs. E. G. White [sic], a Seventh Day Adventist visionary—unlikely fare for a woman whose father was born in Missouri and whose mother had immigrated at age three.

There were even religious publications for more specialized target groups such as the youth. The *Abendschule* (Evening School), which moved to St. Louis from Buffalo in 1856 shortly after its founding and persisted until 1940, presented family entertainment from a conservative Lutheran point of view. Both the title and the prospectus of the *Deutsch-Amerikanische Jugendfreund*, launched in 1890 by the German Evangelical Synod, reflected the dual role of the ethnic press:

If I call myself German-American, I do so because I want to wake and nourish in you the love of German language and customs, to guard and keep the German heritage of our parents, the sense of reverence, truth, and righteousness, to waken and implant in your hearts the German industriousness and love of singing.

And the Friend of Youth calls itself American because after all it has to do with young America. To be sure, we Germans have the unfortunate tendency that we easily throw overboard our God-given distinctiveness and with the adoption of the English language here deny our German essence. That ought not so to be. It is my firm conviction that we can only be good Americans if we are and remain good Germans.

While the prospectus put most of its emphasis on the German half of the combination, its monthly offerings during the first year present a very different picture. Although its editor, Gottlieb Eisen, had immigrated from Switzerland as an adult, only rarely did the magazine's content reach back across the Atlantic, for example, with an occasional personal anecdote about Bismarck. Overwhelmingly, however, the *Jugendfreund* presented American themes, which, except for the language they were expressed in, could have just as well appeared in any publication aimed at native youth. Daniel Boone, Abraham Lincoln, Thomas Edison, Benjamin Franklin, John C. Fremont, George Bancroft, and Green Mountain Boys—these were the figures that populated the pages of the *Jugendfreund*. Nor was the new American nationalism lost on the editor, as exemplified by pieces such as "The Armaments of our New Battle Fleet," or a translation of Edward Everett Hale's Civil War allegory, "The Man Without a Country." The latest figures on circulation were 4,600 from 1905, a gain of eight hundred from a decade earlier, but the *Jugendfreund* ceased publication in 1915, whether because of declining readership or the age of its editor, who died three years later.

The mainstream German-language press often devoted one of its entire pages to serial fiction, the majority of it imported rather than local in its production and subject matter. Many of the novels set in the Old Country were trivial potboilers by deservedly forgotten authors, but some papers also featured works of higher quality. From its main title, the weekly *New-Yorker Criminal-Zeitung und belletristisches Journal*, founded by Forty-Eighter Rudolph Lexow, might suggest sensationalistic crime reporting, but the second half of its name was not a mere afterthought.

It also reported on literature, art, music and theater, not to mention politics. In 1853 it even carried an article by Karl Marx. Some respectable German literary offerings found their way to rather obscure American destinations. In faraway rural Texas, Dr. Hermann Nagel subscribed to the *Criminal-Zeitung* before the Civil War. His son Charles related that he read Friedrich Gerstaecker's tales of hunting on the Arkansas frontier in German, presumably serialized in a newspaper as well. In fact, Gerstaecker was probably the most widely published author in German-American newspapers, nearly twice as popular as Charles Sealsfield in any case. Gert Goebel in his 1877 immigrant memoir mentions Gerstaecker casually as if he needed no introduction, and Gerstaecker certainly offered the most realistic portrait, given his extensive travels in frontier America. He stayed for a time with Pastor Gustavus Klingelhoeffer, who had established a German colony west of Little Rock in the 1830s. Gerstaecker's works, whose titles translate to *The Regulators in Arkansas*, *The River Pirates of the Mississippi*, and *Rambling and Hunting Trips Through the United States of North America*, were all three serialized in the St. Louis *Anzeiger des Westens* in the 1850s. In 1868, just two years after it had first appeared in Germany, the county-seat weekly *St. Charles Demokrat* presented Gerstaecker's "Martin," a tragic tale of insanity and murder on the Arkansas frontier.

Gerstaecker may be considered a middlebrow adventure writer, but some highly regarded works from the Old Country also found publishers on the American side. In 1857 the *St. Charles Demokrat* serialized Jewish novelist Berthold Auerbach's *Barfüßle*, a tale of his Black Forest homeland, only a year after its original publication. In November 1866, the St. Louis *Westliche Post* was serializing the novel, *Die Geschworenen und ihr Richter*, a three-volume work that had been published in 1861 by Levin Schüking, sometimes dubbed the "Westphalian Walter Scott." Immigrants were familiar enough with Goethe's melodramatic "Erlkönig" that it was parodied in a comment on national politics in 1863 Missouri, and in opposition to the Bennett school law in 1890 Wisconsin. Heinrich Heine's *Lorelei* was another popular subject for parody. Immigrant audiences were especially fond of writers like Heine from the liberal side of the political spectrum. The 100th birthday of the "freedom poet" Friedrich Schiller, known for his drama of Swiss liberation *William Tell*, was celebrated across German America in 1859, not only in major cities like Chicago, Baltimore, and New York, but in more than twenty locations in the Empire State and smaller cities like Columbus, Ohio, and even Mobile, Alabama. In San Antonio, it was the occasion for laying the cornerstone of the German-English School. Dramatist Gerhard Hauptmann's socially critical play *Die Weber* was published by a St. Louis labor paper only four months after it was first staged in Berlin, and was still presented on stage in Chicago and New York in the 1890s. Favorites among the poets were Hoffmann von Fallersleben and Ferdinand Freiligrath, who promoted a liberal vision of national unity. Indicative of the latter's popularity, New York publisher Friedrich Gerhard in 1858–1859 put out a six-volume authorized edition of Freiligrath's collected works, including both his own poetry and his translations from British and American poets. Later Gerhard launched an eleven-volume *Deutsch-amerikanisches Conversations-Lexicon* (1869–1874) edited by Alexander J. Schem, a remarkable work catering to the needs and interests of their fellow immigrants, though not a commercial success.

Immigrant readers were discriminating in their tastes. Beginning in 1893, Karl May enthralled readers in the Fatherland with tales of frontiersmen and noble savages in a Wild West that he had never seen (leaning heavily on Gerstaecker), although his royalties did finance a trip to the Northeast near the end of his career. But his implausible work was roundly ignored by German Americans, never serialized in any of their newspapers, and except for two heavily abbreviated juvenile adaptations from 1898 with the German elements removed, never translated during May's lifetime.

Sometimes German literature reached its readers directly rather than through newspapers, or it was presented on stage. In his rural Texas youth, William Trenckmann had devoured the democratic radical Fritz Reuter's Low German memoir, *Ut mine Festungstid*. Less than ten years after it appeared in Germany, the play *Inspector Bräsig*, based on another Reuter work, was held over by popular demand, as reported in 1871 by the *Washingtoner Post* in a Missouri town with only 1,400 German natives.

There was no German immigrant writer who achieved the status of O. E. Rölvaag or Abraham Cahan portraying their compatriots in their heritage languages. Friedrich Gerstaecker and Charles Sealsfield were really sojourners rather than true immigrants. Sealsfield came over twice in the 1820s and again in the 1850s, and apparently acquired U. S. citizenship, but most of his time in America predated the mass immigration of the 1830s, and his work scarcely touched on the immigrant experience. The most prominent second-generation literary figure, Theodore Dreiser, grew up with some knowledge of German and based his novel *Jennie Gerhardt*, and to some extent also *Sister Carrie*, on his own conflicted family experience, but he wrote exclusively in English. Essayist H. L. Mencken, an avid correspondent and promoter of Dreiser, was of the third generation, but still had a better command of German than Dreiser, who once sent him a letter from Germany for translation. However, Mencken, too, admitted, "alas, my German is dreadful." But it was better than that of Kurt Vonnegut, who grew up without the language of his immigrant grandfather, and devoted little of his attention to ethnic themes.

For the most part, German-American literature of the immigrant generation was genre literature of the second tier, often written by newspapermen and reflective of current events, but seldom deemed worthy of English translation. Eugene Sue's 1842 sensation, *The Mysteries of Paris*, which Karl Marx called "a slap in the face of bourgeois prejudice," inspired a whole array of imitations in the German-American press. St. Louis editor Heinrich Boernstein's 1851 anti-Jesuit potboiler appeared in English the following year as *The Mysteries of St. Louis* and was also translated into French and Czech, but made such little impact that only rare copies survive. Serialized in 1854–1855, Emil Klauprecht's *Cincinnati, oder Geheimnisse des Westens* (*Mysteries of the West*), finally saw its translation in 1996. Ludwig von Reizenstein's bizarre and controversial *Geheimnisse [Secrets] von New Orleans*, first serialized in the antebellum *Louisiana Staatszeitung*, did not appear in English until the twenty-first century. Adolph Douai's turbulent *Fata Morgana*, about a group of Texas Germans who fled to Mexico in the face of Know-Nothing agitation, won the contest for publication by Boernstein in 1858 but has never appeared in English. Forty-Eighter Reinhard Solger's *Anton in Amerika* was judged the best German-American novel at its appearance in 1862. It presented a humorous display of ethnic dialects in German and English, not to mention ethnic stereotypes, but it had to wait until 2006 for its first English translation. August Siemerling, who edited the *Freie Presse für Texas*, in 1876 authored a Civil War novella, *Ein Verfehltes*

Leben, reflecting his Unionist sympathies. It won a nationwide contest sponsored by the *Cincinnati Volksblatt* but was only translated in 1932, and distortedly at that.

In a later era, *Wochenblattmann* William Trenckmann drew upon his earlier school teaching experience in authoring a play, *Der Schulmeister von Neu-Rostock* (1903), and in 1907 serialized a roman à clef, *Die Lateiner am Possum Creek*, based on the experience of his family and neighbors, showing the plight of German Unionists in Texas. But despite its historical value, it took more than a century to find an English publisher. Trenckmann also promoted a hometown author who was anything but conventional: Clara Matthaei, who defied social prejudices to marry a Mexican immigrant. Writing under the pseudonym Walther Gray, she authored two autobiographical novellas, which were serialized in Trenckmann's paper in the 1920s, presenting "the paradox of a strict localism of setting combined with an exceptional broadness and nonconformity of outlook." But these too only appeared in translation in 1997, and even within the German-language community, neither of these writers attained any receptivity outside Texas.

Although they worked primarily as journalists and translators rather than novelists, there were a couple of women who figured prominently as immigrant writers with national and international visibility. Mathilde Franziska Anneke came to Wisconsin with her husband Fritz in the wake of the failed 1848 Revolution. In 1852, she founded the *Deutsche Frauenzeitung*, which she continued until 1854 after moving to the East Coast. Most of the Civil War she spent in Switzerland, supporting the antislavery cause with her writings. After her return, she helped establish and run a German girls' school for eighteen years, based on Friedrich Froebel's principles, all the while continuing to support the women's suffrage movement. Without the benefit of having been there, she also wrote *Uhland in Texas*, a Civil War novella that the *Illinois Staatszeitung* serialized in 1866. Like Anneke, Ottilie Assing made her mark primarily as a journalist reporting on America to German papers during the Civil War era. From a secular, emancipated Hamburg Jewish household where she was introduced to some prominent literati, Assing had already established herself as a journalist when she emigrated in 1852. She quickly set herself up as Germany's leading source on the Black race and the abolitionism movement, and formed an intense friendship with

Frederick Douglass, whose second autobiography she translated in 1857. They continued their journalistic collaboration for the Black cause during and after the Civil War, until Assing's permanent return to Germany in 1881.

Assing's translation of Douglass was not an exception; there was probably more such work done from English to German than in the opposite direction. Within a year of its publication, *Uncle Tom's Cabin* was presented in German translation to readers in Louisville, Kentucky, and Hermann, Missouri—two of the few places it was serialized in any language anywhere in the slave states. German papers often offered selections from popular American authors, including James Fennimore Cooper, Henry Wadsworth Longfellow, Edgar Allan Poe, and the western tales of Mark Twain and Brett Harte, the latter both translated by Udo Brachvogel. For example, Twain's 1878 essay "About Magnanimous-Incident Literature" in the *Atlantic Monthly* appeared almost simultaneously in translation in the *Belletristisches Journal*. An analysis of the Sunday literature sections of the *Milwaukee Banner und Volksfreund* and its successor the *Freie Presse* from 1879 to 1885 found nearly seven hundred literary pieces, of which sixty-three serialized. But only a dozen were novels, all written in Germany except for one adaptation from an Anglo-American source. Including the shorter pieces, most were written *auf Deutsch* in Europe, but there were fifteen translations from American works and thirty-six from other European languages, whereas only twenty-two could be identified as original pieces by German Americans.

Ethnics made more significant contributions in theater and music, in the latter case also impacting the larger society. Even more important were the Germanic components of American Christmas customs, far outweighing the British input. After all, "O Christmas Tree" is a translation of the original "O Tannenbaum." German political refugee Charles Follen introduced the decorated evergreen to Puritan Boston in 1835. A Missouri German from that era reported that his frontiersman neighbor was unclear on the month, much less the date of Christmas. The Texas legislature was in regular session on December 25, 1861. Texas German William Trenckmann related how his parents managed to improvise a Christmas tree in 1863 despite the privations of the Civil War, and the astonishment it evoked with their enslaved Black neighbors who had never seen anything like it before. Digitized Texas newspapers reveal just how foreign the custom was. There were only two mentions of Christmas trees in the 1840s, just four in the 1850s, and only ten in the 1860s, nearly all from literature or reports from afar, compared to nearly five hundred in the 1870s. Santa Claus developed out of a multiethnic collaboration, but cartoonist Thomas Nast created his visual image, showing him distributing presents to Union soldiers at Christmas in 1862. On the facing page, he shows Santa driving reindeer before his sleigh and climbing into the chimney, on the periphery of a scene from the home front. Nast would go on to a brilliant career of political cartooning, creating the elephant and donkey as symbols of the Republicans and Democrats. *Harper's Weekly* ran his images of Santa annually until 1886. But only in 1889 did President Benjamin Harrison erect the first White House Christmas tree.

Germans made other contributions of more serious art. Albert Bierstadt, who arrived as a toddler but went back to Düsseldorf to study art, is known for his majestic western landscapes. Emanuel Leutze followed a similar path in becoming a painter of inspiring patriotic scenes. His masterpiece, "Washington Crossing the Delaware," was actually painted in Düsseldorf before he returned to the United States in 1859. Brothers-in-law Hermann Lungkwitz and Friedrich Petri took refuge in Texas in the aftermath of the 1848 Revolution, where Lungkwitz became a well-known landscape painter and Petri an accomplished portraitist. Genre painter Charles Felix Blauvelt, the son of an immigrant but American-trained, in 1855 showed two marginalized figures: "A German Immigrant Inquiring his Way" from an elderly Black laborer. Since lithography was invented in Germany, immigrants were often the ones who established the craft in America. Germans comprised three times their share of engravers in 1870, producing many of the early cityscapes and making paintings popularly accessible.

Although a German sojourner in 1832 characterized America as a "land without nightingales," immigrants quickly set out to change that, promoting music on both an amateur and a professional basis. It did not take long after a settlement was founded for Germans to establish a choral society (*Gesangverein*). Philadelphia's dates from 1835, Baltimore's from 1836, and Cincinnati's from 1838—all the first of their kind. New York followed suit with its *Liederkranz* in 1847, and the next year Buffalo, Pittsburgh, and Cleveland were added to the list. In Texas, New

Braunfels had a *Gesangverein* by 1850, five years after its founding. San Antonio's was organized in 1847, took on the name *"Beethoven Männerchor"* in 1867, and is still thriving and under that name and singing in German 150 years later. Even after 1945, some photos on the wall of its hall and beer garden were still captioned in German. Before long, these local societies were organizing state and regional choral competitions and festivities known as *Sängerfeste*. There were national festivals held every year from 1849 to the Civil War, and on a biennial basis from 1868 through 1890, continuing thereafter triennially until World War I. The next national *Sängerfest* was held in Chicago in 1924, commemorating the seventy-fifth anniversary of the national organization, and a two-day festival was held in conjunction with the 1936 Texas Centennial Exposition in Dallas.

Texas German singers made another largely unheralded contribution: Hermann Seele, the leader of the New Braunfels *Gesangverein*, produced a spirited translation of the National Anthem, "Das Star Spangled Banner," in 1851. It shows up on a handsome Union recruitment broadside published in New York during the Civil War, and in an 1890 Lutheran songbook for its youth. It was still being sung in the bilingual public schools of Indianapolis until 1917.

In German Texas, along with the music tradition, a distinctive type of dance-hall architecture developed, not derived from Anglo culture but unlike anything in the Old Country either. Regardless of what kind of Verein sponsored them—whether choral societies as with the Liedertafel in Sealy and Harmonie Hall in Shelby; agricultural societies such as the Germania Farmer Verein's Anhalt Hall or the Cat Spring Agricultural Society (the oldest in Texas with its 1856 founding); athletic clubs such as the La Bahia Turnverein near Burton or the Turnverein Pavilion in Belleville; the Lindenau Rifle Club near Cuero or the Round Top Schützen Verein—these halls, often shaded by ancient live oaks and fitted with outdoor barbecue pits, were distinguished by their natural ventilation from the days before air conditioning, their clear-span dance floors, and sometimes by their geometric architecture. Texas once claimed more than one thousand such dance halls, though some were sponsored by other groups, such as the Czech secular and Catholic societies SPJST (Slavonic Benevolent Order of the State of Texas) and KJT (Katolická Jednotá Texaská, or Catholic Union of Texas) that followed in the

German wake. Whatever the official purpose of their sponsoring organization, in the course of time, music, dance, and conviviality became their main rationale for existence. My Missouri hometown of Augusta has a Harmonie Verein Hall, complete with dance floor and stage from 1869 and an octagonal gazebo bandstand from 1890. Ironically, in the wake of World War I, the Verein rented and later deeded its hall to the local American Legion, whereby in honor of a local doughboy killed in action, it received a new but equally German name, Harry H. Haferkamp Post 262. It still serves as a venue for various community events, but it cannot match the longevity of Texas *Vereinsleben*. The New Braunfels Schuetzen Verein, forced to move five times by the growth of the city, sports a clubhouse from the twenty-first century, but from its founding on July 4, 1849, it persists as the oldest continuously operating shooting club in the United States. Another Hill Country institution, the Boerne Village Band, founded in 1860, celebrates its heritage as the oldest German band outside of Germany. La Bahia Turnverein has another distinction: It kept its minutes in the German language until 1955.

Germans also spread their musical culture in the United States on a professional basis. It was probably no coincidence that among some 1,800 inhabitants of Texarkana in 1880, it was one of the forty Germans, Julian Weiss, who took future ragtime composer Scott Joplin under his wing and taught him piano. As early as 1870, the census shows that German men made up more than five times their share of professional musicians compared to the overall population, and over three times their share of musicians and music teachers ten years later, and still close to three times their share in 1890, the highest concentration of any immigrant group. Germans were often among the founders and principle supporters of orchestras around the country. When the New York Philharmonic Society gave its first concert in 1842, more than one-third of its musicians were German. By 1865, it was more than 85 percent; by the 1890s, it was 95 percent.

Germans also played a crucial role in its leadership. Leopold Damrosch was first recruited from Germany in 1871 to lead the *Männergesangverein Arion*, a male choral group, three years later founded the Oratorio Society mixed chorus, and then in 1876 was named conductor by the Philharmonic Society. His son Walter, who arrived in America at age nine, stepped in to conduct *Tannhäuser* in 1885, in the wake of his father's illness and impending death. The younger Damrosch went on to a brilliant New York career in conducting, even forming his own opera company for a time. Among the Wagnerian operas he conducted was the first American production of *Parzifal*, but he also premiered French, Russian, and American works, including some of his own composition. He broadened American interest in classical music through radio and by leading orchestral tours into the heartland. But he also exported American culture, leading the Symphony Society of New York on a major European tour. Walter Damrosch and his brother Frank were among a group of eleven musicians who wrote a letter on April 1, 1933, coming to the defense of Jewish musicians in Germany, which only resulted in Hitler banning his works.

Music and theater went hand in hand, most obviously with opera but also in general, often sharing the same venues. Milwaukee, the most German city in America, fancied itself the "German Athens," boasting theater productions in the heritage language from 1850 until 1931. The city's Mozart Hall and its Academy of Music building both hosted German theater presentations along with music performances, as did the Grand Opera House, built by two Swiss immigrant brothers, which began operations in 1871. When it was badly damaged by fire in 1895, it was rescued and expanded by a Milwaukee brewing magnate and henceforth bore the name of Pabst Theater. Milwaukee was second only to New York in such cultural offerings, but there were over eighty cities with active German stages up to 1918. The size of this audience is indicated by the American tours of the Viennese "operetta queen," Marie Geistinger, who played a dozen cities in the 1881–1882 season and appeared in twenty-six cities in fifteen states from coast to coast the following season.

Like Geistinger's performances, the great majority of plays presented in German on American stages were imports from serious and popular German playwrights or translations of English dramas, but there were some sixty that were written in America, often treating themes of immigrant life, past and present. They reached back from Jacob Leisler in the colonial era and Peter Muhlenberg and Baron von Steuben in the Revolutionary era, to dramas exploring slavery and the Civil War. But most was lighter fare, such as Wilhelm Müller's prize-winning comedy, *Im gelobten Land* (1882), an America that did not always turn out to be quite the Promised Land that immigrants imagined. Both Müller and

Ludwig August Wollenweber explored the struggles of "Latin farmers," whose classical education did little to fit them for agriculture, in comedies titled *Ein Lateinischer Bauer* and *Die Lateiner am Schuylkill Kanal*, the latter apparently based on Wollenweber's own greenhorn experiences.

Serious German theater was undermined less by the repressions of World War I than by competition from more trivial offerings on the immigrant stage, like the 1882 St. Louis piece *The Emigrants*, that played on the mutual incomprehensibility of greenhorns' standard German and the hybrid jargon of their Americanized hosts, who had translated their name from Schneider to Taylor. It is replete with bilingual puns such as "Schoppen," with the newcomer looking forward to a pint of his favorite beverage only to be subjected to a shopping spree by the womenfolk of the family. Milwaukee's German theater was experiencing a decline in popularity by 1910, with rising deficits forcing curtailments in the number and frequency of performances. New York was hardly different; before the war's outbreak in Europe, a 1912 *Staats-Zeitung* cartoon lamented Germans' sparse attendance at the Irving Place Theater. One of its actors, Adolf Philipp, had struck out on his own and achieved popular success in the heart of Kleindeutschland presenting "American musical comedy in German" with the insight that "Germans don't care for the high-brow drama any more than the Americans." One example, his 1893 farce, *Der Corner Grocer aus der Avenue A*, had a run of over seven hundred performances. By contrast, the Irving Place Theater cancelled its lease in early 1918. Despite a sold-out farewell performance of Lessing's enlightenment appeal for tolerance, *Nathan der Weise*, its promise of a *Wiedersehen* in a new location went unfulfilled. But Philipp, who now switched to a patriotic theme in English, fared no better. Thereafter, except for a brief upsurge in the mid-1920s, the only Germanic language heard on the New York stage was Yiddish, although to some extent it did share actors and audiences with German theater.

Similar tendencies were evident in the German-language press as well, more than a decade before the Great War. Both the size of the readership and the ethnicity of the content began to dwindle almost immediately once mass immigration dried up with the Panic of 1893. In the mid-1880s, almost 80 percent of all foreign-language newspapers in the United States were German. As the number of German papers reached its peak in 1894 of nearly eight hundred organs, (including ninety-seven dailies), they still constituted two-thirds of the foreign-language press. In the state of Wisconsin alone, there were over one hundred different German journals appearing in more than fifty different towns. But from this point on, the German-language press embarked upon a slow but inexorable downhill slide. Even in such a heavily German city as Milwaukee, the combined circulation of German newspapers declined from ninety-two thousand in 1884 to fifty thousand in 1910, and more significantly, from double that of the English competition at the earlier date to merely one-third as much at the later one.

In 1912, just before the outbreak of World War I, some six hundred German journals still constituted over half of America's foreign-language press. There were still more than five hundred German periodicals in operation when the United States entered the war in 1917, but even by the end of the conflict, only seventy-four of them were exempted from the onerous requirement to submit English translations of all their war news. Relief was hard to come by, and probably had more to do with the political connections of the publisher than the attitude a given paper took toward the war. The very first permit was issued to William Trenckmann's *Wochenblatt*; it was his good fortune to have been a college friend and classmate of Postmaster General Burleson at Texas A&M. However, despite publishing a twenty-two-page special issue promoting Liberty Bonds in April 1918, the Republican-leaning *Seguiner Zeitung* was still subjected to the translation requirement until peace was officially signed in June 1919. Likewise, other papers such as the Chicago *Vorbote* still had to file English translations right down to the end, as did German papers in St. Cloud and New Ulm, Minnesota; Jefferson City and Hermann, Missouri; and Detroit, Michigan. The combination of wartime censorship and curtailment of mailing privileges, intimidation, and loss of advertising revenue had brought the number of German papers below three hundred by 1920, only one-quarter of all the immigrant press. Even then, there were still twenty-nine German dailies, almost twice as many as in any other language, with a combined circulation of 1.5 million.

Already before the Great War and increasingly thereafter, content in the German-American press was becoming more Americanized, and also more standardized. Forty-Eighter editor Wilhelm Rapp had argued that through the "arduous and mostly unappreciated work of the German press, the American national character was gradually being refined through the assimilation of German customs and attitudes." But most observers saw the opposite tendency. When criticism of the foreign-language press welled up in the 1880s, Germans such as the *New Yorker Staats-Zeitung* editor argued that "the daily papers printed in the German language are not German papers, but American papers printed in the German language. They represent American interests as completely as the papers printed in the English language." With the break of diplomatic relations with Germany in 1917, another New York paper, *Deutsches Journal*, actually bore this assertion on its bilingual masthead: "an American Newspaper printed in the German language for American citizens." A Texas weekly, the *Giddings Deutsches Volksblatt*, waited until it received its wartime translation exemption before posting on its masthead: "This is not a German paper but an American newspaper published in the German language," its motto until its demise in 1949.

Not only was content becoming less ethnic; it was becoming less localized as well. As early as 1883, there were Chicago and Philadelphia firms that supplied pre-set "boiler plate" articles of general interest. The German Press and Plate Company, a consolidation of two predecessors, was organized in Cleveland in 1893 with $100,000 in capital, furnishing auxiliary matter to German papers throughout the country until 1954. For example, the *St. Charles Demokrat* in 1911 ran an extensive article on Indian Cliff Dwellings in Colorado. The next year it ran "Die Straphangers" by Lewis Allen. It and other German papers from Minnesota to Ohio regularly presented essays of social commentator and advice columnist Dorothy Dix—all far from the experiences of its readers, and no doubt acquired as boiler plate. Although he promoted cultural preservation, editor William Trenckmann, too, was at home in the modern world, not bound by conservative convention. In the 1920s, under the headline "The Sexual Education of the Youth," he editorialized that this was "absolutely appropriate," though he preferred that it be done by parents rather than in schools. In the wake of America's first Red Scare, he reminded readers of "how much we have stolen from the Socialists, and what hearty thanks we actually owe them." His *Wochenblatt* also presented translated material from the American mainstream—for example anecdotes from Andrew Carnegie's autobiography. After more than forty years at its helm, Trenckmann sold ownership of the paper to a Minnesota publishing syndicate, though he still edited the local news page until shortly before his death two years later in 1935. His paper outlived him by five years.

Such consolidations were common in the later years of the German-language press. Starting out with his *Tägliche Omaha Tribüne*, Bavarian immigrant Valentine Peter came to dominate German publishing in the entire Great Plains region, starting before World War I to absorb various small weeklies and their circulation lists. By the 1930s his papers had a combined daily circulation of more than thirty thousand, and came to be centrally published in Omaha, with much identical national and international material, varying only by the local coverage. The last German daily of the Peters' enterprise turned semiweekly in 1950, but at the founder's death in 1960, there were still seven papers in the chain, which finally sold out to a Canadian firm in 1982. It consolidated them into the *Amerika Woche*, based in a Chicago suburb, which still survives today. Also still persisting is the Interstate Printing Company that Peter founded in 1917, now in the hands of the fourth generation, the oldest family firm in Omaha.

A number of German papers or their publishers crossed over to English. Hermann, Missouri, had a German weekly since 1843, but its publisher in 1874 added the English *Advertiser Courier* to its offering, with overlapping but not identical content. Joseph Pulitzer, a Jewish immigrant from Hungary, was hired in 1868 as a reporter for the St. Louis *Westliche Post* by its co-owner and coeditor Carl Schurz. By 1872 Pulitzer had worked his way up to managing editor and co-owner, but he sold his share in 1876, and two years later founded the *Post Dispatch* before moving on to greater feats of English publishing in New York. The *Westliche Post* itself produced an English-language offshoot, the daily *St. Louis Times*, which lasted from 1907 to 1932 but did not outlive its German parent. Austrian Jewish socialist editor Victor Berger published the daily *[Wisconsin] Vorwärts* (Forward) from 1892 to 1911, supplementing it with an English-language weekly, the *Social Democratic Herald* (1901–1913), and then established the English-language daily *Milwaukee Leader*, which he continued to publish from 1911 until his death in 1929, though the *Vorwärts* lived on under a new editor. Another socialist weekly in St. Louis, one of a dozen journals around the country bearing the name *Arbeiter Zeitung*, gave rise to an English counterpart, the *St. Louis Labor*, but the German version still attracted over 40 percent of the combined circulation as late as 1922. The *Baltimore Journal* switched to English in 1913, but went under the next year. The German Catholic Ritter family, which achieved notoriety for flying the German flag over its New York headquarters before American entry into World War I, was one of the founders of the contemporary Knight-Ritter publishing chain in 1974, remaining involved in its management until its sale in 2006. Ritters were not the only German Americans to attain prominence in the English-language press. Otto Fuerbringer became assistant managing editor of *Time Magazine* in 1951 and its managing editor from 1960 to 1968. Dubbed the "Iron Chancellor," he came from a long line of Lutheran ministers that started with the Saxon colony in Missouri and included his father, both of his grandfathers, and three of his uncles. However, one could debate whether Fuerbringer's editorship indicated mainstream acceptance of German Americans or merely the conservatism of the Eisenhower era and the magazine's owner, Henry Luce.

German-to-English transitions were probably even more common among smaller weeklies than with big city dailies; the *Neu Braunfelser Zeitung* was only one of many journals that went this route. One step along the way was often a bilingual transition phase, where part of the paper was printed in German and part in English, usually with similar content repeated in both parts. This gave a duplicitous publisher the opportunity to play both sides of the street. The editor of the bilingual *German-American Advocate* in Hays, Kansas, noted in November 1882 the prospect of a new saloon opening soon in town. On page one for his English readers, he appended the comment, "May the gods forbid." German readers were informed of the same prospect on page four, but this time coupled with the hopes not of divine interdiction, but for half-price beer at the opening celebration.

The final issue of a German paper often elicited poignant memories, sometimes from editors, at other times from subscribers. On September 7, 1918, the Davenport *Demokrat* announced that it was suspending publication "for the duration of the war." The notice stated that it took this step "reluctantly, but voluntarily." The German-language press "has proven to be an important factor in the Americanization of German

immigrants. In general, it kept itself loyal. . . . Unfortunately, a pronounced prejudice has developed in this country against everything that
is written or printed in the German languages. . . . It is on account of this
prejudice that we have reached the decision to take the abovementioned
step." Hardly two months later, the war ended, but the *Demokrat* never
reappeared.

One can taste the regret in the farewell message of John H. Bode in the
final issue of 1916 to his St. Charles Missouri readers: "I did not 'actually'
have the intention at the end of this year, to cease editing the 'Demokrat,'
which I have headed since 1864, without interruption, and never 'sat out'
a week during these 52 years." But rising costs and poor prospects of additional revenue brought him, "although with reluctance, to decide to take
the step of ceasing publication of the 'Demokrat' with this issue." The
war had dried up immigration from Germany for the foreseeable future.
"When German schools little by little go under, when German churches
find themselves induced to preach in the English language, when English Sunday schools, English youth organizations are introduced, so as
not to be forced to shut their doors entirely; when one further considers that . . . there are here, as everywhere, Germans who can't anglicize
themselves fast enough, . . . then the days are also numbered for German
papers. So, this 'Demokrat,' founded by the unforgettable Arnold Krekel
on January 1, 1852, will 'make its last appearance' with this issue."

Across the river in St. Louis, the German press held out longer, though
only two German dailies outlived the *Demokrat*. The Catholic *Amerika*
succumbed in 1924. The venerable *Westliche Post*, too, was fighting for
its life, having lost ten thousand subscribers between 1912 and 1920, its
circulation down to just eighteen thousand by the latter year. Not all the
loss could be attributed to the world war, of course; there was a downward trend before 1914, but advertising, in particular, was impacted by
the war, and even more with the loss of beer ads as a result of Prohibition.

When the *Westliche Post* ceased operations as a daily on June 19, 1938,
one sad fifty-year subscriber wrote a letter that translates thus: "I was
born in the year 1857, that is together with the WP. In 1888 I came to St.
Louis and have, since then, read the Post daily, deriving much pleasure
from seeing the year of my birth [on its masthead]. And now the paper is
dying, but so long as I live, and so long as the paper is published, I want it
in my home. Things are not better for me; everything I had I lost in 1929.

Best regards, an old subscriber." Although a weekly edition continued, it lasted only a few more months. As the *Post's* biographer writes, "For the first time in 103 years St. Louis was without a reputable German paper."

The same trends could be observed nationwide; the dying *Post* was survived by just a dozen German dailies. Most were in the biggest cities; Philadelphia was the only one with two competing papers, though surprisingly the eight thousand German immigrants in Rochester and a mere three thousand in Omaha managed to support dailies in their mother tongue. Small-town papers show an even greater tenacity in view of the size of their immigration population, evidence that German language competence and use extended into the second and even third generations. Gasconade County, the most heavily German in all of Missouri, counted only 616 natives of the Fatherland in the 1920 census, but the *Hermanner Volksblatt* was still publishing a weekly run of one thousand. It finally succumbed in 1928; two years later, the census found a mere 361 German natives in the county.

The Texas record is even more remarkable, as is evident from the 1940 census data on mother tongue. It was the only state where second-generation speakers of German were outnumbered by those in the third and subsequent generations. Three German newspapers in the Lone Star State were still in operation at the end of World War II. The print run of the Fredericksburg paper was more than four times the number of German natives in the county, but that pales by comparison with New Braunfels and Giddings, both of whose German weeklies enjoyed circulations that were ten times the size of their county's German population. The *Neu Braunfelser Zeitung* celebrated its centennial in 1952 before finally switching entirely to English in 1957, the last German newspaper in Texas. But by another measure, Fredericksburg holds the record for language persistence. Both communities were settled by a colonization society, with county populations more than 85 percent of German origin. But Fredericksburg and rural Gillespie County, located farther from the main routes of transportation than New Braunfels, still had a majority of 57 percent claiming German mother tongue in the 1970 census, with some of its speakers of the fifth or sixth generation in America. Not until the year 2000 did Spanish speakers outnumber German speakers in and around Fredericksburg.

6

German Niches in the American Economy

Most German immigrants were motivated in whole or in part by economic opportunities in America, often touted in letters home by family or friends who had gone before. Although the German image is dominated by Midwestern farmers, the reality is somewhat more complicated. The most frequent occupation reported by Germans in both the 1870 and 1880 census was indeed that of farmer, outnumbering common laborers two to one in the latter year. Yet Germans were not as concentrated in the farm population as the average American. Just over 30 percent of Germans were employed in the agricultural sector in 1880, compared to nearly half of the general population. Moreover, the nearly three hundred thousand German men earning their living from agriculture in 1880 were considerably outnumbered by the almost 370,000 employed in what the census called the "manufacturing, mechanical, and mining industries." From decade to decade, across the nineteenth century and into the twentieth, Germans did steadily expand their foothold in the farm population. By 1900 they were close to parity, and in 1950, the second generation, born in America of German parents, was 50 percent above the national average. As the farm population shrunk, German Americans managed to hang on better than other groups. By 1980, when the census first tallied ethnic origins regardless of generation, Germans had the highest proportion of farmers of any group besides Norwegians. In a farm population of 5.6 million nationwide, over one million were "single ancestry" Germans, who together with "mixed ancestry Germans" totaled over two million living on American farms.

There are a number of factors that explain this German agricultural progress, among them more diversified and less risky farming practices, greater use of family labor (especially that of women, which will be treated in the following chapter), and different approaches to generational succession compared to Anglo-Americans. But probably the biggest factor was the land hunger on the part of the rural lower classes in Germany and the way that they equated land ownership with security when it became attainable in the New World, an attitude they passed on to their descendants.

Germans who settled in rural areas often wrote home in praise of the egalitarian American society, especially those with roots in northwest Germany, which was characterized by a polarization between a group of rather prosperous landowning farmers kept stable by impartible inheritance and a growing agricultural lower class of tenant farmers, *Heuerleute* in the regional parlance, eking out a living from a combination of agriculture and cottage industry. They had no land and little security, and were obliged to work for the landowners whenever called upon. Resentments of the rural lower class continued to echo through their letters home for nearly half a century.

In the 1850s, one immigrant from this class spelled out his grievances in a letter from Missouri: "If I and Wilhelmine [his wife] would have stayed with you, you know what my lot would have been, namely a poor tenant farmer, how they get along you also know. Here I needn't pay any land rent, any house rent, no money for wood or for cropland, and also don't need to buy bread. Here I stay year in, year out with my family, here I hitch my own team to the wagon or plow and sow my fields as good as I want and can." He goes on to comment on the pace of work: "Here I don't need to do nearly as much work, especially hard work; threshing is left to the horses. I don't need to spin and work flax, here you only have to work by day . . . and no landowner will order you to work or put you out of your house" [that is to say, a tenant's cottage].

Writing from Illinois during the Civil War, another immigrant applies American terminology to the old homeland: "Anybody that wants to work can get along much better than in your slave-land, . . . if the tenant farmers and servants knew how it is in America then not a single one would stay there." He then lists a half-dozen or more one-time neighbors, perhaps expecting skepticism from his readers: "Those were all tenant farmers from Germany and now they're farm [owners], we found things better than we would have thought, we're not thinking of going back to Germany and I've written you the truth just as true as my hand has written it."

As late as 1867, an immigrant writing from my home county of Missouri echoes similar sentiments: "Dear friend, believe me, I've thought of you quite often, and I have thought of Germany quite often, but I have never yet thought that I wished I had stayed in Germany. Because here there is no pressure from the landowning farmers, for here a common man counts for as much as the rich and big shots, and everyone can undertake what he wishes, because it's a free land here."

Even the son of a small-scale but indebted landowner reflected such class tensions. Writing on the eve of the Civil War, he contrasted his situation with that of the local bailiff's son, noting that in Germany "he was looked up to, and I was dirt on the street in his eyes, and here it is the other way around, because here nothing counts but education."

The egalitarian ethos of Americans and the lack of social distinctions come up repeatedly in letters back to Germany. Perhaps it was merely a cliché, which one pious immigrant to Missouri repeated in 1851, "In this free land you don't have to take off before anyone except the Lord God." But that same year, a better educated immigrant wrote from Wisconsin, where his brother served as Justice of the Peace, with more concrete examples: "such differences in ranks are unknown here. You don't have to be ashamed to do any kind of work, and it often happens here that someone does a kind of work that he would not have done under any circumstances in Germany . . . . We really find this amusing. Last summer for example Louis (JP) was called out of the hayfield in order to perform a marriage for 2 young people. Later people came to get an arrest warrant from him to have someone arrested because of a fight, while he was at work in the cow barn. A third called him from felling a tree in order to have a land deed certified, and so on. Just like you see a merchant splitting wood or cleaning out his stables."

Despite minor reservations about America, another immigrant wrote from rural Illinois in 1864: "They're of the opinion here that the war will be over around springtime. I can't write you anything else good about America, except for the good custom that the servants here are respected just like the masters themselves. Also, they all eat here at the same table with the masters. They only eat three times a day here, but so as if it was a wedding over there."

This was just one of many points about which there was a broad consensus among immigrants who wrote home to Germany. At the most
basic level, nearly everyone agreed that common folks had more and better food than back in Germany. Even during the severe depression of the
1890s, one farmer wrote from Minnesota: "One thing I'm sure of, that
we live better here than the farmers in Germany who have three times
as much money as I do. . . . Anyone who isn't able to eat meat 21 times
a week if he wants to is in bad shape." Or as an immigrant to Michigan
wrote back in those innocent times when eating wasn't sinful and choles-
terol had not yet been discovered: "Here there's more grease on top of the
dishwater than there is on top of the soup in Germany."

An immigrant farmer in Missouri, writing in 1851, seems to have
encountered disbelief on the German side: "The reader should not get
upset, meat is eaten at every meal. On winter days you fry sausage in the
pan in the morning when you're having coffee, and everyone can have it
like this here, even if he didn't have a dime of money left when he arrived
in this country. . . . Dear reader, whether you believe it or not, it is indeed
the truth. America is a land that leads honorable, hard-working people
out of poverty into prosperity, from 'small bites' to 'eating your fill.'"

Fifteen years later, his opinion was echoed by a woman writing from
rural Illinois: "When I think back on Germany, I'm often astonished that
in Germany the farming folks have to slave away so awfully hard, and
some of them still don't have that to eat what the livestock eats over here.
When we arrived here, we thought at first that is was just like there was
a wedding feast here every day. Now we've gotten used to it, and the
men still have to slave away awfully hard, but now it only goes from 7 in
the morning till 6 in the evening."

Almost all German letter writers agreed, however, that the pace of
work was faster in America; there is testimony of this from both rural
and urban settlers, in the early as well as the late nineteenth century,
though some, especially if they had a background in cottage industry,
did remark that the workday was shorter in America. For example, a
farmer's son wrote from rural Ohio in 1834, "The Americans want to see
a lot of work done in a day, and anyone who thinks he can get by easy
shouldn't come here. The Americans are strong and quick, they can do
more in one day than the Germans." Still, most of them were also of the
opinion that this hard work paid off, as a wagonmaker wrote from rural

Illinois in 1866: "Everything here is different from Germany and faster. You also have to work hard here, but if you're careful with your money, you can certainly earn a lot."

One immigrant with roots among agrarian proprietors injects a note of caution in his description of American opportunities in a letter from Ohio written on Christmas Day of 1840: "You wanted to know how such poor families get along here, they rent a room or chamber and work at day labor in the rain, snow, and cold wind and when such people are lucky, in 4 to 6 years they can maybe earn enough to buy a 40 acre piece of bush, then they have to work 5 more years before they get anything done and that is hard work, a weak man can't get through it." But most writers stressed the opportunities, and the fact that arduous labor had been the tenant farmer's lot all along.

That is what one of them told a Protestant pastor in the 1830s just a few years after his arrival in Missouri: "In Germany, I didn't have as much property as I could hold in my hand, and dared not hope, no matter how hard I worked and saved, ever to acquire any property. What you see here belongs to me. I have had to work terribly hard, that is true, but I have something to show for it."

Catholics in the area fared just as well. Johann Hennerich Buhr had left his hometown in 1833 with the parting shot: "The landowning farmers are eating up the tenants"; in America he acquired landholdings that would have put him near the top of his home village. The 158 thalers that he took along he had increased eighteen-fold by 1860 to 2,817 thalers or $2,000. According to the agricultural census, he only owned one horse (still more than 99 percent of the tenant farmers back home); but in addition he had two mules, three milk cows, four draft oxen, six other cattle, seven sheep, and thirty swine. Before emigrating, his only livestock had been two cows. He owned 120 acres of land, fifty of them in cultivation, which would have placed him in the top 10 percent of the landowners back home.

Early arrivals such as these fared best, but experiences such as theirs were in no way atypical. Land ownership was not restricted to those who could trade small, expensive plots in Germany for large and cheap pieces of American public land. One transatlantic tracing study found that German background had no effect on whether someone acquired land in America, but only on the size of their holdings. Regardless of whether someone was of landowning or tenant origins, 80 percent of both groups had become landowners by 1850, after a decade or so in America; in fact, a higher percentage of German immigrants owned land than their Anglo-American neighbors. In Germany, the social gap between landowners and tenants was such that marriage across that divide was almost unthinkable, and was itself cause for immigration when unequal couples fell in love. Examples of this have come to light from Ohio to Missouri. On the American side, this was no obstacle, as shown by the intermarriage between my landowning Groenemann ancestors and a Gausmann of tenant-farmer origins.

Immigrant farmers encountered unfamiliar crops and methods of cultivation in America. Even a familiar word like *Korn* had a different meaning. In Germany it meant rye, the leading crop with fifteen million acres in 1895, followed by oats with ten million, potatoes with 7.5 million, and only then wheat with five million acres. The acreage planted in corn (maize) was insignificant, not even half of that devoted to vineyards in Germany. In U. S. fields by contrast, corn overshadowed all other grain crops, with nearly double the acreage and four times the yield of wheat. Oats was only half as prominent as wheat, while rye was insignificant.

A Missouri immigrant who arrived in 1833 struggled to find the vocabulary to describe corn, but his neighbors who had immigrated a year earlier had obviously learned quickly: "They had their fields in such good shape already, the trees chopped down, and dragged out with the oxen, and plowed up around the stumps, . . . and already had such fine crops on it, they were 5–7 foot high but they get to be 11–13 foot, and it gets 3–4 cones on it, and in each cone 500–600 grains, as big as the horse beans in Germany, and they don't know what fertilizer is." Corn was finding its way onto immigrant tables as well as their fields; another new arrival in the same county wrote home in 1861: "Corn, that is Turkish wheat, . . . that's the most important thing in America, man and beast live from it." Another term for the grain common among southwest Germans was *"Welschkorn"* (foreign corn). But whatever they called it, German immigrants quickly became proficient at growing corn. Even an amateur such as Latin farmer Friedrich Muench claimed never to have suffered a crop failure, not even in his first year. Despite their inexperience, Germans in his area of Missouri were just as likely to grow corn as their American neighbors. Other studies of German agricultural practices in areas as varied as Michigan, Wisconsin, and Texas have found that the similarities with those of Anglo-Americans far outweighed the differences. The practices of Germans were most distinctive in matters involving their own stomachs. They planted more potatoes, but were quite skeptical toward the American sweet potato. Germans had a reputation for higher productivity due to greater use of animal manure. "Prayer and manure will not be in vain"—such was the pragmatic piety of a Low German proverb. The punch line, whether explicit or implied, was that "manure will help for sure." However, the agricultural census returns show little difference in the per-acre yields between the two groups, possibly because Anglo-Americans had arrived earlier and settled on better land. An early settler remarked about fellow Germans on the Ozark fringes, "These guys will clear any land where the rocks aren't lying three feet deep."

There were some forms of specialty agriculture where Germans stood out. They were heavily overrepresented among dairymen, as well as gardeners and vine growers. Wisconsin, which dubs itself "America's Dairyland," was also the most heavily German state of the Union. On the urban fringes, Germans frequently engaged in truck gardening. The wine industry is especially indebted to German immigrants.

The leading historian of winemaking in America made an educated guess that "there were more growers and winemakers of German descent, both in California and in the rest of the country, than of any other origin before Prohibition." Only in New York did a wine industry develop without significant German influence. New Jersey native Nicholas Longworth developed the wine industry in Cincinnati in the 1830s, but he relied heavily on German labor and German customers, even giving his Catawba wines German names. By the 1840s, the Queen City was heralded as the "Rhineland of America," but its vineyards largely succumbed to disease, compounded by the Civil War. From the 1860s on, the Ohio wine industry migrated to the vicinity of Lake Erie, again carried on largely by Germans, some of them refugees from Cincinnati. The city also played midwife to the Missouri wine industry, centered around the town of Hermann, which produced nearly half of all the wine in the state before the Civil War. The first grapevines planted in Hermann around 1840 were largely obtained from Longworth. The town celebrated its first wine festival in 1848. By 1855, the hills around Hermann were planted with five hundred acres of grapes, and its wine was exported as far away as Cincinnati. A bit farther downstream on the north side of the Missouri, the Augusta area was developing a wine industry, led by Latin farmer Friedrich Muench, who in 1859 authored a treatise on viticulture that went through several German editions as well as a translation titled *School for American Grape Culture*. In 1861, Michael Poeschel founded the first commercial winery in Hermann, which had one thousand acres of vineyards by the end of the Civil War. Poeschel's enterprise grew into the largest winery outside California before Prohibition.

Lest one romanticize these immigrant artisan winemakers, it is well to remember Gert Goebel's critique in his 1877 memoir of the practice of "gallizing," adding sugar to the fermentation process: "an attempt is made to justify 'gallizing,' namely the desire to remove the so-called fox taste from the wine. . . . This 'fox hunt' was now often pursued with such energy that not only was the fox exterminated, but the character of the wine and its distinctive flavor was sacrificed in the process, so that almost no difference could be detected anymore . . . except for the red or white color." Reporting on his 1867 visit, Friedrich Gerstaecker was charmed by the town of Hermann: "I suddenly stood in the middle of a friendly little German town, as if it had conjured up the homeland out of the ground especially for me." But he also criticized "gallizing," going on to say that he didn't believe the United States would ever yield a *famous* wine and earn the title of a wine land, but it was at least capable of producing "a good, drinkable, and also healthy product."

Illinois rivaled Missouri in wine production, and there, too, many of the initiators were German, especially in the Latin farmer settlement in and around Belleville, among them Forty-Eighter Friedrich Hecker. In California wine country, Italian names have predominated for the last century, but they only became prominent after 1880. Many of the pioneers were German, including the founders of the state's first wine company in 1854, musicians Charles Kohler and John Frohling. Ironically, neither had even seen a vineyard before. Similarly in Missouri, neither Michael Poeschel nor Friedrich Muench hailed from wine country in Germany. The same was true of George Husmann, the son of one of Hermann's founders and another of the pioneers of Missouri wine. Education, access to information, and adequate initial capital were more important than previous experience with winegrowing. The scientific disposition and willingness to experiment on the part of German vintners worked to the benefit of winegrowers not only in Missouri, but also those in France, and later in California, where Husmann moved in 1881.

A specter was haunting Europe after 1867, not the specter of Communism but some unseen foe that was causing grape stocks to wither and die. Missouri state entomologist Charles V. Riley identified the microscopic *phylloxera* louse that was causing the havoc. The solution proved to be grafting French vines onto resistant American rootstocks. The three most important suppliers of these vital rootstocks were all Missouri nurserymen and vintners: George Husmann; Isidor Bush, a Jewish immigrant from the Austrian Empire who learned viticulture in America; and Swiss immigrant Hermann Jaeger, who was later awarded the French Legion of Honor for his part in saving the French wine industry.

Another aspect of Germans' modernization in American agriculture was their quick adoption of mechanization; its advantages were one of the standard refrains of immigrant letters back home. The son of a landowning farmer wrote from Nebraska in the late 1860s to correct a stereotype: "In Germany they often say, whoever doesn't want to follow the plow back there has to pull it over here, but that's a big mistake, because here the horses have to do the work and we go and sit on the machines, here they've even got riding plows. Horses stack the hay, they have many kinds of harvesting machines, . . . now they've invented one that ties the bundles, for if we didn't have all these machines, we couldn't pay such high wages." Over the course of time this mechanization only increased, as is reflected in another letter written from Illinois. In 1895, after ten years in America, the writer reported that he owned and farmed a 160-acre square of level land: "Last year I and my [16-year-old son] August did it all by ourselves, because here everything is done by machine. We don't need to use a scythe, then August gets on the self-binder and in five days with 3 or 4 horses cuts 50 or 60 acres of grain, that's how it goes with grass too but we only hitch up 2 horses, and because I don't have a hired hand any more we don't milk as many cows . . . I only keep 6 now." It is apparent how Americanized his attitudes had become in his reactions to a letter from Germany in 1892, at least as far as agriculture was concerned: "My sister wrote that Karl Wattenberg bought 7 acres near you for 1800 [marks?], tell him he's much too dumb, for that money you could get 160 acres here and 3 times as good a land, then he could keep 5 horses and go driving whenever he wants to, to church or to town—walking is not in style here." That was true in the 1830s in Missouri, as an immigrant reported in his first letter home: "We still haven't found any beggars in all America, here they all ride on horseback, the women as well as the men, one neighbor rides to the other, you hardly see anyone walking." Twenty years later in another Missouri county, it was much the same: "If you want to go somewhere, you bridle the horse and saddle up and ride, even if you're just going to your neighbor's. In Germany that would be considered arrogance, here it's the general custom, here everyone rides, young and old, man and woman."

Although a scholarly investigation of the subject is still lacking, it seems likely that German immigrants played an important role, directly and indirectly, in promoting the growing exports of American agricultural machinery to Germany. As early as 1880, the brochure of one Berlin foundry featured a number of American implements, including plows, horse treadmills, a grain cleaning mill, and a chain pump. U. S. exports surged in the 1890s, and by 1910, some fifty thousand foreign reapers were being imported into Germany annually.

The era of mass German immigration from 1830 to 1893 was also the era in which the United States surged to world leadership in industrial production, so it is worth examining to what extent the two developments were interrelated and where in U. S. industry Germans played important roles. Despite their image as capable farmers and their progress in the agricultural sector during this period, German immigrants were most heavily represented in U. S. industrial production. Germans were half again as likely to be employed in manufacturing as the average American. But the question still remains just where in the manufacturing sector Germans were concentrated, and at which level.

With the help of the 1880 U. S. Census, one can identify German concentrations in individual occupations, in this case considering both German immigrants and their American-born offspring. The results confirm some ethnic stereotypes. Men of German birth or parentage made up less than 11 percent of the male labor force, yet they dominated some occupational specialties to the near exclusion of everyone else. Over 80 percent of all brewers in the country were German, a feat even more impressive given the large number of workers in the branch—over fifteen thousand. More than three-fourths of all pork butchers and sausage makers in the country were German, bringing to mind Cincinnati's early nickname of "Porkopolis." Teenage immigrant Oscar Mayer was then employed as a butcher; three years later he and his brother established a Chicago meat market that grew into a nationwide business that remained in family hands until 1981. Germans made up a solid majority in several other branches of the food industry: sugar refining, vinegar making, and in the huge contingent of bakers and confectioners. One of the latter, starting in Belleville, Illinois, in 1869, went on to invent corn candy, and was celebrated as the supplier of jelly beans to the Reagan White House, bearing the Goelitz family name over four generations until 2001. Steinway pianos and Martin guitars come to mind when one sees that 55 percent of piano-factory workers and over 60 percent of the small group of musical instrument makers were of German background. This group also constituted half of all the country's eighty thousand tailors. There is no doubt that many of these ethnic niches reflected a transatlantic transfer of skills. One young tailor's wife related how her husband had been hired right off the boat upon arriving in New York in 1854, and advised her unmarried girlfriends toiling away in the steep vineyards of the Moselle, "Burn up your grape baskets and get yourself a tailor, even if he's just a windbag."

Even an unskilled newcomer to industrial work appreciated the higher wages he earned, writing in 1882 less than a year after arrival in Pittsburgh: "Here you work harder than over there, but when it's payday and you get those lovely dollars counted out in your hands, the hardship is forgotten, you get fresh courage, here they always say *Gohätt, Vorwärts* in German. I'm only sorry that I spent the best years of my life in the German land of Egypt so miserably and painfully, for nothing."

Germans with artisan skills fared even better, and some of their occupational concentrations stand out even in states where they constituted just a small minority. In Texas, where less than 6 percent of the labor force was German in 1870, they actually outnumbered natives in the baking trade, and among brewers they held a huge—almost three-to-one—advantage without even taking the second generation into consideration. It is no coincidence that the last independent brewery in Texas bears the name of Spoetzl, or that a worldwide fruitcake exporter in Corsicana, Texas, can trace its origins back to German immigrant August Weidmann, who, together with an Anglo partner, founded the Collin Street Bakery in 1896.

Even where they did not constitute a majority, Germans showed impressive concentrations of 40 percent or more of those working in a number of large trades, including cigar makers, cabinetmakers, and upholsterers. Further up the production chain, nearly two-fifths of the country's butchers were German. Not only did Germans produce most of the country's musical instruments; they made up 36 percent of those playing them professionally. Besides brewing the great bulk of the beer, Germans also sold much of it: 44 percent of the saloonkeepers and one-third of the bartenders were German. These two job descriptions are among the few instances where the occupational categories allow a rough distinction between ownership or management as opposed to labor. Not until 1910 did the census distinguish between employers, employees, and those working on their own account. Thus, the term "brewer" in 1880 would probably encompass everyone from Augustus Busch on down to his journeyman brewmaster, as well as small, family enterprises like that of Heinrich Kreische.

A broader classification of occupations by industrial branch further confirms the above information. Germans not only dominated brewing, they constituted 70 percent of all those employed in the entire beverage industry. They made up a solid majority of those involved with bakery products as well. They also dealt in food and drink on the retail side, comprising one-third or more of those involved in eating and drinking establishments and liquor stores. Close to two-fifths of all tobacco and furniture manufacturing was carried on by Germans, and almost half of all clothing stores were run by them. But the question remains, how many of these skills were transplanted?

Paradoxically, German Americans were more urbanized than either the compatriots they left behind or the American population in general. So one cannot simply assume that immigrants were transferring skills across the Atlantic; many were new recruits to urban and industrial life. Often, as was the case in agriculture, they commented upon the degree of mechanization in American industry. Already at the outset of mass immigration in 1833, a German farm-owner's son wrote from St. Louis: "Our Heinrich is . . . in a mill, and earns per month 12 dollars with board, that's done differently here than in Germany, here you don't need to pour the grain into the mill, that is all done by machines. He doesn't have to do more than to put the flour in barrels, and then it goes away by ship.

We like it here quite well, therefore I bid you (my loved ones,) you could live much better here." A cooper writing from rural Indiana in 1883 was equally impressed by mechanization (even if he couldn't spell "machinery"), but he saw it as negative: "all the *machinri* wrecks everything, too much is being made, everything is cheap, wages are pushed down, won't be getting any better, more and more keeps getting invented, not much work is done by hand any more, the *machün* does everything." Mechanization came early to the textile industry. One immigrant advised his brother-in-law in 1845, "With your occupation I would not advise you to come here, for there is not much spinning done here, and most of the clothing is of cotton, which is grown a lot in America, and is all spun in factories." But some, such as Martin Weitz, a handloom wool weaver from an impoverished mountain village in Hesse, transitioned easily from artisanship to industry. Immediately upon arrival in 1854 he went to work in a *"fectori"* in Astoria, New York, and then in Rockville, Connecticut, tending power looms. Still, there was a higher degree of transatlantic continuity with both labor and management in the textile industry of New England than was usually the case.

When one examines the urbanization rates of German immigrants of various origins, it appears that urban and industrial background plays somewhat of a role, though by no means a stringent one. Even including U. S. towns as small as 2,500 as the "urban" threshold, only natives of Berlin and Hamburg were more than two-thirds urbanized in America. Excluding city-states, Saxony was the most heavily urbanized and industrialized state of origin in Germany, but its immigrants were only slightly more urban than the average German in America.

One instance where occupational background did play a significant role was in the Saxon immigration to New England. This was a relatively uncommon destination for Germans; in 1880, Chicago claimed ten times as many Germans, and New York twenty times as many as Boston. But of the few Germans who did settle there, many did so because of industrial specializations. Nationwide, there were roughly equal numbers of Saxons, from the most industrialized state in Germany, and Mecklenburgers, from the most agricultural. But in New England, Saxons outnumbered Mecklenburgers by a factor of twenty-four. Saxons made up 14 percent of the Germans in the New England states, compared with only 3 percent nationwide. For an explanation, one need look no further than the textile industry, where one finds Germans involved in a transatlantic transfer of skills at both the top and the bottom of the industrial hierarchy. Two similar case studies make this abundantly clear. In Holyoke, Massachusetts, where a Westphalian industrialist had established a woolens factory, nearly half of the German immigrants originated from the Saxon textile district around Glauchau und Werdau, west of Chemnitz. The textile factory towns of Manchester, New Hampshire, and Lawrence, Massachusetts, exercised a similar pull on immigrants from German textile regions. More than one-third of the Germans there originated from Saxony or Sachsen-Altenburg, and another 17 percent came from Silesia. These and a couple of other places of origin, all characterized by a strong textile sector, accounted for nearly three-quarters of the German population of these towns. Saxons were responsible for barely 3 percent of total German immigration, but approximately 35 percent of the Germans in Manchester and Lawrence, and no less than 46 percent of those in Holyoke.

Particularly in the case of Holyoke, it is evident that a German employer attracted fellow ethnics with experience in the textile industry to run his mills. The Stursberg family of Lennep, Westphalia, had been heavily involved in exporting products of their woolen mills to the United States, but with the political and economic shifts of the Civil War, they faced protective tariffs and a weakened U. S. currency. In response, they transferred the bulk of their operations to the Germania Mill in Holyoke in 1865. Although they managed to recruit some workers from their home region in the Wupper Valley, they soon derived the bulk of their labor force from Saxony, where the woolens industry was facing similar problems. The German population of the mill town skyrocketed from just thirty-six in 1865 to nearly six hundred a decade later, seven-eighths of them concentrated in the Third Ward near the gates of Germania Mill.

Manchester was dominated by the Amoskeag Mills, with some fourteen thousand employees, the largest industrial establishment in the U.S. or the world at that time—not the environment where one might expect immigrant entrepreneurship to thrive. But there is ample evidence that within this complex, "the growth of gingham weaving at the Amoskeag owed much to German managers and workers," many of whom arrived with industrial experience and several of whom attained supervisory positions. At least one worker with German training came up through the ranks to become an entrepreneur himself: Abraham Olzendam, founder of the Hosiery Company that bore his family name. He grew up and was trained as a dyer in the textile town of Barmen, and immigrated to the United States in 1848 at age twenty-six. Initially, he worked his trade in Massachusetts, moving in 1858 to Manchester and establishing his own hosiery factory in 1862. It apparently flourished from the start, for during the Civil War he was among the select group earning enough to pay income tax, and he went from reporting no property in the 1860 census to claiming $5,000 worth of real estate and $25,000 worth of personal property a decade later, when the census listed him as a hosiery manufacturer. He continued to lead this enterprise successfully until his death in 1896.

Another significant concentration of German industrialists employing fellow immigrants was in the northern Queens communities of College Point and Astoria, New York. Already in 1854, Conrad Poppenhusen had established his factory manufacturing hard rubber combs in College Point and built up a paternalistic company town for his largely German labor force, which numbered around one thousand. One historian describes it as "a typical German industrial town similar to the Ruhr region." Of some 1,200 families resident in 1880, nearly three-fourths were headed by Germans. Poppenhusen's philanthropy was so appreciated by his fellow Germans that they tolerated his dislike for beer. In nearby Astoria, the Steinway piano manufacturers, fleeing labor agitators and the crowding of Manhattan, purchased four hundred acres and erected a new factory after the Civil War. Steinway, too, financed workers' housing and public facilities, even sponsoring a German-language teacher for the local public school. More than four-fifths German, this area was even more homogeneous than College Point. Steinway and Poppenhusen were only the most prominent among German industrialists in the area; their neighbors included the Hugo Funk Silk Mill, the Samuel Kunz Mill, and another rubber company run by I. B. Kleinert, and, last but not least, brewer Adolph Levinger. But ethnic homogeneity and employer paternalism did not necessarily guarantee tranquil labor relations. Steinway was faced with a strike when he attempted to impose a significant wage cut in 1870, and he ended up backing down, though he did prevail against the eight-hour-day movement later in the decade.

Labor organizers had an easier job when they did not need to bridge ethnic divides, and piano workers were in a strong bargaining position because of their specialized skills.

Germans, bringing with them many artisan skills, were clearly at an advantage over groups such as the Irish, who were much more concentrated in unskilled labor. But it remains to be seen whether this proved to be of long-term benefit, particularly in the next generation. Two studies of nineteenth-century social mobility, one set in Philadelphia and another in the small New York town of Poughkeepsie, came to similar conclusions: Artisan skills often provided a fast start down what proved in the long run to be a blind alley, particularly for the subsequent generation. Another initially positive characteristic of German communities had similar ironic consequences: their institutional completeness. As a pioneering study of Milwaukee observed, in that city, "Germans had the size and range of occupations and achievement within their numbers to support a potential community in the full sense of the word, one performing community supportive functions largely independent of the wider Milwaukee society." Such internal divisions made it "possible to live a German life as if in a microcosm of a whole society." One of the markers of genuine entrepreneurship was the ability to break out of this ethnic cocoon and participate fully in the larger society. But this was the exception rather than the rule with German immigrants in the late nineteenth century.

For much of the nineteenth century the boundary between artisanship and industry was still rather indistinct. A study of Detroit in 1880 found that, as in Milwaukee on the eve of the Civil War, "the very presence of both German employers and German artisans shows that at least a significant part of the German community was independent economically." As late as the turn of the century, among Detroit workers, "the Germans were most likely to be employed within their own community, . . . many working for large industrial concerns but as many being independent craftsmen, often employing a few men of their own. . . . Some German entrepreneurs would hire only German employees, but some would also hire . . . other ethnic groups." Although such enterprises could occasionally serve as a springboard and allow their creators to break out of their ethnic cocoons, such opportunities were relatively scarce, and becoming much rarer by the automobile age of the 1920s. A profile of 121 of

Detroit's leading industrialists at the turn of the twentieth century finds that, in a city where German immigrants and their children made up 30 percent of the population, only 10 percent of the entrepreneurs employing one hundred or more people were German Americans. Even of those, only half "had entered the world of the Anglo-Saxon business elite" with respect to their residences or club memberships. By contrast, "Most of the large German employers who produced mostly consumer products such as beer, clothing, or furniture operated within the confines of the [heavily German] east side only, not in the city at large."

Occasionally, an immigrant enterprise succeeded in making the transition from what was basically a small artisan-scale operation serving an ethnic enclave to a more industrial mode of production serving a broad, multiethnic customer base. Although every company history is a story unto itself, one such instance, the milling concern that was founded by immigrant Carl Hilmar Guenther and survived as a family-owned enterprise into the twenty-first century exemplifies many of the characteristics that contributed to long-term entrepreneurial success. Equipped with a thorough training in milling when he left Germany in the fateful year of 1848, Guenther was propelled less by any political motivations than by a sense of adventure combined with sober economic calculations. Arriving young and unencumbered, he could operate with an optimal degree of flexibility. Although Guenther enjoyed the German sociability in and around his first destination of Racine, Wisconsin, within two years he had located some 1,300 miles to the southwest in Fredericksburg, Texas, which still offered German *Gemütlichkeit*, but where his milling skills were in much shorter supply. By the time he turned twenty-five, Guenther was in the midst of designing and building a mill from the ground up, putting into practice what he had only learned in theory, and taking charge of activities he had only experienced as a subordinate in the Old Country. But when the first water flowed down the millrace, the mill "worked so well that it seemed as though it had been running for years." It became a thriving enterprise, but in 1859, faced with competition from a steam mill in town, Guenther relocated to San Antonio, which was four times larger than Fredericksburg but not as well served with mills.

In his old location, Guenther could operate largely in German; after two years in Fredericksburg he put off his brother's request for a letter in English, "for I still use the dictionary." Within a few months of the move to San Antonio, he reported that his firstborn son Fritz, at age two-and-a-half, "speaks very distinctly, but occasionally mixes Spanish, German, and English all together," perhaps unsurprisingly, since the three cultural groups were represented in the city in roughly equal proportions. Guenther reached out to all three, importing wheat via oxcart from as far away as Mexico, and marketing his products across the whole ethnic spectrum and beyond. This was evident in the names under which his product was sold. "Pioneer Flour Mills" was one of its most prominent brands, although the Guenther name and portrait remained prominent on the labels. On tortilla flour sacks, he added "El Viejo" ("the Old Man"), so that there was no mistaking among Spanish-speaking customers. Marketing kept pace with technological innovations in the milling process. A name like "Dewey's Success" in the wake of the Spanish-American War shows an increasing identification with the dominant culture. By the eve of World War I, Pioneer sold a half-million pounds of flour to the U. S. Army, and during the war bought $50,000 worth of Liberty Bonds, a San Antonio record.

Guenther's labor force also became increasingly multiethnic over time, including many Hispanics, but management of the enterprise remained in German (and family) hands through 1982. Still, one can observe an increasing engagement with the dominant culture. All of pioneer Guenther's eight children married within Germanophone cultural circles. They had received a fully bilingual education in the two-way immersion program of the San Antonio German English School. The younger Guenthers participated enthusiastically both in the ethnic *Vereinsleben* and the multiethnic San Antonio Fiesta. By the third generation, Guenthers were studying at faraway elite institutions such as Washington University in St. Louis and Stevens Institute of Technology in New Jersey. It was this combination of persistence and adaptation that allowed the Guenther enterprise to celebrate its 150th anniversary in 2001, the oldest surviving family-owned business in Texas.

When profiling prominent German-American industrialists and entrepreneurs, it is important to weigh just what were the relative contributions of Germany and America to their varied achievements. The range is quite varied. In some cases, the German experience was little more than a bad dream, a prime example being John Jacob Astor, who owed little more to Germany than the determination never again to be so poor as he was there. Or to take a less familiar example, Jacob Haish was one of the first successful inventors and manufacturers of barbed wire, and bequeathed his hometown of DeKalb, Illinois, $150,000 when he died at age ninety-nine. But he arrived from Württemberg with his parents at age nine, so his skills were obviously developed on the American side. He struck out on his own at age nineteen, married the daughter of his Yankee boss, and later employed Swedish servants in their household.

John Pritzlaff presents a similar case, although he was nineteen when he emigrated from Pomerania in 1839 with one of the first groups of Old Lutherans. His background as a poor shepherd boy had next to nothing to do with the job he obtained in a Milwaukee hardware store after four years of knocking about—unless one considers counting sheep as good practice for counting change. He worked seven years for Yankee bosses before starting his own business in 1850, initially with a German partner whom he soon bought out. Building up a large trade "with all classes, but more particularly with his countrymen," Pritzlaff expanded beyond local and ethnic circles to become one of the leading hardware wholesalers in the Midwest with four hundred employees; his firm's imposing building still stands today. He was succeeded by his son Fred, who headed the concern until his death in 1951, 101 years after the company's founding. Although both generations of Pritzlaffs were active participants and major benefactors of the Missouri Synod Lutheran Church reflective of their heritage, there was little about their business enterprise that could be traced to their German origins.

More often, however, one sees with immigrant entrepreneurs a symbiosis of the two cultures. Immigration often involved a transfer of skills and technology, and sometimes capital, to more promising surroundings. Germany contributed good technical training, but America provided a more conducive and less restrictive environment in which to nourish ideas and enterprises. The brilliant, eccentric "Wizard of Schenectady," Charles Steinmetz, had received an excellent German technical education, earning a doctorate at the University of Breslau by age twenty-three. It was not lack of opportunity, but Bismarck's persecution of socialists, that brought him to the New World. Nonetheless, the supportive scientific and technical milieu that he encountered here furthered his talents and allowed him to make pathbreaking contributions in the theory and practice of electrification. The benefits of transplanting were even more apparent with John Roebling, the father not only of the Brooklyn Bridge but also of the steel-cable suspension bridge in general. He immigrated at age twenty-five with less than $400 to his name, but the technical training he brought with him was much more valuable. He had already been exposed to iron-chain suspension bridges at least on a small scale before he left. But on the German side, all his ideas remained theoretical because, as Roebling himself so pungently remarked in his diary, nothing could be done in Germany without "an army of councilors, ministers, and other officials discussing the matter for ten years, making long journeys, and writing long reports, while the money spent on all these preliminaries comes to more than the actual accomplishment of the enterprise."

In general, ambitious young men were afforded much greater autonomy with less experience in America than back in the Old Country. The technologically backward situation of the Confederacy during the Civil War presents an extreme case of a broader tendency. Heinrich Stähler, who immigrated in 1860 after studying metallurgy at the mining academy in Berlin, happened upon a unique opportunity to apply his theoretical knowledge to practical problems in the copper district of east Tennessee as a result of the Civil War. In less than two years he advanced from being a laboratory assistant to directing a copper refinery. In November 1862, Stähler proudly reported to his parents, "Since Trippel [his previous boss, a Swiss immigrant] left I have been the sole head of the largest copper works—perhaps not in all America, but at least the largest in the Confederate States." Although Stähler's sympathies were "more for the Union," this opportunity was simply too good to pass up, as his letter of May 1863 indicates: "I would really like to run a refinery like this at home in Germany someday, but unfortunately, there's no chance." With the approach of Yankee armies in late 1863, Stähler crossed over into Union lines and, despite numerous job offers, he returned to Germany where his fiancé was waiting. As it turned out, his American experiences and a subsequent sojourn in Sweden helped launch Stähler's career as a successful manager and industrialist in Germany after all. But it required the proverbial "oxen tour through the provinces" to accomplish it.

Heinrich Steinweg presents a similar case of frustrated ambitions, although he was considerably older when he immigrated and became Henry Steinway. He was an accomplished, prize-winning piano maker in Germany, but he had a serious problem: *Kleinstaaterei*, which subjected his products to high tariffs and severely restricted his marketing potential outside the not-so-grand Duchy of Braunschweig. Steinweg had even tried selling a piano by lottery as a way of dodging trade restrictions. His first American piano was number 483 in his career. Moreover, he and his sons continued to innovate in the United States; his first cast iron single-frame piano was built in 1855, five years after his arrival in New York. This design was exported back to Germany to the one remaining son who carried on the family business there.

There is another well-known musical instrument firm that is even older, but whose German roots are for the most part a well-kept secret: Martin guitars. It, too, is a story of German obstructions and American opportunities. Its founder, Christian Frederick Martin Sr., hailed from a family of Saxon cabinetmakers and had apprenticed with a famous guitar maker in Vienna. Attempting to establish himself back in Saxony, he became embroiled in a jurisdictional dispute between the cabinetmakers' and violin makers' guilds, which precipitated his emigration in 1833. After a few years in New York City, he moved his family and business to Nazareth, Pennsylvania, in 1839, where they have been ever since. His success was due to both German and Austrian technical training and further innovation in America; the x-brace system distinctive to Martin guitars was not invented until the 1850s, for example.

In some instances, it is difficult to determine just how much the German background contributed to entrepreneurial success. One such case is the brothers Julius and Carl Wesslau, who established a very successful cabinetmaking and furniture business in New York's *Kleindeutschland*. But circumstantial evidence suggests an important German role. Wesslaus no doubt brought with them a thorough training as craftsmen, for they were at least the third generation in their trade, and their father's journeyman wanderings had taken him all across central Europe from Osnabrück in the northwest to Vienna in the southeast. But since the father survived until 1869 and four siblings remained behind, his sons probably brought along little or no capital besides human capital when they emigrated in the early 1850s from Jüterbog, a small city fifty miles south of Berlin. Although they located in the heart of the German community on the Lower East Side, there is evidence the Wesslau brothers quickly reached out beyond the city and its German community. With the Civil War looming in December 1860, Julius wrote, "Our main business was with the South, and up to now we've lost about 600 dollars, and we may lose most of another 1,500 dollars, and we've let half of our workers go, and if things don't get better soon we'll have to send more away." Wesslaus seem to have adjusted to the new situation rather quickly, reporting by October 1862, "Our business has done rather well this year, and it is quite possible that we'll make up what we lost last year." Soon, the brothers were complaining about income tax, which was imposed on only a select group of high earners. By war's end they reported, "people think we're rich, and maybe we are, if 40 thousand dollars means being rich."

One important question is where immigrant entrepreneurs managed to obtain capital and credit, given the scarcity of both during the American take-off period. When Pritzlaff started his hardware business, his American employer lent him the original capital at 7.5 percent interest, and that was probably a preferential rate based on years of faithful employment. In letters from the young state of Wisconsin and frontier Texas, Hilmar Guenther complained about interest rates ranging from 12 to 20 percent, for loans of only three- or six-month durations. In both Fredericksburg and San Antonio, he was able to draw upon family capital, all told some 6,600 talers ($4,712), and was happy to pay 5 or 6 percent interest against his future inheritance. Even in the financial center of New York, an ambitious immigrant complained in an 1860 letter about 6–7 percent interest rates, and hoped to obtain a family loan from Germany at 5 percent. Anyone who could draw on capital or inheritance from the Old Country was at a distinct advantage, though the extent of transatlantic (or intraethnic) capital mobilization bears further investigation.

As with sources of labor and capital, for immigrant entrepreneurs in the consumer goods branch, one can pose a similar question on the marketing side: to what extent was the enterprise restricted to an ethnic niche; to what extent did it reach out to a larger customer base, particularly among Anglo-Americans? Most brewers probably started out serving primarily fellow ethnics. Germans viewed the right to drink beer as practically a constitutional right, and reacted vehemently and sometimes violently against any attempt to restrict it. Chicago experienced a "Lager Beer War" in 1855 when a Know-Nothing mayor attempted to drastically raise the fees for saloon licenses. But over time, immigrant entrepreneurs, especially the more successful ones, broadened their customer base. In 1874, journalist Edward King, reporting on his journey through the former slave states, remarked upon a cultural symbiosis that was taking place in St. Louis: "At the more aristocratic and elegant of the German beer gardens, . . . many prominent American families may be seen on the concert evenings, drinking the amber fluid and listening to the music of Strauss, of Gungl, or Meyerbeer." He goes on to say that they "no longer regard the custom as a dangerous German innovation," and he found in St. Louis "many of the hearty features and graces of European life, which have been emphatically rejected by the native population of the more austere Eastern States."

Clearly, brewing was an imported craft that catered to, or perhaps helped to create, a general American demand. Ironically, however, there were a number of successful immigrant brewers with backgrounds relatively unrelated to the brewing industry. This holds true for stonemason Heinrich Kreische, who by the late 1870s had the third-largest brewery in Texas, and machinist August Schell, of New Ulm, Minnesota, whose enterprise has survived to the present, the second-oldest family-owned brewery in the nation. Although this lack of brewing experience may not have been typical, it holds true also for the largest and best-known German-American brewing establishment, Anheuser-Busch, another firm that maintained family ownership into the twenty-first century. Neither of its founders arrived with a background in the brewer's trade. Eberhard Anheuser had amassed a fortune in soap making before 1859, when almost by happenstance, he first acquired a struggling brewery of which he was a major creditor. His son-in-law Adolphus Busch, who had previously been in the brewery supply business, handled the marketing side of the Anheuser brewing concern. Busch's main innovations were the pasteurization and rail shipment of beer as early as the 1870s to places as far away as Texas and Colorado. Miller Guenther served Anheuser bottled beer at a company picnic in San Antonio in 1875, and once the town of La Grange gained a railroad connection in 1880, within a year brewer Kreische was serving the imported product along with his local brew. What Anheuser and Busch owed to Germany was something perhaps more important than a craft. Both brought with them good educations and business training, as well as some capital, and they maintained transatlantic connections throughout their lives. The German language and culture gave brewers like these easy access to the immigrant expertise they needed. German ethnicity also provided access to a ready-made customer base both in towns like La Grange and New Ulm and the city of St. Louis, though successful brewers quickly branched out beyond this base. Furthermore, German brewers could draw upon a large ethnic network heavily involved in the wholesaling and retailing of alcohol.

Particularly in the case of second-generation German entrepreneurs, one might wonder what they could possibly owe to the Old Country unless they took over a family enterprise. Three prominent examples of international success, William Boeing, Hermann Holerith, and Edward Stratemeyer, from their beginnings addressed a national market outside of any ethnic niches. Even so, they show a rather broad range of German identity and influence of their ethnic heritage. The German roots of Boeing aircraft might appear rather tenuous, given that the firm's founder William Boeing was not only American born, but involved himself in a totally different branch of industry than his father. The latter had immigrated to Michigan and become rich in the lumber business by a classical American method: marrying the boss's daughter. But since she was Austrian born, and since their son was schooled in Vevey, Switzerland, it is safe to assume that he had a command of the German language, and that his technical training had a significant European component.

The German connections are less direct with Hermann Hollerith, the inventor of the punch card and the father of modern data processing, who first visited his ancestral home as an adult promoting his new invention. His father, a Heidelberg professor and a refugee of the 1848 revolution, had died when Hermann was only seven. But growing up in the heavily German city of Buffalo, Hollerith was exposed to the German language and culture, which left its mark on him. In fact, his "precise Germanic ways" sometimes caused him to be mistaken for an immigrant. Although he married outside the ethnic group, his wife had spent a year in Austria, and even the family cat was named Bismarck. Hollerith's Swiss brother-in-law was one of the first to provide financial support for his invention, and his father's Forty-Eighter network proved helpful on several occasions, possibly opening the door to his first appointment to the U. S. Census Office under Interior Secretary Carl Schurz, who as a young revolutionary had survived the Prussian siege of Rastatt along with the elder Hollerith.

The opposite extreme of ethnic identity is represented by Edward Stratemeyer, who read the pulse of the American psyche so well that the quintessential figures of American juvenile fiction that he and his ghostwriters created—Tom Swift, Nancy Drew, the Hardy Boys, and the Bobbsey Twins—long outlived him and dominated the youth market for most of the twentieth century. Although both of his parents were born in Germany, Stratemeyer's self-identity was purely Anglo-American. He even launched the most un-German book series imaginable about "the great modern movement for temperance" in 1915, though it never caught on with the public. Particularly in the books that Stratemeyer authored himself before establishing his "fiction factory," he spread the message that "Anglo-Saxon blood is bound to rule the world." With stereotypical names like Hans Liederkranz and Fritz Stimmermann (two fictional corrupt saloonkeeper politicians), whatever German characters appeared in his early novels were just as unflattering and hackneyed as any of the other racial or ethnic groups he portrayed. Although it seems probable from the punning names he used, it is difficult to determine whether Stratemeyer even knew the German language. But in this instance, German ethnicity was practically irrelevant to his career: an American entrepreneur with a German name, one might say.

The progression from artisanship to entrepreneurship is nicely illustrated by the generations of the Nieburg family, even though it ended up in somewhat of a blind alley. Friedrich Nieburg immigrated in 1854 at age eighteen, apparently trained as a wagon maker, and initially started out combining his trade with farming. Later, he pursued wagonmaking full-time, and by 1880, he was assisted by two hired workers along with his three teenage sons. After their father's death in 1889, the sons went into partnership forming the Nieburg Manufacturing Company, which produced "a good line of carriages and spring and farm wagons," according to an 1895 "mug book." Their increased division of labor indicates they were moving beyond the artisan stage. The eldest son, Charles, who had ventured outside the ethnic enclave, was responsible for management and bookkeeping in the family firm. The middle brother, Otto, was head of the iron works and blacksmith shop, and the youngest son, William, was foreman of the woodworking department. The dawn of the automobile age posed daunting challenges to an enterprise of this nature, and it would have required a major mobilization of capital as well as a shift in the product line to remain competitive. Instead, the Nieburg brothers appear to have resigned themselves to supporting roles. In 1913, the firm, still designated as "Nieburg Mfg. Co.," was selling Reo and Chevrolet cars. But by 1940, Charles was the proprietor of a farm machinery business, brother Otto finished out his career owning a garage and car dealership, and William ended up in the furniture and mortician business, succeeded by his son Julius. All three thus maintained their self-employed, middle-class status, but they did not achieve the breakthrough to genuine entrepreneurship beyond the local level.

Not that it would have been impossible: another Westphalian wagon maker who arrived in the Midwest only nine years earlier and started out very similarly managed quite a successful transition to the automotive age. Knapheide Manufacturing Company is now in the sixth generation of family ownership. Its current address, 1848 Westphalia Strasse, reflects the roots and the founding year of Herman Heinrich Knapheide's enterprise in Quincy, Illinois. Compared to the Nieburgs' location, Quincy was a bigger town with both river and railroad connections, and Knapheide got off to a quicker start. By 1870, he was worth $14,000 and employed six men and two youths, producing a wagon every week. When the second generation took over after 1890, the enterprise was exporting its wagons to markets as distant as South America and Africa. But Knapheides embraced the automotive age in a very different way than Nieburgs, installing the first truck bed on a Model T Ford as early as 1910. In the twentieth century, the firm increasingly specialized in steel truck bodies, and by the 1970s they were the largest producer of farm truck bodies nationwide. The differing responses to the end of the horse-and-buggy era as much as anything explains the contrasting trajectories of two superficially similar family firms, though it took constant readjustments to keep the Knapheide enterprise viable into the twenty-first century.

The era from 1840 to 1893 in many respects marked an optimal period for German-American entrepreneurship. It was both the period of heaviest German immigration and the era in which the United States took over first place among industrial nations. From that point on, aspiring German-American entrepreneurs faced an increasingly challenging business climate in general, and some additional obstacles specific to their own ethnic group. For one thing, there was a much smaller pool of newly arrived Germans in the labor force. In the wake of the Panic of 1893 and the resultant depression, the United States underwent a wave of business consolidation, and embarked on industrialization of an ever larger scale with the dawning of the automobile era. Detroit, with its concentration on heavy industry and auto manufacturing, presents an extreme case of a general tendency, as one historian writes: "The German community, which was still a cross-class community in the 1890s, economically based on independent small enterprises," had by 1920 "disappeared under the pressures of industrialization, and of the ideological trauma associated with the First World War." Across the nation, the industry hardest hit was the one most heavily dominated by Germans. As St. Louis historian James Neal Primm pungently remarked, "World War I and its illegitimate offspring, the Prohibition Amendment, ruined the beer industry." Another of the Great War's illegitimate offspring, immigration restriction, left Germans relatively unscathed compared to other nationalities. But the constellation of factors favoring German-American entrepreneurship, often with its roots in ethnic communities and initially based on fellow ethnics as workers and customers, would never again be as favorable as it had been in the years between 1830 and 1893.

7

Women's Roles and Women's Work

Paid and Unpaid

GERMANY HAS THE REPUTATION as a highly patriarchal society, where women had few rights and little to say. But in northwestern provinces such as Westphalia and Hanover, the agrarian society had a surprisingly matriarchal aspect. In this region of indivisible inheritance, the family name was essentially also the farm name, and if a man married into a farmstead (e.g., when his in-laws had only daughters), the husband took on his wife's maiden name. Although the passing down of the man's name had been prescribed in the Prussian General Law Code of 1794 for the eastern parts of the kingdom, a special ruling was made in 1828 to continue the old custom for Westphalia. It was not until 1919 that bridegrooms there were required to retain their original names, and even thereafter, exceptions were sometimes made. Around 1979, I happened to meet one Friedrich Hohenschwert (born in 1921 with the name Heuwinkel), who had married into a farm and taken on the name of his wife, who had lost all four brothers in World War II. By then, it required a special authorization for what had been customary practice throughout the previous centuries.

Such evidence notwithstanding, the stereotypical German woman of the nineteenth century, and by extension her overseas counterpart, was restricted to the narrow sphere of *Kinder, Küche, Kirche* (children, cooking, church). That may have held true for the urban bourgeois, but this alliterative array overlooks another important realm of women's activity that extended beyond the appropriate female sphere in Anglo-American culture: *Kuhstall* (cowbarn), and into a variety of fields, literally and figuratively, on German-American farms. Decade by decade, Germans expanded their position in the farm population, their communities becoming more homogeneous over time, often at the expense of Anglo-Americans whom they bought out. But some of these German property gains were made at costs that were considered unacceptable to most Anglo-Americans. Land was often accumulated at the cost of children's educations, and by putting wives and daughters, as well as sons, to work in the milking barns and out in the fields.

The Yankee viewpoint in this clash of cultures was reflected in an 1890 sketch by agrarian novelist Hamlin Garland, "The Creamery Man":

> She had a little schooling . . . but her life had been one of hard work and mighty little play. Her parents . . . could speak English only very brokenly. . . . Her life was lonely and hard. . . . She knew that the Yankee girls did not work in the fields . . . but she had been brought up to hoe and pull weeds from her childhood, and her father and mother considered it good for her. I'd tell the old man to go to thunder . . . Yankee women don't do that kind of work, and your old dad's rich; no use of your sweatin' around a corn-field with a hoe in your hands. I don't like to see a woman goin' round without stockin's, and her hands all chapped and calloused.

This story had a happy ending, resulting in a mixed marriage after the "creamery man" had been jilted by a "lady" and took a closer look at this outsider.

There is ample evidence from sources both inside and outside the German-American community that this was more than just an ethnic stereotype. A New England woman traveling in Civil War Wisconsin was astonished to see female workers in the fields, and inquired of a woman driving a team hitched to a reaper: "You are not German? You are surely one of my own countrywomen—American?" Indeed she was. But what was an anomaly for Anglo-Americans, was business as usual for German women. From Texas, Friederike Lehmann reported to her husband in the Confederate army that their daughter and son, ages eight and six, were busy picking cotton, along with the young German woman they had hired for the year. Of course, the Civil War was an unusual period when even Anglo women took on field work.

But with Texan German families, nothing had changed a decade later. A journalist touring the South reported in 1875 from New Braunfels how German families—mother, father, and the whole gamut of children, from four to fourteen—were coming in from work. "The women have been afield ploughing, with the reins round their necks and the plough handles grasped in their strong hands. Yet they are not uncouth or ungracious; their faces are ruddy, their hair, blown backward by the evening breeze, falls gracefully about their strong shoulders. Surely, this is better than the tenement house in the city!"

Not far from the big city of St. Louis, a German newspaper reported in 1870: "Our farmers are now diligently occupied with the harvest, and many a pretty farm maiden can be seen in the field 'earning their bread in the sweat of their brow.'" This was a Protestant village; in fact it was home to the first German Protestant church west of the Mississippi. But this work culture was shared equally by Catholics, as a reminiscence from the same county recorded: "Mother was very strong and could well stand hard work. She loved to help Father in the field so they did not have to hire a man. That way they could save money to get a better home and purchase more modern farm machinery. But this was not strange, for at that period of time almost all farm women and girls did hard work in the fields." The writer recalled that he "even saw women plow, harrow and haul wheat to town." That not enough, the woman in question had an infant in tow: "Mother would do her housework and then go out in the field to help. She took my little sister to the field with her, put her down in the shade of a wheat shock and then went to bind a section of wheat. At times she returned to the baby to nurse her and then she returned to her work again. I also saw her pitching wheat and hay while Father did the stacking." Closer to the house, she took on an array of other chores, although she did have her widowed mother-in-law living in the household: "The planting and cultivation of the garden was in itself a huge task which Mother performed. . . . Most women milked the cows, which were not always near the house. . . . Mother was responsible for the preparation and storage of milk. She churned butter in the old-fashioned way, which was a tiresome task done by working a plunger up and down. . . . It was also Mother's task to care for the young chicks and other fowl and gather their eggs." When the writer was twelve, his mother died at age thirty-five, so at first glance one might suspect that hard work killed her. In fact, it was probably an epidemic, for her husband passed away just five days later.

Immigrant Randolph Probstfield was in many respects an assimilated, progressive farmer, as his anglicized name would indicate. He was even elected to the Minnesota State Senate in the 1890s on the Farmers Alliance ticket. But in 1875 he cut his barley with a scythe while his wife bound the sheaves, despite her pregnancy, which ended in a miscarriage. When their daughter was only sixteen, she plowed with a team of four horses or a double yoke of oxen. She may have borne the greatest responsibility since she was the oldest, but there are also records of her younger sisters plowing, and the entire family turning out to weed crops.

But beyond the realm of work, Anglo-American standards were making themselves felt also in German communities, as is related in a bit of transatlantic gossip written from rural Indiana in 1868: "Here you have to treat a woman like a woman and not like a scrub-rag, as I've seen it so often in Germany that a man can do whatever he wants with his wife. Whoever likes to beat his wife better stay in Germany, here you can't get by with that or you soon won't have a wife any more, that's what happened to Carl Wihl." Not everyone was happy with this enhanced female status. One Catholic farmhand wrote from Civil War Iowa, "I do go dancing, but I don't like it half as much as in Germany. . . . You have to take a girl with you, and they are so lazy here, they won't walk for even half an hour, instead you have to get a wagon and pick them up."

Girls could afford to be choosy. One obvious reason why young single German women immigrated was that the sex ratio was in their favor, though not overwhelmingly so. In 1850, just under 57 percent of Germans in America were male; by 1900 it was down to 54 percent. The male surplus was much higher among Germans at other immigrant destinations. America was one of the few places to which single women would risk traveling along. Despite a relatively balanced sex ratio, women's chances of marriage, even without a dowry and in otherwise challenging circumstances, were much better than back home. In 1853, when a young servant girl in New York ended up with "a baby son . . . for whom she had a father all right but no husband," her brother-in-law was primarily concerned only about the fact that "it will make it very hard for her to find a match." If unwed motherhood was considered highly scandalous, one might have expected her to cut all ties with her home village and pose as a young widow. But instead she kept in touch, and within less than three years, she had not one but two offers of marriage from other hometown immigrants, though they were far off on the Indiana frontier where they could shoot deer out their log-cabin window. Still, as one of her brothers reported in 1882, she was "doing very well, last year she built another new house, she has 7 well-brought-up, Christian children."

Better marriage chances were not the only reason young German women were motivated to emigrate. Immigrants brought with them from Germany the tradition of working as servants in the households of others, which normally began right after confirmation around age fourteen. Many of them worked somewhere nearby in the surrounding rural neighborhood, but particularly from locations near cities, and increasingly with the improvements in transportation in the nineteenth century, many peasant girls served in the households of the urban bourgeoisie. This custom was transplanted practically intact to America.

In the immigrant generation, servant girls often reported both a more egalitarian work climate and an easier job than back home. This was particularly true of women who came from areas of Northwest Germany with a tradition of cottage industry. Later, in hindsight, immigrants sometimes romanticized these crafts. A 1916 photo from a celebration at the Lutheran church in St. Charles, Missouri, showed young women in traditional folk costumes seated at spinning wheels; a 1919 history of Quincy, Illinois, portrayed an old German couple seated before their hand-loom. But in the Old Country the arduous work of spinning and weaving continued on into the night the year around. One immigrant to rural Illinois encouraged his sister-in-law in an 1866 letter: "Wouldn't you like to come to America? It would be 10 times better for you. You wouldn't have to spin in the winter and work like a dog, you would just have to cook a little and the rest of the time you could go for a walk." Two sisters who escaped a similar background of rural poverty and began as servants in the city of Indianapolis reported back regularly to their brother and their illiterate parents. Writing in 1867, one of them advised a friend back home, "If Loise doesn't want to do any more spinning and weaving then she should come over here." Her sister added with a touch of schadenfreude, "I am very happy, I never have to spin or weave, I can go to bed at 6 in the evening." A year later one of them wrote, "I'd like to hope that you are as contented as I am, if you were to offer me my own farm I wouldn't take you up on it," a very strong statement given that a rise to farm ownership was virtually unthinkable for a tenant family

like hers. The next year, she remarked to her friends, "it's a stark contrast with servants and maids, since they have a lot more rights here than
over there, when I'm done with my work then I go anywhere I want to,
and they can't even say one word about it." Most surprising is perhaps
what she reported after being off work for three weeks with illness while
employed in an Anglo-American lawyer's family: "I didn't have to leave
the family I work for, they didn't want to let me go. . . . The lady took
care of me like a real mother, for it's just like I were her daughter, I've
been with them for a year and 5 months."

Given their background in rural poverty, one might write off these
women's comments to low expectations. But a very similar tone perme-
ates the letters of Wilhelmine Wiebusch, who had served in the big city
of Hamburg before going into domestic service in New York in 1884.
Here is how she characterizes her employers: "The family is remarkably
friendly . . . the lady herself speaks broken German, we can make ourselves understood quite well with her, . . . You should just hear us speaking English, we just rattle off what we hear, whether it's right or not,
the lady says sometimes she almost dies laughing at us." Although Wiebusch does not mention it, judging by their names her employers were
apparently Jewish. Her letters relate a lively social life off the job, enjoying dances, balls, and theater visits. When she married, four years after
arriving, she reports among her "lovely presents" a "silver fruit basket,
silver sugar bowl, and silver butter dish from my last employer." By the
1900 census, she was employing a domestic servant herself. A Philadelphia immigrant of the same era was fortunate enough to find a German
employer who not only took her along to church, but even invited her
along to the German theater.

Nearly half of all German women listed with an occupation in the
1880 census worked as domestics. Every census of female occupations
from then on through 1950 shows German women overrepresented in
the category of domestic service. In the late nineteenth century, they were
less likely to work as servants than Irish or Scandinavian women, but
by 1950, second-generation German women had a higher proportion
employed as domestics than any ethnic group except Mexicans. Although
newly arrived immigrants often started out as servant girls, in the hinterlands of major urban areas, a tradition of domestic work in the big city
continued across several generations.

A study of the German Lutheran village of Block, Kansas, illuminates the role that domestic service played in the life cycle of rural young women. More than three-fifths of the generation born in the first two decades of the twentieth century worked as "hired girls," half of them in the nearby county seat like some women of their parents' and grandparents' generation, the other half in Kansas City, sixty miles or ninety minutes away by train or car. Working in the big city, where their earnings were their own, brought young women greater autonomy and more exposure to the outside world. Those who had this experience married two full years later than their peers who did not. Barely one-third of those who had worked in Kansas City returned to their home village, though some did return to the county rather than remain in the city. Even with those back in Block, there was evidence of lasting influence from the city. The naming patterns of children increasingly reflected that of the dominant culture, and the congregation's Ladies Aid society switched its minutes to English in 1934, two years earlier than the all-male voters' assembly.

Similar patterns were evident in the hinterlands of St. Louis from the immigrant generation on, as an 1877 memoir reported: "The older children, girls as well as boys, were very often sent to St. Louis in order to earn something, and with the money that these children were able to save, one forty-acre plot after the other was purchased, until out of these little farms big ones had grown . . . these young people never had to wait long for a job; . . . the girls hired out as housekeepers, cooks, or nursemaids." According to this observer, domestic service promoted acculturation; these young women "through their residence in the city frequently became very skilled in all the undertakings that belong in the feminine department. The mother may have often been proud when the daughter on a visit to the parental home set on the table a dish which the Frau mama had never heard of or seen before." This continued into the second generation and beyond, and extended across the Mississippi into the Illinois hinterlands. In 1900 there were more than nine hundred Illinois natives of German parentage working as servants in St. Louis; there were no doubt many more from rural Missouri, but they cannot be easily identified in the census.

Sometimes domestic service led to permanent migration; in other cases, women returned to rural areas, often when they married. In my own family, two of Conrad Weinrich's sisters who immigrated in the

1830s worked in St. Louis and settled there permanently after marriage. In the third generation, four of my father's aunts worked in St. Louis; one died young, but the other three married Anglo-Americans, whereas their three brothers remained in the rural community where they had grown up and married within the ethnic group. Despite a high school education, my paternal aunt also worked as a "maid" in St. Louis and settled permanently there. My mother, her mother, and both of her godmother aunts worked as domestics in the city; all but one of the four returned to the farm after marriage. As was the case in Block, Kansas, this work was facilitated by networks of friends and relatives with roots in the rural community. My grandmother, serving in St. Louis at age seventeen in the 1910 census, worked next door to a woman seven years older from back home, who had almost certainly arranged her placement. Domestic service had developed into a normal stage of the life cycle for many rural German Americans, a pattern that only faded in the wake of World War II, when better paying "Rosie the Riveter" jobs became available to women like my mother.

But what of the other half of employed German women who were not domestics? The occupation where German women stood out most of all was that of midwife. In 1880, German women made up 3 percent of the female labor force, but 27 percent of all the nation's midwives. This was a transplanted skill; German immigrants thought of this job as a profession, for which women were trained and licensed in the Old Country. They advertised in German-language newspapers and in city directories, often mentioning midwifery schools in their ads. German women also were concentrated in several important occupations where German men likewise stood out, particularly as confectioners and in dressmaking and tailoring, and to a lesser extent in cigar making. Many of these were no doubt family enterprises, and probably reflected Old World training as well. Germans were also much more likely than other women to be working in the grocery and dry goods business, not to mention saloon-keeping, although their numbers were rather small. German women in artisan and shopkeeping families undoubtedly contributed more labor than is indicated by the census. In a rare instance, the 1860 census taker in Femme Osage Township, Missouri, recorded women's occupations as "farmerin" or "laborerin," mostly for family heads but occasionally for others, adding the German feminine ending "in" to English occupations.

Of those designated "farmerin," two happened to be my immigrant ancestors, widows Gausmann and Toedebusch. More typical is the contrasting case of Angela Heck. She wrote home from New York during the Civil War: "We bought a sewing machine for 100 talers. It sews as much as three men can sew by hand. We can earn 12 talers every week. We always have lots of work but because of the war food is very expensive." Notwithstanding the "we," no census lists her as doing anything besides "keeping house," although her daughter is listed as a "tailoress" in 1875. But in reality, German women like her contributed significantly to family income, especially in the artisan and shopkeeping sector.

German men, in particular, were of the opinion that the position of the female sex was better in the New World. A laborer wrote home from Pittsburg in 1881: "As a man here things are the opposite from over there, here the woman rules the roost, if a man comes home drunk and his wife reports him he gets put in prison, the first time for 5 days and then longer and longer if he does it again, if he beats her and she reports it he gets punished and she doesn't need any witnesses." Another immigrant wrote from his Missouri farm shortly after the outbreak of the First World War: "Because the war started during harvest time and the men had to go off to war right away, who did the work [in Germany]? Women and children and old folks; I've often wished that many of our women and girls were there now, . . . that would cure them of their extravagance, . . . if they had to work like in Germany that would cure them of it. . . . I'd like to go to Germany and bring back a dozen girls from there, they do more work in 2 days than the ones here in a week." This conservative outlook was shared by a Louisville Catholic newspaper: "The long store bills, the over-salted soups, the burnt up beefsteaks and the neglected, wayward children are sufficient proof for a man that he didn't marry a woman, but rather a 'Lady'" (the last word in English also in the German original).

Children, too, enjoyed much more independence from their parents, something that not all Germans welcomed. Writing from a Union Army camp in Wisconsin, a university dropout weighed in on American youth: "The children are free citizens of the United States and they want to be treated accordingly by parents and teachers . . . and when the boys have grown up, they are raw, course, ignorant louts, more or less well-trained, depending on their money, but . . . with no respect for authority

or sense of morality. The only thing they learn is how to make money."
One might attribute this to class prejudice, but it is echoed by a common laborer writing from Pittsburgh in 1882: "the children of the poorer
classes are very badly brought up, some don't go to school at all are cocky
and rude, run around on the streets till 10 or 11 at night, some can't write
their own names."

Thirty years later, a farmer from northern Germany reported with
astonishment from his western farm: "By the way, it is the custom here
that parents have nothing to say about their children's marriages!" This
is confirmed by what another German wrote from rural Iowa, that his
oldest daughter was about to get married. "Friedrich Schlueter's son [an
acquaintance from back home] also would have liked to have had her,
but since he lives 100 miles from here she wasn't much inclined, although
we would have welcomed it. Talking them into it, which is almost the
fashion over there, is out of style here in this free land. Wealth is simply
not taken into consideration here when marrying." Another immigrant,
still traumatized a half-century later by the forced marriage of his sister
that he had witnessed as a twelve-year-old, confirms this marital freedom but views it much more positively in a letter to his nephew: "The
daughter who is married, married the man who asked for her hand, he
wasn't my choice, I never would have chosen him, but I couldn't get your
mother's fate out of my mind. None of my children will be 'forced onto
or apart from' anyone. The only freedom I permit myself with regard
to marriage—if I am asked—is to speak my sincere opinion and judgment about it, without threat, dis- or persuasion." One beneficiary of this
freedom, engaged to an Anglo-American, wrote from New York City in
1860: "The father of my bride . . . does not approve of our engagement,
and for now I will not be able to count on financial support from this
source. That isn't the custom here anyway. . . . If we lived in Europe, he
might be able to keep me from marrying his daughter, but here in the
land of freedom, parents can't block marriages." Men like him who took
American brides were considerably wealthier on average than those who
married fellow Germans.

Despite a considerable surplus of immigrant males, mixed marriages
with Anglo-American women such as that above, or with other immigrant groups, were fairly rare during the first generation, and even into
the second. Nationwide in both 1880 and 1900, 73 percent of people born

in America with a German father also had a German mother, and about 85 percent of those with German mothers also had German fathers. Most intermarriage was apparently with the American born, because it was quite rare with the Irish, the next largest immigrant group at the time. Of people with any German parentage, less than 2 percent had one German and one Irish parent in 1880, and just over 1 percent in 1900. Rates of endogamy were slightly higher for Irish men in 1880, though in 1900 the differences were slight for men, and Irish women were actually more likely than their German counterparts to marry outside their group.

Many apparent outgroup marriages were, in fact, with second-generation Germans. One immigrant wrote home from St. Louis in 1891: "Why do you keep asking if my wife is German? Of course she was born here, but she speaks German just as well as any of you and is proud of her German heritage." This was a common occurrence. A study of marriage patterns in Cincinnati in 1880 (the first time the census also identified the second generation, tallying not just people's birthplace, but also that of their parents) found a high degree of in-group marriage among both Germans and Irish. Only about 4 percent of immigrant men from either country married immigrants from a different foreign country. Sixty percent of Germans and 72 percent of Irish married immigrants from the same country. That left nearly one-quarter of the Irish and over one-third of the Germans who married American-born women. But when one looks at the parents of these "American" women, over 80 percent of Germans' wives and almost 60 percent of the Irishmen's wives were in fact the second generation of the same ethnicity. So when this is taken into account, 89 percent of German men and 86 percent of Irish men married within their own groups. With old stock Americans it was only 75 percent. Immigrant women were even less inclined to marry across ethnic lines, at least in the case of Germans. Some 92 percent of immigrant women married other Germans, or German Americans of the second generation. With immigrant Irishwomen, it was 81 percent; with American women, just over two-thirds. Even with the second generation, over three-fourths of German men married within their own group, though with Irish Americans it was just under 60 percent. So at least in Cincinnati, Germans were the least likely of the three ethnicities to marry outside their group.

St. Louis showed a similar pattern. In 1860, an overzealous census taker recorded not only the state but also the town of birth of most residents of the heavily German second ward. An analysis of German men with no children born abroad, most of whom married after arrival, showed that only 4 percent of them married U. S. natives, and some of them may have been of German parentage. Seven percent married other Europeans, but 89 percent married other Germans. In fact, 59 percent married someone from the same German state, including 14 percent with partners from the same German town, while 40 percent married someone from a different German state.

In rural areas the ethnic and regional endogamy was even greater. In two counties of Missouri with nearly equal numbers of Germans and Anglo-Americans, only 1 percent of German women and 4 percent of German men married outside their own group according to the 1850 census. Of course, some were already married when they arrived, but even among couples with no foreign-born children, only 7 percent of German men and not even 3 percent of German women entered mixed marriages. There was also less of an intra-German melting pot in rural areas than in the cities. Of immigrants from the tiny principality of Lippe-Detmold (roughly the size of an American county), 70 percent of those in rural Missouri married partners who were also from Lippe. Although Mecklenburg was more than ten times as large as Lippe, only half of the Mecklenburgers in Chicago married partners of the same origins. But regardless of where they found husbands, most German women ultimately married.

In contrast to the Irish, domestic service was normally a stage in the life cycle, not a lifelong career for Germans. The great majority of them were married by the time they were in their thirties, with a mere 4 percent remaining single at this age according to the 1880 census; with Irish women the figure was four times as high. By contrast, 89 percent of the immigrant generation was married (Irish: 72 percent), and another 5 percent widowed (Irish: 9 percent). Divorce was a negligible quantity in both cases. Not much had changed by 1900. At age nineteen, when service rates peaked, just over one-quarter of German women were employed as domestics (Irish: 46 percent). By the time they reached their thirties, only 7 percent of German women remained single, and less than 2 percent were working as servants, a stark contrast with Irish women, for whom the figures were 23 percent and nearly 11 percent, respectively. These patterns weakened somewhat for second-generation Germans, 17 percent of whom remained single in their thirties, but a mere 1 percent worked as domestics at this age. By all indications, German immigrant culture was quite family oriented. If it was also patriarchal, German women did not appear to object, or at least did not avoid marriage or seek partners outside their ethnic group. But perhaps the reality is somewhat more complicated than the image.

In some instances, the patriarchal reputation is deserved. The Lutheran body with the strongest German heritage, the Missouri Synod, has an exclusively male clergy to this day. Beyond that, it forbids women to serve as church elders, the highest lay office. Even the right of women to vote in congregational assemblies is not guaranteed, though it has been allowed by "local option" since 1969. But as late as the 1980s, this emancipatory measure sometimes led to splits in congregations and secession movements, and the issue of women's suffrage has continued to be the subject of discussions and task forces in the Synod into the twenty-first century. But more telling than this conservative church body is an organization that should be a best-case scenario of female emancipation.

The North American Turnerbund (NATB), the umbrella organization of German athletic clubs, took a progressive position on slavery, race, and equal rights, but even a group such as this was ambivalent at best toward the women's movement. Although the issue was raised as early as 1871 in the national assembly, it took until 1894 for a proposal to be entertained to accept women as equal members, only to see it rejected as a "nice, but highly impractical expression of feelings," although it was recommended that local clubs discuss the issue. Finally, in 1904, the national organization recommended that local clubs accept women as equal members, but left the decision up to the locals. However, until then, women were largely relegated to auxiliary organizations in support of their male counterparts, as they were in most other German-American institutions. This held true even for socialists, as one scholar observes: "Before World War I, female self-assertion or even militance was neither common nor acceptable to German-American socialists in their everyday culture."

With respect to feminist journalism, Mathilde Franziska Anneke published the first German-language feminist newspaper in 1852, only three years after the first such journal was published in English in the United

States. She and another Forty-Eighter, Amalie Struve, who had actively participated in the revolution alongside her husband, were among the leading German proponents of voting rights and educational opportunities for women. But Struve died in 1862, and there were few new recruits to the cause among her ethnic sisters. One of them, Mathilde Wendt, published a feminist New York weekly, *Die Neue Zeit*, touting, as its title implies, a new era. But she reported in 1870 that only three others among the three hundred German newspapers and journals nationwide supported the feminist cause: the *Neue Welt* (New World) in St. Louis; the *Columbia* in Washington, DC; and Karl Heinzen's *Pionier*, which promoted a variety of radical causes from its fourth home of Boston. All appeared weekly, and Wendt's paper succumbed after only three years, though a struggle for editorial control played a role in its demise. But its St. Louis counterpart was similarly short-lived, and the *Columbia* lasted just a decade. Heinzen persisted with his *Pionier* for more than a quarter-century until shortly before his death in 1879, but feminism was only one of his many causes.

To the end of the nineteenth century and beyond, as the Anglo-American feminist and suffrage movements gained strength, little had changed with their immigrant sisters, to judge by publications with "Frauen" in their titles. One of the few that suggests a feminist bent was the *Chicagoer Frauen-Zeitung*, 1893–1898, a supplement to the *Freie Presse*. Milwaukee supported a monthly *Frauenvereins-Bibliothek*, but only for two years, 1907–1909. Two other publications with "*Frauen*" in their titles reflect very traditional roles, one in Boston, supporting Methodist missions, and another in St. Louis, *Frauenfleiss*, a supplement to the conservative Lutheran *Abendschule*, literally promoting female diligence at sewing and knitting.

But there were exceptions. Writer Dorothea Boettcher, who immigrated in 1876 at age twenty-four, shatters many of the stereotypes of German women. She supported herself as an editor and contributor to German newspapers in Chicago, such as the *National Zeitung* and the *Chicagoer Freie Presse*. In 1893, she led a mass meeting of some six hundred women defending German instruction in the city's public schools and was appointed to deliver the protest message to the school board. She was also an accomplished poet who published an anthology of her original work and translations in 1895. She was a leading member of the Columbia Damen Club, which was "the first and only German women's association which promoted purely intellectual aims." But these clubwomen looked to the women's movement in Germany rather than their Anglo-American counterparts for inspiration. As a study of Chicago women observes, "German-American women held ethnicity over gender by following their men in their distaste for the temperance movement," although Boettcher herself returned to her native Mecklenburg in 1902 before the campaigns for temperance and women suffrage reached their peak.

German-American men's opposition to the suffrage cause was complicated by the movement's association with the temperance crusade and the fear that Anglo-American women would take away their beer. German culture viewed alcohol differently. No respectable native-born woman would be seen in a saloon, but German beer gardens were often family affairs. Immigrants and their children comprised seven-eighths of all female saloonkeepers in the country in 1890; Germans alone accounted for almost one-third of them. Both supporters and opponents of women's suffrage assumed that the first thing women would do if they got the vote would be to outlaw the saloon. But ironically, with the anti-German sentiments whipped up by World War I, the Prohibition Amendment became law before women achieved the right to vote nationwide.

Even on the suffrage issue there was no unanimity. There was reportedly a *Frauen-Stimmrechtsverein* in St. Louis in 1871, and a year later, a *Deutsche Frauen-Stimmrechtsverein* was founded in New York. It is unclear how long either persisted; both were associated with freethinking circles. A 1913 article on Wisconsin suffragists reported that "some of our best workers are German," going on to state that "the Germans are not so universally opposed to the cause as many people think." Granted, suffragists' expectations were low; they considered it a positive sign that the issue lost by less than a 2:1 vote in Milwaukee. Mathilde Anneke stands out as one of the first supporters of women suffrage all the way back in the Civil War era. Oshkosh immigrant Sophie Gudden, from a bourgeois Munich family, campaigned for women's suffrage and various progressive reforms in both German and English. But they are two of just a half-dozen German speakers, two of them Jewish, included on a list of some seventy-five prominent suffragists in a state that was one-third German.

Particularly among second-generation Germans, however, there were some men who flatly contradicted the patriarchal image and women who shattered submissive stereotypes. Texas editor William Trenckmann, for instance, had a very egalitarian marriage. Having taken over the cooking as a teenager after his mother died, he reflected, "This practice period certainly did me no harm. In the case of all marriages except the very wealthy ones, circumstances occur when it is exceedingly advantageous if the husband can occasionally take the place of the wife." He shared major decisions and newspaper-editing tasks with his wife, whom he often referred to as "the editress," and who was not afraid to criticize his "tapeworm sentences." They moved the family and their newspaper to Austin in large part so that their two daughters could receive a university education. Both of these women went on to active professional lives in teaching and journalism, respectively. Trenckmann also mentored an unconventional young woman from his hometown and serialized her novellas in his *Wochenblatt*.

Mathilde Dallmeyer, the daughter of a prosperous merchant in the Missouri state capital, first gained prominence as a speechmaker and fundraiser in support of the American war effort during World War I. She ardently supported women's suffrage among other civic causes, and after its successful campaign in 1919, attended the first Republican National Convention to which women were admitted. She had clearly moved beyond ethnic circles both geographically and socially, later marrying an Anglo-American, adopting his Presbyterian denomination, and settling in his hometown of Kansas City.

Similarly unconfined by narrow sex roles was Dr. Melinda Knapheide Germann, daughter of a prominent wagon manufacturer in her birthplace of Quincy, Illinois, although she remained in the German Methodist congregation of her parents and married another German American. A high school valedictorian, she studied medicine at the local college and continued her education abroad in Zurich, Paris, and Vienna, facilitated by her fluency in German. A 1919 local history characterized her as "not only one of the earliest physicians and surgeons to practice medicine in Quincy, but in point of ability and attainments . . . among the first in the profession, irrespective of sex." Beyond her medical achievements, she was the first woman ever elected to the city's board of education in 1912, and in 1917 achieved a similar first on the county board of supervisors.

Her immigrant parents also belied the German stereotype: "I owe much to my parents for their good judgment and foresight. Their ideas were that their daughters should have a profession or business by which they could be financially independent." Her own daughter, with "many of the ideals and ambitions of her mother," followed in her footsteps as high school valedictorian, Phi Beta Kappa at Vassar, and the top female graduate of Johns Hopkins Medical College, which immediately appointed her to its hospital staff.

There were many ways beyond *Kinder, Küche, und Kirche* to be a woman in German America.

8

German Political and Military Roles in the Civil War Era

St. Louis Germans made national headlines on May 10, 1861, with the capture of the secessionist state militia at Camp Jackson, foiling the governor's attempt to cast Missouri's lot with the Confederacy and helping to secure the state for the Union. Some of these German "Wide-Awakes" had been active in the 1860 election, protecting Republican candidates and voters, and had continued to drill through the winter and spring. In cooperation with several Anglo Unionist politicians, they prevented the federal arsenal in the city from falling into Confederate hands. Three of the four Unionist regiments that disarmed Camp Jackson were commanded by Forty-Eighters, refugees of the failed German revolution of 1848. Many of the men in their ranks were Turners, members of athletic clubs that were hotbeds of revolutionary idealism. They saw the struggle against slavery as a continuation of their struggles for a united and democratic fatherland. Friend and foe considered Missouri Germans the state's most decisive Unionists. One southern belle wrote from the city ten days after the Camp Jackson affair, "my blood boils in my veins when I think of the position of Missouri—held in the Union at the point of Dutchmen's bayonets." This image reflected upon Germans' reputation nationwide, but in fact their record varied widely from place to place and among various subgroups of immigrants.

The activism and visibility of German immigrants was most pronounced among the Forty-Eighters. The early 1850s saw the arrival of several thousand of these German political refugees. Well educated and articulate, they provided an important stimulus to immigrant cultural life and political participation. They nearly doubled the size of the German-language press in just four years, started the Turnverein movement that combined physical training with radical ideology, and flocked to the newly founded Republican party that reflected their ideals. Even in the abolitionist hotbed of Boston, where the German community was quite small, it was the Turners, led by arch-radical Charles Heinzen, who rallied to protect abolitionist Wendell Phillips when he was threatened with mob violence in 1860. But the question remains, to what extent the Turners' ideology was shared by the German rank and file.

Numerically, the Forty-Eighters were just a drop in the bucket among the multitude of their compatriots who immigrated during the 1850s, for the first time surpassing the number of Irish arrivals. The years from 1850 to 1860 inclusive brought an influx of over a million Germans and a net increase between the two censuses of nearly seven hundred thousand, more than doubling their numbers. The bulk of the German newcomers had more in common with their Irish counterparts than their Forty-Eighter countrymen. They were first and foremost economic refugees, even if not quite as desperately poor as the average Irishman and blessed with more marketable skills. Still, the distinction between economic and political motives for emigration is not as clear in practice as it might appear in theory. The economic burdens of German lower classes were related to their political impotence and their lack of a voice in village self-administration. For the first time in 1848, not just bourgeois liberals but occasionally also ordinary immigrants commented on the European political situation in their letters home.

Although a few German liberals such as political refugee Charles Follen had been closely associated with the abolitionist movement as early as the 1830s (and lost his position at Harvard College for fear he might frighten away Southern students), most Germans kept their distance. The revivalist tone of abolitionists was especially repellant to freethinking political refugees, even if they pursued many of the same goals relative to slavery. Germans stressed the "rational" basis of their humanitarian antislavery program in contrast to the "fanaticism" of their religiously motivated Anglo-American counterparts.

Germans' reservations toward antislavery reformers had other grounds as well. Reforms usually came in a package that included the temperance movement or outright prohibitions on alcohol, laws enforcing the Puritan

Sunday and forbidding what most Germans considered to be innocent pleasures of beer gardens and brass bands, and injected a militantly Protestant tenor into public institutions such as schools. Although many Germans shared an aversion to slavery with the "Conscience Whigs," who made up one wing of that party, by all accounts, German Whigs were a scarce commodity. According to one estimate, only 20 percent of nineteenth-century immigrants in New York voted Whig. If anything, the party fared worse with Germans in the Midwest, as contemporary political activists testified. According to Gustave Koerner, the German Whigs in Wisconsin could practically be counted on one's fingers. Editor Heinrich Bornstein claimed there were only three German Whigs in all St. Louis; voting patterns confirm that this was only a slight exaggeration.

Yankee reform impulses that originally found their vehicle in the Whig party took on a more explicitly antiforeign tone in the so-called Know-Nothing movement, which sprung up out of its ashes in the mid-1850s. Since this movement operated as a secret society rather than a conventionally organized political party, there was considerable overlap between it and the newly formed Republican Party. By 1860, the Republicans had outmaneuvered the nativists and established themselves as the majority party in the North. Nativists usually had nowhere else to go except to join the Republican fold, but they no longer set the tone. However, their subterranean presence, stronger in some states than others, gave pause to many religiously conservative Germans.

Whig and Republican faith in both national and individual improvement went so far that they were not always willing to leave things to chance or personal choice. Not just southern slaveholders, but also many impoverished immigrants, Catholics, or tipplers (sometimes all wrapped up in one) felt threatened from the do-gooder zealotry of Republicans and their inclination to force self-improvement also onto those who didn't realize they needed it. Whigs and Republicans had taken the lead in humanitarian areas such as asylum building and school improvement, but they had often given these new institutions an unmistakably Protestant tone, to the point of reading the King James Bible in schools and proclaiming the Pope as the Antichrist.

One Luxembourger editor captured the sentiments of many other German-speaking Catholics: "it was only natural that they turned to the Democrats, who were conservative in their principles, well-disposed towards immigrants, opposed to centralization, and supported by other fellow Catholics." They remained Democrats, "not because they were friends of the slaveholders, no, but because they did not like the elements that had combined to form the new Republican Party. Instinctively . . . they stood in opposition to the party of centralization and Puritanism."

Ethnic cheerleaders have continued to echo John Peter Altgeld's 1890 claim that the "freedom loving Germans" unanimously supported Lincoln and proved decisive for the outcome of the 1860 election. In fact, anti-immigrant tendencies within the Republican Party and anticlerical sentiments of its most articulate German leaders, especially the Forty-Eighters, alienated many rank-and-file voters of Catholic or conservative Lutheran backgrounds. However, it would be erroneous to replace ethnic determinism with religious determinism and assume that voters followed religious leaders unquestioningly. One Catholic scholar wrote that for her coreligionists, "To join the Republican party was tantamount to joining forces with the devil," and a Lutheran journal found the leaders of the Missouri Synod "Republican neither by inclination nor in party affiliation." In fact, the Synod's founder, C. F. W. Walther, denounced the liberal St. Louis *Anzeiger des Westens* as "Satan's press." But the laity often saw things differently. One German left the Catholic seminary in Cape Girardeau, Missouri, for Milwaukee, in protest over the Rebel sympathies of an Irish-American professor. Similarly, on the Lutheran side, Walther was challenged by laymen in his own St. Louis congregation for his views that slavery was divinely sanctioned. Another charter congregation of the Missouri Synod, New Melle, voted about 80 percent for Lincoln, raised a whole company of Unionist Home Guards, and later sent its captain, Conrad Weinrich, to the state legislature as a Radical Republican after the war.

But Germans did not uniformly support Lincoln in the North, and some of the places where they did were safely in his column anyway. Wisconsin Republicans converted few Lutherans and virtually no Catholics to their cause, but they didn't need them. Perhaps Altgeld was not exactly wrong, he just overgeneralized from his Illinois perspective. Lincoln had to convert his home state from the Democratic column in 1856, and his winning margin there in 1860 was one of the smallest anywhere in the North. Here, the German role was indeed crucial. Illinois, along with Missouri, was the state where Lincoln fared best among Germans, generally, and Catholics, in particular. Lincoln had distanced himself early on from nativism in his 1855 letter to his friend Joshua Speed, and wrote in 1859, "I have some little notoriety for commiserating the oppressed condition of the Negro; and I should be strangely inconsistent if I could favor any project for curtailing the existing rights of white men, even though born in different lands, and speaking different languages from myself." It is important to remember that Lincoln was a politician as well as a statesman; in 1859, "Honest Abe" purchased a silent partnership in his hometown German newspaper to keep it in the Republican fold.

Three main factors influenced the degree of Republican success in winning over Germans, and particularly the Catholics among them. The first, which was seen above in the case of Lincoln, was the degree to which Republicans at the state level reached out to ethnic voters or remained tainted by nativism. The second factor was the local presence of Catholic cue-givers who were friendly to Republicans. Thirdly, internal strife among Catholics between Irish or French bishops and German parishioners sometimes conditioned the latter to vote Republican.

German Catholics tended to be more conservative than Protestants or especially freethinkers, and radical Forty-Eighters particularly aroused their ire. Writing back to Germany in 1863, one Catholic coal miner called the Civil War "a nice present from Europe that the dear 48ers, those heroes of freedom who have broken with God and their respective monarchs, have brought into this beautiful country." But there were exceptions, especially among more prosperous elements. The aspiring Chicago merchant John Dieden was an ardent Catholic, but was nonetheless well disposed toward liberalism on both sides of the Atlantic. His admiration for the much maligned Forty-Eighters shows through in an 1860 letter he wrote to his cousin back in the Rhineland: "Since the Revolution in Germany in 1848, the position of the Germans in the United States has really improved remarkably, since in that year many intelligent and educated people left the old fatherland, and many of them had to leave because of their rulers." Dieden naturally welcomed the election of "Lincoln, the man of freedom, the enemy of slavery, the man of equal rights."

In places where influential Catholic opinion makers supported the Republicans, they made substantial inroads and probably attracted a majority of Catholics. They almost had to in St. Louis, where some

80 percent of the Germans voted for Lincoln. In fact, the more educated Catholics were on the whole much friendlier toward the Republicans and their program. Important liberal Catholic cue-givers included Cook County Sheriff Anton Hesing in Chicago, lawyer John B. Stallo in Cincinnati, Dr. Bernhard Bruns, who founded Westphalia, Missouri, before moving on to Jefferson City, and jurist and publisher Arnold Krekel, the leading German Republican in St. Charles County, Missouri. All four of these Catholics were present at the 1860 Republican convention: three of them as delegates, Hesing providing "muscle."

Charges of anticlericism were not so damaging when leveled against someone such as Krekel, founder of a German-language weekly in St. Charles. He had been careful to maintain his distance from Heinrich Boernstein, a St. Louis Forty-Eighter editor notorious for "eating Catholic children for breakfast," and denied charges that "when Boernstein takes snuff, I sneeze." Krekel was not a practicing Catholic—an 1885 county history recorded his espousal of Darwinism and denial of divine origins of Scripture—but he could point out that he was brought up in the Church and still had parents, brothers, and sisters worshiping at its altars. Local Catholics were not likely to forget the early years of settlement when priests had held services in the Krekel family's barn. And like the candidate he was supporting in 1860, Krekel was a self-made man, having split rails at twenty-five cents per hundred to earn money for college.

It was often such liberal Catholics, not all of them as radical as Krekel, who led their German coreligionists into Republican ranks. Internal Catholic controversies sometimes eased their task. In Osage County, Missouri, where practically all the Germans were Catholic, Lincoln outpolled Stephen Douglas and got over one-quarter of the total vote, thanks above all to Dr. Bernhard Bruns, a practicing Catholic of liberal views. His writings showed sympathy for the 1848 revolution, and he wrote contentedly in 1860, "We Republicans have worked faithfully since the Chicago convention and elected our candidates. For that the German element deserves the honor. Unfortunately the arch-Catholics were against us. Now they are on the side of the disunionists." Catholic internal conflicts may have aided his cause; he and his local parish had been the scene of several disputes with the clergy, one of them culminating in a successful lawsuit against the priest (so much for lay deference to the Catholic hierarchy). Another such example is Buffalo, New York, where a majority of

Germans, among them many Catholics, swung to the Republican side. Buffalo had been the scene of a particularly bitter controversy from 1843 to 1855, pitting an Irish bishop against German and Alsatian lay trustees who wanted to retain title to parish property. Similarly, John B. Stallo had represented Cincinnati's first German Catholic parish, Holy Trinity, in a trusteeship dispute with Irish Archbishop Purcell.

One strong piece of evidence against religious determinism is the fact that Germans of the same local origins and religious affiliation ended up supporting different political parties depending on where they happened to settle. Even with identical backgrounds, immigrants were more likely to become Republicans if they settled in Missouri or Illinois than in Wisconsin or rural Ohio. German Catholics in Missouri were probably more Republican than German Lutherans in Wisconsin. Crucial for the partisan alignment of immigrants was the degree to which the local Republican party was dominated by nativist and temperance elements. Not that Germans were unmoved by the issue of slavery, and especially its expansion. But, as one county newspaper editorialized at the height of the nativist crisis in the words of an old German proverb, "The shirt is closer than the coat" to one's own hide. Combatting nativists had to be the first priority, for if they prevailed, immigrants would be crippled in their ability to fight for their own rights, not to mention the rights of anyone else.

In Wisconsin, Democrats had ingratiated themselves with Germans during the territorial period by supporting "alien suffrage" provisions that allowed them to vote before they were even naturalized. The new Republican Party made things worse by passing two prohibition bills in 1855, only to see them vetoed by the Democratic governor. An attempt to make good by nominating Forty-Eighter Carl Schurz as lieutenant governor in 1857 backfired when he was defeated by nativist defections, even as much of the ticket triumphed in a very close election. In 1859, the Republicans had no Germans on their state ticket at all. Wisconsin finally came around in 1861, electing Edward Salamon, who moved up to the governorship in 1862 when his predecessor died.

By contrast, Illinois Republicans reached out earlier with the sanction of prominent Germans who were former Democrats, foremost among them Gustav Korner, whom the Democrats had elected lieutenant governor in 1852. This office became almost a reserved seat for Germans.

Francis A. Hoffmann, a former Lutheran minister, was nominated in 1856 but had to withdraw when he discovered he did not meet the residency requirements. He was again nominated in 1860 and this time elected. Minnesota Republicans, who also were able to attract a majority of their state's Germans in 1860, matched their Democratic opponents in placing Germans on their ticket. Michigan Republicans finally saw the wisdom of German nominations in 1859, but this apparently helped them more in Detroit, where they elected a German as mayor that year, than in rural parts of the state.

The Republicans made greater efforts than the Whigs ever had to meet immigrants, and particularly Germans, halfway. By 1860, *New Yorker Staats-Zeitung* publisher Oswald Ottendorfer was one of only a handful of Forty-Eighters who remained a loyal Democrat. There was a prominent German presence at the 1860 Republican Convention, including earlier immigrants as well as Forty-Eighters, a few Catholics as well as Protestants. The convention, with four Germans on the drafting committee, enacted a party program containing several "Dutch planks," in particular one opposing any tightening of naturalization laws such as nativists had demanded, and had actually enacted in Massachusetts. A number of German-language orators, headed up by Carl Schurz but also including prominent earlier political refugees such as Friedrich Muench and Gustave Koerner, were sent out on the campaign trail to bring the Republican message into ethnic communities.

Republicans expended scarce political resources on Germans, dishing out a number of political plums such as various European consulates as well as military appointments to men such as Carl Schurz. This might appear puzzling in view of their mixed voting record. Democrats retained a majority of German voters in Wisconsin, Iowa, Indiana, and in New York City, Albany, and Philadelphia. In Indiana, a state where Republicans were strongly tainted by nativism and prominent Catholic Republicans were rare, the Catholic stronghold of Dubois County gave Lincoln his lowest support statewide, a mere 18 percent. But Republicans won greater or lesser majorities among the Germans of Missouri, Illinois, Minnesota, and the cities of Brooklyn, Buffalo, and perhaps Pittsburgh. Michigan Germans presented a contrast between Republican Detroit and Democratic outstate. In Ohio, one could see a clear contrast between rural areas, and also Cleveland, where Republicans did not nominate a single Catholic between 1855 and 1860, German or otherwise, as opposed to Cincinnati, where the Fifth Ward in German "Over the Rhine" went from a three-thousand-vote Democratic majority in 1855 to a Republican majority of 1,739 votes for Lincoln, obviously including many Catholics. Across the North, Germans were probably the social group that underwent the greatest shift in a Republican direction during the 1850s, even in the states where a majority of them remained Democrats.

The differing political affiliations of Germans in various states clearly affected the degree to which they supported the Union military cause. These categories overlapped with religious confession, but far from completely. In fact, the overall level of German representation in the Union forces was so high as to make it doubtful that a segment as large as the Catholics (at least one-third of the total) engaged in widespread slacking. Nor was it merely poverty that compelled Germans to enlist in the Union Army, as was demonstrated by the counter-example of the Irish, who were considerably poorer yet served at lower rates.

Information on the ethnicity of soldiers was compiled by B. A. Gould of the U.S. Sanitary Commission, who then set up "quotas" for each nationality group based on its share of the population. According to his figures, Germans were the group most overrepresented in the Union Army (except for Canadians, many of whom were not permanent U.S. residents). Germans surpassed their quota by almost 50 percent, British by 19 percent, Irish by only 4 percent, while native white Americans were 8 percent under quota. Gould's findings are confirmed by local data that measured war service directly. According to the 1865 New York state census, in Buffalo only 9 percent of the Irish of military age had seen Union service, as opposed to 10 percent of the natives and 16 percent of the Germans.

Although Germans generally complied, if sometimes reluctantly, with Union conscription laws, there were several cases of collective resistance, one serious enough to cause arrests. Not coincidentally, this took place in Wisconsin, where Germans largely stuck with the Democratic Party, and where it was necessary to impose a draft in 1862 to meet the state's troop obligations. As the drawing was about to get under way in Port Washington, the Ozaukee County seat, local Luxembourgers and German Catholics revolted. A drunken mob of about two hundred people seized and destroyed the draft lists and drove off the officials in charge, wrecking the house of the head of the draft committee and four others who were associated with him. Eight companies of federal troops were immediately sent and remained for more than a month, allowing conscription to be carried out peacefully. Eighty-one persons were arrested and held at military stockades, though eventually they were set free without prosecution. There were several other incidents of draft resistance in Wisconsin German communities, including at least two that led to the sending of troops. But nowhere did German resistance approach the magnitude and virulence of the largely Irish 1863 draft riot in New York, a heavily Democratic city, which left more than one hundred dead in its wake.

The effects of politics on recruitment become especially apparent in state-level contrasts. Though Wisconsin Germans outnumbered those in Missouri by 40 percent, and made up twice as large a share of their state's population, they supplied barely half as many troops, or possibly even fewer. Union muster rolls include over 950 men named "Schmidt" or "Meyer" in Missouri, but fewer than 250 with these names on Wisconsin's rolls. Some Missourians may be counted double in both three-month and longer-term regiments, but this at least confirms Missouri Germans' role as Unionists of the first hour. The legend of German "Wide-Awakes" saving Missouri for the Union at the outbreak of the war is only a slight exaggeration, though they did have the help of a handful of Anglo political and military leaders. Of the five three-month regiments recruited at the outbreak of the war, four and a half were German. As late as the Battle of Pea Ridge, Arkansas, securing Missouri for the Union in March 1862, at least one-third—and, by some estimates, nearly half—of the Union soldiers involved were German.

By contrast, in Wisconsin, the most German state of the Union, of the first twenty regiments only the 5th Militia and the 9th were overwhelmingly German, though the 18th and 20th were both more than half. Some of the units raised later by conscription were of little use for the war effort. The mostly German 34th Wisconsin, consisting entirely of nine-month draftees, could be trusted only for garrison duty, never heard an enemy shot, and still saw almost 30 percent of its men desert during its short term of service. There can be no doubt that political affiliation played heavily in such varying enthusiasm for the Union cause.

Immigrants in general, and Germans in particular, were an essential component of the Union Army, about one-quarter of which was foreign born. Germans alone constituted about 10 percent, some two hundred thousand in an army of two million. Although Rebels denounced them as hirelings and Hessians, most "Yankee Dutchmen" had immigrated well before the war's outbreak and knew what they were fighting for, or against. There was, however, one group of some 1,077 men recruited under deceptive pretenses in Germany and given free transport in 1864, but this was a major exception. As one Catholic German in the War Department remarked, "I admit there are some clumsy oafs who get fooled by recruitment officers. That's their own fault. Should watch out." Overall, German immigration was quite low at the war's outset and fell even lower during the conflict.

Immediately, in response to Lincoln's call for troops, and sometimes even before, ethnic pride merged with political convictions in the campaigns to raise German regiments. As Forty-Eighter August Willich put it, "Germans will really prove they are not foreigners." All the states of the Union with sufficient numbers of Germans produced such regiments. New York, Pennsylvania, Ohio, Indiana, Illinois, Wisconsin, and Missouri all fielded multiple ethnic German units. Although efforts to form a First German Regiment from Kentucky failed, its recruits helped make the 6th Kentucky Infantry nearly half German, and the 4th Kentucky Cavalry had three German companies. Men sometimes served out of state in order to fight alongside fellow Germans; the 32nd Indiana had an entire company from Cincinnati, and some additional Kentuckians from Louisville. Two companies of the 12th Missouri came from the "Latin Farmer" colony of Belleville on the Illinois side. A number of Turners from Illinois joined the 17th Missouri, another Turner unit, after their three-month terms with the 6th Illinois expired. All told, there were more than thirty regiments that were wholly or predominantly German, accounting for perhaps one-sixth of the Germans in blue. Another thirty regiments were roughly half German, but together they accounted for at most one-quarter of the Germans in the Union forces. The rest fought in units where they made up a small ethnic contingent of 5 to 15 percent, often concentrated in one "German company" for ease of communication. But even at higher levels, the Eleventh Corps was heavily German and popularly identified as such.

The Union Army made major efforts to meet Germans halfway. Many of the recruiting posters for ethnic regiments were in German, which is perhaps not surprising because it was usually German-American politicians, many of them political refugees, who took the lead in their formation. Germans received as many appointments as officers as they deserved, or perhaps more, including four to the rank of major general, though not as many as they thought they deserved. German was commonly used as the verbal and written language of command in ethnic regiments through mid-1862, and in some instances as late as the end of 1863. A New York City publisher of patriotic music even put out, along with many English marching songs, a handsome color broadside of "*Das Star Spangled Banner*," the national anthem in the 1851 translation of a Texas German, flanked on the one side by a soldier in a Jäger uniform and a Tyrolian hat and on the other by a Black man throwing off his shackles.

In general, "Yankee Dutchmen" managed to give their units and camps an ethnic flavor that often caught the attention of Anglo-Americans. Even before they were in the field, the Cincinnati *Commercial Gazette* remarked, "In two respects the Germans take to life at Camp Dennison like ducks to water: lager beer and military drill." The 9th Ohio was so appreciated by their compatriots in eastern Maryland that "38 barrels of beer were sent by railroad as a gift from the German beer brewers of Cumberland." A soldier of the 32nd Indiana reported from north Alabama in August of 1862: "We have built bowling lanes on which 12-pound cannon balls substitute for the wooden ones. . . . Gymnastic scaffolds were built in front of the headquarters, on which several men execute the most difficult things with an ease and deftness, which causes with us, but even more with the Americans, astonishment and admiration." An artilleryman at a quiet post guarding the Baltimore and Ohio Railroad described his battery's typically German diversions: "Many of the young men expressed interest in starting a four-part singing group. . . . I must confess that we have all been very satisfied with the results and have spent many a happy hour singing. We also set up an area for gymnastics in order to pass the time as well as possible." Even in the Rebel army, Texas Germans stood out: "The other evening we were singing some chorales, and it didn't take 10 minutes before we were completely surrounded by Americans who came to listen to our singing."

The 9th Ohio was so proud of its record that in 1894 it commissioned a professional writer to produce a regimental history: auf Deutsch! Surprisingly, its commander Robert McCook was adored by his troops although he understood little of their language, but he was the law partner of a prominent Cincinnati German Republican, John B. Stallo. The 9th Ohio had another German oddity that set it apart: instead of a traditional chaplain, it had a defrocked priest who served as a freethinking lecturer, and could also grab a rifle when needed. The 82nd Illinois was another of a handful of regiments with a Forty-Eighter rationalist "chaplain" whose first address "was a very liberal speech without the slightest religious reference." These two units had something else in common: both were Turner regiments, largely recruited from German athletic clubs. The 82nd Illinois had another distinction; it was ranked among the three hundred "fightingest" regiments in the Union Army. The fighting capacity of Turner units should not be surprising; their recruits were physically fit and had a head start on training, and they were ideologically motivated, imbued with the spirit of Forty-Eight. In fact, all five of the German regiments ranked among the "fightingest" were Turner units, including the 9th Illinois, the 32nd Indiana, the 12th Missouri, and the most distinguished of all, the 26th Wisconsin, which ranked sixth overall in its fighting capacity. In addition, there were ten other regiments among the "fightingest" that were half German, or in the case of the 15th Missouri, a mixture of German and Swiss. So overall, Germans held their own among the "fightingest," standing out neither negatively nor positively compared to the rest of the Yankee army. Their record varied widely from unit to unit.

Ethnic visibility was of course a double-edged sword; the decisive record of Missouri Germans at the outbreak of the war to some extent rubbed off on the whole group. But the experience of the Eleventh Corps at Chancellorsville led to charges of "cowardly Germans" and "Flying Dutchmen" also being applied to the group at large. As far away as Tennessee, a German captain in the 37th Ohio protested to the *Nashville Union* for calling his men "Dutch cowards." Most scholars agree that the failure at Chancellorsville rests primarily on the shoulders of its Yankee commander, General Oliver O. Howard, who deployed his troops poorly and ignored the entreaties of his subordinate Carl Schurz to reposition them, with the result that they were overwhelmed by Stonewall

Jackson's audacious flank attack. The Eleventh Corps was in fact only half German, and while some units resisted better than others, this hardly depended on ethnicity. Further evidence of resistance was the number of the Corps killed and wounded in the battle, which outnumbered by half the tally of those missing and captured. But Howard blamed his troops for his own mistake, and as the *Pittsburger Demokrat* complained, "For the idiocy of the commanding generals the poor Corps must now take the fall."

Something else that left Germans vulnerable to criticism was the presence of a number of "political generals" in their ranks. In the enormous military buildup required by the Civil War, there was no alternative to placing into command many men who lacked previous military experience or training, among them a number of Germans. Given the political nature of the conflict, political and regional (and in the North, ethnic) considerations figured heavily in many appointments on both sides, even up to the rank of general. This led rivals to raise acrimonious charges of incompetency on the part of "political generals," charges that were not entirely groundless but certainly exaggerated.

Whatever drawbacks political appointments had from a military standpoint, from the viewpoint of patriotism and national morale, they integrated important ethnic constituencies into the Union cause. Even in the case of Peter Joseph Osterhaus, one of the most competent German officers, Lincoln stated that his promotion to major general in 1864 was based "on what we thought was high merit, and somewhat on his nationality." Whatever the shortcomings of the hapless Alexander Schimmelfennig—chosen by Lincoln over several other German nominees primarily for his conspicuously ethnic name, and singled out by one historian for making a "real ass" of himself—he was not a rank amateur. Trained as a Prussian officer, he had fought on the revolutionary side in 1848 before emigrating. But he never lived down spending most of the Battle of Gettysburg in a pigsty.

One biographer describes Carl Schurz as "a competent officer who had risen too high too fast." The second half of the characterization would apply equally to fellow Forty-Eighter Franz Sigel, a prime beneficiary of ethnic lobbying though not an amateur soldier. He had graduated at the top of his class at the military academy in Karlsruhe and served four years in the Baden army before casting his lot with the 1848 Revolution.

Sigel was probably the Forty-Eighter with the most military training and battlefield experience in Germany. This, along with his devotion to the revolutionary cause, won him a place in the hearts of German Americans and assured him a position of command at the outbreak of the Civil War. He spent the first year of the war in the Missouri-Arkansas campaign as a brigade and division commander, punctuated, as was his whole career, by quarrels with superiors and threatened and actual resignations. The political lobbying of German Americans as much as any military achievements led to Sigel's promotion to major general and transfer to the eastern theater. Sigel was a good administrator and a master of orderly retreat, but despite personal bravery in battle, he showed timidity of leadership and proved to be neither a competent and dependable subordinate nor someone capable of independent command. He was no match for Stonewall Jackson, and when he proved equally unsuccessful against Jubal Early, he was removed from command in July 1864.

Lincoln's appointment of Sigel as a brigadier and even major general made sense on military as well as political grounds. What is less understandable is the continued uncritical enthusiasm of German Americans for Sigel, especially given the superior record of other compatriots such as General Osterhaus, or even Schurz. But as late as August 1864, one German soldier wrote "since we were under the command of the popular and beloved Sigel, we felt confident we would accomplish great deeds" when they embarked on the 1864 campaign. "We all felt sorry for Sigel, since shortly thereafter he was relieved of his command and has probably ruined a career that had been so promising." Native Yankees saw it differently, as one wrote retrospectively: "Osterhaus is the only German General that was consistently successful during the whole civil war . . . he was very popular with his troops."

General Henry W. Halleck was often accused of prejudice against Germans, and he did include Sigel in his statement, "It seems but little better than murder to give important commands to such men." But the other four he singled out were Anglo-Americans; what the five had in common was that none were West Pointers. Halleck was a conservative Unionist suspicious of abolitionists, regardless of ethnicity. But he himself was of German ancestry, and was a close confidant of immigrant Francis Lieber, whom he commissioned to write General Orders No. 100, a pioneering code of military conduct.

Nevertheless, perceptions of ethnic discrimination in military appointments and the slow process of emancipation had alienated some German
Americans from Lincoln. They formed an important component of the
political forces that opposed the president from the left and attempted to
nominate a more radical candidate in 1864. Some of these tensions went
back all the way to the beginning of the war, especially in Missouri, a
slaveholding border state. There conservative or pragmatic Unionists
had clashed with idealistic abolitionists over a number of issues. Missouri
Germans were outraged and almost rioted in St. Louis when the president rescinded General John C. Fremont's emancipation order in 1861
and removed him from command. In June 1862, when a convention of
"radical emancipationists" met in the Missouri capital, one-third of the
delegates were German; a similar convention in September 1863 had a
German majority. The following month, German delegates from fourteen states met in Cleveland to push their radical agenda. Beginning in
March 1864, a number of German-language newspapers endorsed Fremont for the presidency, and in May, a convention in Cleveland nominated him as candidate. But what had started in Missouri as a Radical
Emancipationist Party took the national stage as the Radical Democratic
Party, making concessions to the Democrats with an opportunism that
contrasted with Lincoln's statesmanlike pragmatism. Lincoln's differences with the radicals were more about timing than about ultimate goals.
After the visit of a largely German delegation from Missouri in 1863, the
president characterized such radicals as "devils . . . to deal with," but conceded that "their faces are set Zionwards." In September, Fremont withdrew his fading candidacy, and many German radicals gritted their teeth
and supported Lincoln, or at worst stayed home. But this may explain
why the number of German votes for Lincoln—besieged from the right
as well as the left—failed to increase between 1860 and 1864, and the percentage support in German areas actually declined slightly. Milwaukee
was one of only two big cities where Lincoln lost ground between elections. The only congressional race Wisconsin Republicans lost in 1864
was the 4th District, which included the heavily German counties north
of Milwaukee that had been the scene of earlier draft resistance.

The North was not the only place where Germans were confronted
with the issues of secession, civil war, slavery, and nativism; there was
also a small but significant ethnic presence in the Confederacy, and

more in the loyal slave states. Two prominent German names in Southern leadership circles, immigrant Christopher Memminger as Confederate Secretary of the Treasury, and immigrants' son John A. Quitman as Governor of Mississippi and one of the leading "fire-eaters" (radical secessionists) until his early death in 1858, might lead one to believe that Germans in the South identified easily with the slaveholding aristocracy. But it is questionable to what degree either of these figures shared or identified with German culture. Quitman's "mother" tongue was Dutch; his mother was from the Dutch West Indies, where his father, a pastor born and trained in Germany, spent twelve years, met his wife, and adopted the custom of slaveholding before settling in New York, where John was born in 1798. Groomed for the ministry, John no doubt understood German, but he soon turned his back on the Lutheran confession and his father's ambitions, settling at age twenty-three in Mississippi.

Although born in Germany, Memminger was probably less exposed to its culture than Quitman. He immigrated as an infant with his grandparents and widowed mother, and after her death, was placed at age four in a Charleston orphanage. Taken in at age eleven by the future governor of South Carolina, Memminger went on to a successful career in law and finance. He was so assimilated to an Anglo-American world that letters from his German relatives had to be translated into English. In general, Germans of a bourgeois background like these two, especially when they migrated alone and settled in areas without a substantial German presence, were the ones most likely to adopt the Southern way of life.

They were the exception; Germans were among the few outspoken critics of the "peculiar institution" actually living in the slave states. Radical Forty-Eighters in 1853 authored the Louisville Platform calling for the abolition of slavery along with other drastic reforms. Texas Germans in conjunction with their 1854 *Sangerfest* adopted resolutions calling for compensated emancipation, which were picked up by Forty-Eighter Adolph Douai in his *San Antonio Zeitung*. These radicals were not typical of the Germans of their states; in fact, Douai had to move north after his newspaper lost support. But many Germans had similar reservations about slavery even if they did not express them so openly, realizing that the First Amendment offered little protection in the South when the subject of slavery was involved. A German translation of *Uncle Tom's Cabin* was serialized within a year by the *Wochenblatt* in Hermann, Missouri, one of the few newspapers in a slave state to risk it. Even in the most German county in the state, it earned the editor threats of violence. In the next county over, Friedrich Muench was another target of intimidation, editorializing in 1862 against "the shameful fact that we were not free men in this so-called free country as long as the slaveholders could control us at a whim. . . . Were we allowed to tell the slaves . . . that we regarded them as *human beings* and that they had human rights too? Yet even if we said nothing whatsoever . . . were not these grand gentlemen suspicious of our inner thoughts because we seldom stood out as *praisers* of the institution." Paradoxically, even Muench resorted to purchasing a Black domestic, raising the question of how much Germans in the slave states conformed to local customs, particularly in Missouri and Texas where they had the largest presence.

There were some important distinctions between Germans in east and west Texas as far as slavery and secession are concerned. Eastern settlements were older, their immigrants more acculturated to American values, their local economy well suited for plantation agriculture and slavery. The Hill Country west of Austin, by contrast, was more recently settled. With its semiarid ranching economy it had very few slaveholders, Anglo or German. A frontier region, it was exposed to dangers of Indian attacks should federal military protection be withdrawn—a consideration that also promoted Unionism among Anglos in the Hill Country. But even in plantation country, Germans stood apart from their fellow Texans on the issues of the Civil War era. In three counties where Germans made up one-third or more of the white population in 1860, they constituted less than 5 percent of the slaveowners there, with less than 2 percent of all slaves. Nor was this merely the result of poverty. At every level of wealth from bottom to top, a much higher proportion of Anglo-Americans than Germans owned slaves. For example, among people with $3,000 to $6,000 worth of property, more than half of the Anglos but hardly 2 percent of Germans in these three counties were slaveowners. Those who had been of the servant-keeping class back in Germany were the most likely to become slaveholders, but even in the richest category, people worth $15,000 or more, only half of the Germans, but 92 percent of the Anglos owned slaves.

Similar tendencies can be observed in Missouri, the only other slave state with a large German population. In two Missouri River counties near St. Louis, Germans and Anglo-Americans were about equal in numbers in 1850, but not even 3 percent of the slaves were in German hands. Nor does poverty provide the explanation here. One-fifth of all Americans without any real estate nevertheless owned slaves, but not a single German. Also among farmers with less than $1,000 in real estate, 28 percent of the natives owned slaves, but only three Germans, not even 1 percent.

The same tendencies held true in five mid-sized Southern cities from Savannah, Georgia, to Baton Rouge, Louisiana. Not only were Germans less likely than native Southerners to own slaves but their rates of ownership were also lower than those of any other cultural group in these locations. If there was a Southern city where Germans were well integrated, then it was Charleston, where they had been around longer and grown more prosperous than anywhere else in the South. But even there, Germans stood apart. Among residents owning property worth $500 or more, with every other group—Southerners, Northerners, other immigrants, even Irish—half or more were slaveholders. With Germans, it was barely a quarter. Regardless of where one looks, and regardless of which comparison group one takes, the tendencies are similar: In matters of slaveholding, Germans brought up the rear. To be sure, for Germans, the acquisition of slaves required an active decision unless they married into a slave-owning family, whereas many of the native born acquired slaves through inheritance. But contrasts of this magnitude could have hardly come about without a conscious decision against human property on the part of most Germans.

Even the few Germans who did own slaves did not appear particularly wedded to the "peculiar institution." The only German slaveowner in New Braunfels, Texas, a prosperous Jewish merchant named Joseph Landa, freed his five slaves immediately in 1863 when he received word of the Emancipation Proclamation, evoking such ill will among his Confederate neighbors that he fled to Mexico and spent the rest of the war there. Ferdinand Flake in Galveston owned a female domestic with three children, but still edited a German newspaper with the telling name of "*Die Union*," and was threatened with mob violence as a result. Missouri presented similar cases: Several Germans who were small-scale slaveowners became leading and even radical members of the Republican Party.

The letters of the Bruns family, founders of the German Catholic settlement of Westphalia, Missouri, gave some insight into the dilemma of slave ownership. Evolving from a Free Soil Democrat to the Radical Republican Mayor of Jefferson City, Dr. Bernard Bruns served as a surgeon in the Union Army and lost a son and a stepson for the Union cause. This may seem paradoxical given that he was a slaveowner and Catholic besides. Part of the explanation is that he was typical neither of Catholics nor of slaveowners. It was no easy decision to become personally involved in slavery. In the case of Dr. Bruns, his wife Jetta was obviously involved in the decision, as is apparent from her 1845 letter to her brother back in Germany: "I'm sorry if . . . you were offended that we had some blacks. Indeed, I do not feel very good about it either. Blacks are frequently good for nothing. But our Mary loves the children and is always very cheerful. I wouldn't do without her for anything. White girls are very pretentious and rarely stay very long." Friedrich Muench's daughter Paulina Busch, another German with a Black domestic, expressed similar sentiments: "I couldn't stand the thought that I should own a slave, but what can you do when . . . you can't help yourself."

In the 1850 census and until they relocated to the state capital of Jefferson City, the Bruns family owned a slave couple with a child. But then Jetta reported something remarkable: "The black folks chose a new master." As suggested above, the scarcity of white domestic servants played an important role in the decision to acquire slaves. Many men from the servant-keeping class in Germany, among them Professor Francis Lieber, felt they had imposed upon their wives enough just by immigrating, without making them do without servants, or trying to get along with white servants who were both scarce and unreliable.

The voting record of Germans in the slave states provides another indication of their attitudes toward Southern institutions and the Rebel cause. In Missouri, Germans were among the few supporters of Lincoln, who came in fourth in the state. In fact, the only counties he carried in any slave state were two German counties of Missouri, rural Gasconade with a majority and urban St. Louis with a plurality, and all but 30 percent of Lincoln's statewide vote came from these and five other German counties. Elsewhere below the Mason-Dixon Line, Germans obviously did not vote for Lincoln, for he was not even on the ballot, and just trying to vote for him meant risking life and limb. In Maryland, a state wracked by nativism, it appears that a majority of Germans voted for the Southern Democrat John Breckinridge, considering him to be the orthodox Democratic candidate, though they soon proved their Unionist mettle when war broke out. Even before, a Baltimore Turner company and another from Washington had guarded Lincoln during his inauguration. In New Orleans, the leading German newspaper supported the northern Democratic ticket of Stephen Douglas; a rival organ backed the moderate Constitutional Union ticket, and its editor opposed secession to the end as a member of the legislature.

Texas put the question of secession up to a popular vote in February 1861, and here, too, Germans stood apart from the Texas mainstream, though not always to the same degree. In an appeal to ethnic voters, the declaration of secession was published in two thousand copies of German translation (and an equal number in Spanish), but these copies largely fell on deaf ears. Across Texas, secession won by a landslide, with less than a quarter of the voters opposing. But two German frontier counties in and around Fredericksburg led the state with a 96 percent margin against secession. San Antonio turned in a razor-thin margin for the Union due above all to German voters. After the election, German city councilmen still resisted for several months demands to turn over seized federal arms to the secessionist state. Even older Texas German settlements farther east in cotton country showed little evidence of Rebel enthusiasm. The 64 percent support for secession in Colorado County, for example, masks an internal polarization. Three German precincts voted 86 percent against, while five Anglo precincts cast all but six votes in favor. Similarly in Fayette County, some Anglos must have contributed to the narrow majority opposing secession because less than half of the voters were German, but a local paper with the telling name *State Rights Democrat* blamed what it called the "sauer-kraut dirt-eaters." Only in Austin County did close to half the Germans vote for Southern independence, still a rather lukewarm result compared to the 96 percent level in six of the county's Anglo precincts.

The stance of Comal County, the only German area of the Hill Country voting strongly in favor of secession, was largely the work of one man, reflecting trust in the advice of the venerable Ferdinand Lindheimer and his *Neu Braunfelser Zeitung*. Rather than touting the merits of the secessionist case, he warned his readers: "When in Texas, do as the Texans do.

Anything else is suicide and brings tragedy to all our Texas-Germans."
Despite the secession vote, New Braunfels was one of the few places in
Texas where Confederate sympathizers were subject to wartime intimidation. Editor Lindheimer's pragmatism was not universally appreciated; his windows were stoned in twice, and his dogs poisoned with
strychnine. Incensed readers at one point threw the press and type of the
Neu Braunfelser Zeitung into the Comal River—but Lindheimer fished it
out of the clear water so that the paper did not miss an issue.

A comparison of military participation rates in the North and South
provides more insight into German attitudes and motivation. There is
a scholarly consensus that Germans were overrepresented in the Union
Army, more so than almost any other nationality, though recruitment
rates varied considerably from state to state. Missouri presents the best-
case scenario, where Germans foiled a secessionist governor and practically dragged the state back into the Union.

A recent study of Germans in the Confederacy (focusing primarily on
the cities of Charleston, Richmond, and New Orleans) estimates their
overall level of military service as close to that in the Union: 16.1 percent
of the South's German population in uniform as opposed to 16.6 percent
in the North. At first glance, this might suggest widespread sympathy for
the Southern cause, but not upon closer examination. Since a much higher
proportion of the military-age population in the South saw service (61 percent as opposed to 35 percent in the North), it is apparent that Germans
in the Confederacy were much less enthusiastic than either their Anglo
neighbors, or their compatriots in the North on the Yankee side.

These three cities pose some interesting contrasts. The German community of Charleston, the oldest, richest, most homogeneous and most
prone to slaveholding of the three, also gave the greatest support to the
Confederacy. But even there, Germans were notorious for their unlaw-
ful sales to slaves and were often fined because of "Negroes loitering"
in their shops and taverns. Richmond's Germans, many recently arrived
and concentrated in the artisan class, were strongly suspected of disloyalty. The most prominent German in the Army of Northern Virginia,
aristocratic cavalryman Heros von Borcke, was not an immigrant at
all, but a soldier of fortune who arrived during the war and returned
to Prussia after the Rebels' defeat. New Orleans had the largest and
most diverse community of Germans in the Confederacy. Despite their

moderate political stance and reservations about secession, they did manage to produce five companies of the 20th Louisiana Infantry to form the Confederacy's only German battalion. But once the Crescent City was in Union hands, it also proved fertile recruiting grounds for the Union Army, whether from economic or ideological motives. If the Schmidts and Meyers are any indication, nearly a quarter of the German Civil War soldiers from Louisiana wore the blue rather than the gray.

Except for Texas, Germans in the Confederacy comprised only a few urban clusters such as these and a negligible rural diaspora. Even in the loyal border states, well over half of the Germans in Missouri and Maryland and almost half of those in Kentucky lived in the cities of St. Louis, Baltimore, and Louisville, respectively. Five Confederate states had no German newspapers whatsoever, and New Orleans was the only city with competing German dailies beyond the duration of the 1860 presidential campaign. From June 1862 on, the *Richmond Anzeiger* remained the only German-language paper in the Confederacy east of the Mississippi. Texas, which was home to more than twenty thousand of the seventy thousand Germans residing in the eleven Rebel states, was the only place in the South where Germans were concentrated enough in rural areas to form a critical mass and maintain an ethnic community life, so that they were a factor to be reckoned with in politics and war.

At the beginning of the war there were some courageous Texas Germans who resisted the Confederacy and sometimes paid for it with their lives. Thirty-six of them who died in the Battle of the Nueces while attempting to escape to Mexico or were executed in its aftermath are commemorated on the "Treue der Union" monument in the village of Comfort: the only such monument to Unionists erected by local residents on the soil of the would-be Confederacy. But it was not only their recruiting grounds in the Hill Country that was placed under martial law, but also the plantation counties of Austin, Fayette, and Colorado because of German draft resistance there. A few German Confederate companies were raised before April 1862 when the Rebel draft set in, but most were formed in response to conscription—for example, the three German companies from these plantation counties in Waul's Texas Legion. With the onset of the draft, Germans from the Victoria area contributed most of two companies to the 6th Texas Infantry, but when they surrendered at Arkansas Post, 162 of its men, mostly Germans and Poles, "took the oath," changed sides, and became "Galvanized Yankees." Judging by common surnames, less than 1 percent of the Smiths and Joneses from Texas served the Union, compared to 11 percent of the Germans from the Lone Star State.

Although the great majority of Texas Germans served the Rebels, many fell into the category of reluctant Confederates, who had doubts about the cause but could find no way to avoid military service. Louis Lehmann no doubt spoke for many when he wrote to his brother-in-law from his farm near Brenham in 1866: "As much as I hated to, I also had to enter the army and fight for a cause that I had never approved." Returning home after a stint as a Union prisoner, he sat out the last six months of the war with, as he put it, "intentional illness." In general Lehmann appeared pleased with the outcome of the war: "the existence of the United States stands more firmly than ever before, the stumbling block of slavery is cleared out of the way," an opinion that most of his German neighbors shared: "No element of the population rejoiced more about peace than the Germans, since they never had any interest in the cause anyhow."

An atypical German in the same county did have a material interest, writing back home in 1861 that he had bought a "slave" or "black man," whom he considered "worth as much as two hired hands." But even he expressed little regret at the demise of slavery, an institution he identified primarily with Anglo-Americans, as he stated in a letter of 1866: "The Americans almost all had Negroes, . . . because whoever had a lot of Negroes, he was rich. They had to do all the work, because the Americans, they don't like to work." Although he justified slavery with the biblical "Curse of Ham," he also remarked with a touch of schadenfreude, "The Americans can't get along with the Negroes now, but they don't like to work themselves."

Even someone as cynical as Georg Schwarting—an antebellum immigrant who by chance spent most of the war back in Germany, and made his way back to Texas as a Union Army "bounty jumper"—expressed his satisfaction with the war's outcome in an 1866 letter to his brother: "The blood was not shed in vain, slavery has ceased. How the Negro will get along as a free laborer, time will tell . . . anyhow they are free, and the 10 bottles of wine that I bet on it with Lönneker I gave away with no little delight. And when you get a chance, you can drink up some of it to the blessings of freedom and the health of the United States."

Deep in the heart of the Confederacy, when the 82nd Illinois "Hecker" Regiment marched into Savannah at the end of Sherman's March through Georgia in December 1864, before the Yankees could even raise the flag, they were greeted by the Stars and Stripes unfurled by the local Turner Society, who called it "the hour of their delivery." They resolved to hold a Turner party to honor their guests, with "the usual Turner festivity and sociability, and singing, gymnastics, and dancing."

July 4, the date of Vicksburg's surrender, was for the most part observed only by newly emancipated Blacks in the South in 1865. The Union Army finally arrived in Texas and proclaimed emancipation on June 19. But Germans and Czechs at New Ulm displayed the U. S. flag on May 20, and marked the Fourth of July with an equally rousing celebration, perhaps unsurprisingly given the draft resistance there. And despite its vote in favor of secession, New Braunfels also showed its true colors that Independence Day with what sounded like a huge sigh of relief. The Stars and Stripes was unfurled from the highest hill, a marching band led a well-attended parade throughout the town, and a number of dances rounded out the evening and lasted into the next day.

Missouri Germans were in the forefront of agitation for emancipation, ahead of Lincoln in that respect, and when it finally became law in 1865, a German immigrant, Arnold Krekel, chaired the convention, and his compatriot George Husmann drafted the ordinance abolishing slavery. The Union was preserved, and emancipation achieved, but it still remained to be seen what position Blacks or Germans would hold in postwar society, and what political roles the two groups would play.

9

Race, Culture, and Politics
in the Late Nineteenth Century

Two important questions faced German Americans in
the aftermath of the Civil War: Would Unionists "vote like they shot"
and continue to support the Republican Party? And what position would
Blacks hold in postwar society and politics? For one village blacksmith in
Missouri who had raised and commanded a Unionist militia company,
the answer to both was clear: "Mr. Weinrich from New Melle, the Radical candidate for the legislature, . . . is said to have recently told some
gentlemen that he regards the Negro as quite his equal in political and
social terms. He also remarked that if four of his five daughters were to
marry white men, and one married a Negro, he would treat his black
son-in-law just like the white husbands of his other daughters."
Incidentally, none of his daughters put him to the test, though one did
try his patience in another way, marrying his employee Fritz Kamphoefner only three weeks before giving birth to their first child. Weinrich's
statement was printed in an antiradical paper and might have been exaggerated, but if it was intended to damage the candidate in the eyes of
his countrymen, it completely misfired. Weinrich reported shortly after
the 1866 election, "We elected the entire Radical Ticket without exception, and the conservatives are hanging their heads. I heard that 2 days
after the election, the barbers in St Charles were charging double the
price to shave a conservative, because their faces are so long now." Judging by his letters, Weinrich's spelling was rather shaky in both German
and English. But loyalty to the Union and decisiveness when the chips
were down were obviously more important to the local German voters

than educational polish. In Weinrich's case, his legislative record provides some evidence that his radicalism was genuine. When new regulations for the state university were being drawn up, there was a motion to delete a clause prohibiting discrimination based on race or gender. Weinrich demanded a roll-call vote in a futile attempt to retain this provision.

After the Civil War, Germans like Weinrich engaged themselves as never before in the politics of Southern states and especially the loyal border states. This held true particularly in Missouri, where a record number of eighteen Germans served in the legislature, all but two of them Republicans. They even elected fellow immigrant Carl Schurz to the U. S. Senate in 1869. From Baltimore, Christoph Barthel proudly wrote home on official letterhead in 1865: "I am the first German to have the honor of being elected to the Legislature of Maryland . . . with a majority of 6,000 votes," naturally, as a Republican. He and three others had founded a "Unionsverein" in 1863, which was also strongly supported by a number of German Jews. In New Orleans as well, Michael Hahn, a German-Jewish immigrant, was one of the state's leading Republicans. Even Texas sent Forty-Eighter Edward Degener, who had lost two sons in the Battle of the Nueces, to Washington as one of the state's first Republican Congressmen. However, four years later the seat was taken over by Gustav Schleicher (the name translates to "skulker"), who in less than two decades underwent a remarkable transformation from a Communist to a Confederate and "Conservative," as Democrats styled themselves back then. Similarly in Charleston, at the beginning of Reconstruction, Blacks could attend the *Schuetzenfest*, and their children participated in their game competitions, but Germans began restricting them in 1870 and by 1873 were offering blackface minstrel troupes for entertainment.

There are scattered indications of rather friendly relations between Blacks and Germans in this era. One immigrant wrote home in 1867 about a slaveowner who had been a neighbor both in Germany and in Texas: "With old Bartels everything is still like before, only their log cabins are increasingly falling into disrepair, and the two old folks now have to work their farm alone, cut off from the world and humanity, enriched from year to year only by a few new wrinkles in their faces." As it turns out, they were neither all alone, nor were they burdened by poverty. A local history related the following: the Bartels were childless and had purchased a slave boy, who learned their language and loved them like a child. After Mr. Bartels died and his wife was bedridden with a stroke for two years until her death, this former slave and his wife faithfully cared for her. The Bartels's will left their entire property to this freedman Henry Williams, who in 1930 was reportedly still in possession of the farm and of a bundle of old German letters, which he greatly treasured. Although the story is tinged with magnolia mythology, it gains credibility from a number of manuscript census entries, which all show Williams as a mortgage-free farm owner, and by the fact that a Texas archive acquired the Bartels's letters from the Williams couple shortly after the story was published.

There are other reports in both Texas and Missouri of Blacks acquiring the German language. However, in the case of the notorious Black Fredericksburger during World War I quoted as saying *"Mir Deutscha müssa zusammahalta"* ("We Germans have to stick together"), German was literally his mother tongue; he was of mixed parentage. What is more surprising is to find similar patterns farther east in Texas, areas that were not so overwhelmingly German: for example in Industry, the oldest German settlement in the state, where a few of the last Black German speakers survived into the twenty-first century. In Missouri, Carl Schurz reported to his wife of his 1867 visit to the village of Augusta in preparation for his Senate campaign: "Of course all the speeches were in German, for in Augusta there are no Americans except the shoemaker's apprentice, who has recently arrived and who is learning German, and several Negro families, among whom the children can already speak German." The town had even briefly integrated its school in the aftermath of the Civil War.

The 1865 Missouri emancipation convention was chaired by immigrant Arnold Krekel, and German radicals were on the forefront of efforts to make the state constitution race neutral, and to extend voting rights to Blacks, initially without success. But along with the 1868 presidential election, Missouri held a referendum on Black enfranchisement. The German-language press in several towns weighed in supporting the amendment—for example, the *St. Charles Demokrat*, which called Negro equality a "boogeyman, with which the Democrats are trying to terrify and intimidate the loyal populous." It was apparently a hard sell with some of their constituency, for rather than arguing for Black suffrage primarily on its merits, German papers mainly attacked its opponents. Both the *Demokrat* and the St. Louis *Westliche Post* placed Blacks in positive comparisons to other groups, the *Post* asking: "Is that justice? The rebels used their intellect only to plunge the country into ruin, whereas the Negro faithfully helped out to save the Union." A week later, the venerable Friedrich Muench posed another contrast in the *Demokrat*: "Even drunken Irishmen and other wastrels with white skin may come to the ballot box; for them a decent black girl would almost be too good." The Irish also served as a whipping boy for the appropriately named Jefferson City *Fortschritt*, whose name translates to Progress: "If the Irishman is an ignorant person and votes for the Democratic Ticket—why shouldn't we Radicals allow the perhaps equally ignorant Negro to vote for the Radical ticket? But as ignorant as the average Irishman the Negro is not." These polemical tones suggest that the rank and file were not as progressive in their racial views as the editor of the *Fortschritt*, which is confirmed by a police report from the previous week's issue: Two men were fined $3 each for "beating up a Negro boy"; their ethnicity is quite apparent from their names: Christ Herchenroeder and John Rockermann.

"No rose without thorns" was the reaction of the *Westliche Post* to the vote on Black enfranchisement; "right remains right, whether it achieves victory on the first attempt or not." If one examines the election returns and compares the number of supporting votes with the number of Republican votes for Grant, it is apparent that less than half of all Grant supporters also favored Black enfranchisement. The deficit was as high or higher in the German wards of St. Louis as in other parts of the city. Also in rural Missouri, Conrad Weinrich's hometown of New Melle cast nearly double the number of votes for Grant as for Black voting rights. Neighboring Schluersburg went 92 percent for Grant but showed a majority opposed to Black voting. The cause fared better in two other German precincts of St. Charles County, probably because of the leadership of local Latin farmers. Femme Osage saw only one-quarter of the Grant supporters defect, and in Augusta, home to Friedrich Muench's brother George, only five of the 146 Grant supporters opposed Black suffrage and another six abstained, while 92 percent held the line. But across the board on the voting rights issue, neither Missouri nor its German population stood apart from other Northern states.

In Jefferson City, Jetta Bruns had rejoiced in Missouri's election of a Radical governor in 1865 and regretted that her husband did not live to see it. Left in tight financial straits, Widow Bruns was assisted by Arnold Krekel, who had bought his house lot from her after moving to the state capital when Lincoln appointed him a federal judge. She turned her home into a boarding house for legislators. Krekel, who was a frequent guest, called it "the Radical corner." Among her boarders were many of the leading German Republicans mentioned above: Friedrich Muench, Gert Goebel, Conrad Weinrich, Gustav Finkelnburg, Gustave Bruere, and others, including a few Anglo-Americans such as the lieutenant governor.

Nonetheless, Bruns expressed reservations about Krekel's racial egalitarianism: "In general the black people are still very shabby, although certainly many of them are also quite respectable. Judge Krekel still endeavors to further the university for them; however, he also goes too far in his estimation of them. It is after all a different race from the white, and equality often leads to unacceptable situations." Along with veterans of the U. S. Colored Troops, Krekel was instrumental in the founding of the Lincoln Institute in Jefferson City. He was one of the six members of its first board of directors, and still presided over the board two decades later, shortly before he died. He lectured without pay in the subjects of government and political economy, and traveled east to raise funds for the institute. Together with Black businessman Howard Barnes, he gave his name to Barnes-Krekel Hall, the school's first women's dormitory. Krekel was perhaps a best-case scenario of German-American racial attitudes.

If there was a worst-case scenario, one might expect it from a Democratic-leaning Catholic paper in a former slave state, such as the Louisville *Katholischer Glaubensbote*. But even there, it is surprising what one does not find: The paper engaged in no essentialist arguments based on alleged biological inferiority of the Black race. Although the church had hardly criticized slavery while it existed, it did not mourn its passing, as an 1866 article shows: "Therefore she joyfully greeted the greatest event that the history of America has to offer, the abolition of slavery." No suggestion that Blacks were somehow created or suited for bondage, rather "It was painful for her that so many millions, who were granted the same mental characteristics as we, and only differ from us in the color of their skin, were treated like a head of cattle, an object for a Jewish profiteer." That a Democratic paper would oppose Black suffrage is not surprising; what is interesting is how it is justified: "It flies in the face of reason . . . to educate slaves politically, before they are educated as persons." Although the *Glaubensbote* opposed immediate suffrage for freedmen, it blamed their shortcomings entirely on environment, stressing their full human equality and strongly supporting educational and religious efforts among Blacks. As late as 1886, the paper stressed that there was "no more inviting field" for the church than work among Black Catholics.

The positions taken during Reconstruction by Germans who had worn the gray also give some insight into their wartime motivations. At the outbreak of the war, there were some courageous Texas Germans who resisted the Confederacy and sometimes paid for it with their lives, and others who voluntarily joined the Rebel ranks. But the majority probably fell into the category of reluctant Confederates like Louis Lehmann, who had doubts about the cause but could find no way to avoid military service.

Lehmann's letters show at best an ambivalence toward Blacks, but in the first Reconstruction legislature his home county, Washington, was represented in the state senate by a freedman, Matt Gaines, and in the lower house by a German, Lehmann's comrade Wilhelm Schlottmann, both, of course, Republicans or Radicals. In the deliberations over a new school law, Schlottmann and a half-dozen other Germans stood united against a clause that would have required segregation in the schools. Although Texas Democrats recaptured the state government in 1873, Washington County remained under Republican control through 1884, upheld by the majority of Blacks, about half of the Germans, and a handful of courageous Anglo-Americans. As long as they held on, Blacks continued to serve as deputy sheriffs and jurors, and received a relatively fair shake in the local judicial system. The Democratic takeover in 1884 could only be achieved through violence and intimidation, and a Republican revival in 1886 was suppressed by stealing three ballot boxes in Republican precincts, lynching three African-American Republicans, and running three white Republican leaders out of the country. At least one of them was German, lawyer and publisher Carl Schurze.

Two years after his departure, Schurze wrote from his California exile to Lehmann's brother Julius, who had helped finance his newspaper: "[I] am afraid the *Mob* will put on the same show in this election that we went through 2 years ago. Violence and intimidation will once again be the main weapons used to intimidate the Negroes and if need be control the *Ballotboxes*. [. . . .] I can imagine that these are just the rascals who are doing their best to play themselves up as friends of the Germans and stir them up against the Negroes, just as they stir up the Negroes against the Germans." Washington County was not unique; one finds a similar pattern in neighboring Colorado County, where Republicans maintained local control until 1890, again through the cooperation of Germans and Blacks. A similar coalition elected a Galveston businessman to the first of two terms of Congress as a Republican in 1897.

Missouri returned to Democratic control via the Liberal Republican movement of 1872, which initially had considerable German support. This led many reformers to desert President Grant and enter into an improbable coalition, as immigrant John Bauer observed from his farm near Kirksville on Election Day: "The Democratic Party has lost every election since the one in 1856; this time they resorted to a major trick & united with a certain small party which has given itself the name / liberal Republicans, / many of these people used to be the worst enemies of the Democratic Party, but since they don't see all their wishes being fulfilled by the current President, they thought that this way they could prevent his reelection, acting out of revenge & envy."

This might suggest that Germans had abandoned Reconstruction and their Black allies, although it would seem strange if many of the same querulous German radicals who had opposed Lincoln from the left in 1864 now opposed Grant from the right. More than race or reconciliation, the issue of corruption was particularly relevant in Missouri where the Whiskey Ring originated. For all their differences with authoritarian Prussia, German radicals still missed the incorruptibility of its bureaucrats. Their fervor for the Liberal Republican movement largely evaporated, however, with the nomination of the eccentric Horace Greeley, an early prohibitionist. Carl Schurze captured their mood on the evening of Greeley's nomination when he sat down at the piano and played Chopin's Funeral March. Mercilessly pilloried by immigrant cartoonist Thomas Nast, Greeley lost in a landslide as Grant was reelected.

The Franco-Prussian War had raised another source of antagonism between German Americans and the Grant administration, which sold arms to French agents until Carl Schurz successfully protested against this breach of U. S. neutrality. A Union veteran from Ohio wrote disgustedly, "Präsident Gränt is also a French-loving sheepheaded idiot." But in Congress, Schurz came under fire for airing America's dirty laundry in full view of foreigners. However, Schurz countered this uncritical nationalism with words that have lost none of the pertinence down to the present: "In one sense, I say so too. 'My country, right or wrong—if right, to be kept right—and if wrong, to be set right.'"

After their flirtation with the Liberal Republican movement in 1872, Missouri Germans largely returned to the Republican fold. Carl Schurz was one of them, and was rewarded with a cabinet appointment by President Rutherford B. Hayes. But many of their Anglo-American allies in Missouri transitioned via the Liberals back to the Democratic Party. Unless they were Catholic, few Germans did, although they were divided like other Republicans on how far they were willing to go in the direction of racial equality.

There is no disputing that the German-Black alliance in the Republican Party was to some extent a marriage of convenience, and that German racial idealism eroded over the decades. But it persisted to some extent well into the twentieth century in Missouri and even Texas. In 1915, when St. Louis introduced by referendum a residential segregation law, Republican Mayor Henry Kiel spoke out prominently against it, and most of the white votes in opposition came from Germans, especially socialists. The law was challenged in the courts by Charles Nagel, a Texas German who had fled with his father via Mexico to Missouri during the Civil War, and had served as a cabinet member in the Taft administration.

Another Missouri Republican, Congressman Leonidas C. Dyer, sponsored an antilynching bill that passed the House in 1922, only to fail in the Senate. Although an Anglo-American, he had grown up among Missouri Germans, studied at a German Methodist college, and represented a St. Louis district with more German than Black voters. (In fact, he was one of only two Missouri congressmen who voted against Wilson's declaration of war.) While not quite a smoking gun, this evidence suggests that the German-Black alliance was still alive at this late date, or at the very least that German Americans were not violently opposed to Black rights. Not even in Texas: the lone congressman in the Deep South to vote in favor of the bill was a Texas-German Republican from a San Antonio area district, Harry Wurzbach, who went on to serve five terms in the House.

Carl Schurz was the only German native elected to the U. S. Senate until Jewish immigrant Joseph Simon was elected in 1898 as a Republican from Oregon, a state with little German population. The next was New York Democrat Robert F. Wagner, who served four terms beginning in 1927 with support from a broad ethnic spectrum, particularly among fellow Catholics. There were only six German immigrants who served as state governors. Two of them were Jewish immigrants elected on the eve of World War I in Utah and Idaho where there was no significant ethnic constituency. But with the other four, ethnicity played a more significant role, especially with Republican Edward Salomon in Civil War Wisconsin and Democrat John Peter Altgelt in 1890s Illinois. Wisconsin also elected inventor and manufacturer Julius Heil to the first of two terms as a Republican in 1939. The other German governor was the above mentioned Michael Hahn in Louisiana. There were probably more German-born lieutenant governors, even if their nominations represented tokenism. Besides Koerner, Hoffmann, and Salamon in the Civil War era, two Forty-Eighters were Republican candidates during Reconstruction: German-Jewish immigrant Sigismund Kaufmann was an unsuccessful nominee in New York in 1870, and Jacob Mueller was elected in Ohio the following year.

From the Civil War to the end of World War II, there were forty-three German immigrants elected to Congress, fifty including German-speaking Austrians. Although they far outnumbered any other nationality without an English-language background, they were no match for the Irish, 122 of whom served in Congress from its beginnings through 1945, whereas the English and Scots together only tallied 105. The Irish figure, of course, also includes many Ulster Protestants. In the German delegation, the entire religious spectrum was represented: thirteen Protestants, seven Catholics, five Jews, and one declared freethinker (though there were undoubtedly more among the remaining seventeen whose religion could not be determined). German Republicans had a slight edge, accounting for twenty-three representatives to the Democrats' eighteen; plus, Minnesota and Wisconsin each elected a congressman from leftist third parties in the 1930s.

Not surprisingly, in view of its population makeup, Wisconsin sent the largest number—seven—of German natives to Congress. Pennsylvania and New York tied for second with five each, followed by Missouri with four. New York City accounted for all five in the Empire State, but St. Louis was close behind with all four of Missouri's German Congressmen, the most from any other city (though one was denied his seat in a partisan vote). All four were Republicans, among them the longest serving of the forty-three: Richard Bartholdt, who advanced, as he titled his autobiography, *From Steerage to Congress* after emigrating from Germany at age seventeen and working in journalism. St. Louis continued to send him to Congress for twenty-two years from 1893 to 1915, and had it not been for World War I, he might well have become Missouri's second German immigrant senator.

In contrast to congressional contests, in mayoral races Germans held their own with Irish Catholics. Despite the reputation of the Irish as born politicians and their advantage of an English mother tongue, it comes as some surprise to learn that more first-generation Germans (twelve) than immigrant Irish Catholics (nine) were elected as mayors between 1820 and 1980 in the fourteen leading American cities covered by the *Biographical Dictionary of American Mayors*. Irish Catholics had a slight edge in the second generation, bringing the totals for immigrants and their children to thirty-nine each for Germans and Irish Catholics. In the third generation, when ethnicity began to fade, Germans again had a slight advantage, twenty-three to seventeen. Because they were more likely to be reelected than Germans, Irish maintained a slight edge in other indicators of political success, such as times elected or total years in office.

Compared to the Irish, the confessional, regional, and occupational diversity of the Germans was just as apparent as their fluctuating political loyalties. It is not so certain, however, that slavish loyalty to one party brought large benefits in terms of policy output or even the makeup of the ticket. Precisely because of the independence of the Germans, political parties could ill afford to ignore their wishes. This was particularly true at the local level, where the leading issues were often in the highly emotional areas of cultural politics, like education and alcohol. Not only in questions of policy, but also in the area of personnel, Germans in local politics came off better than is generally realized. And with respect to the type of individual who presided over city government, the contrasts between Germans and Irish, and the propensity of the latter toward machine politics, can easily be exaggerated. For example, the first Irish Catholic to preside over Chicago was Edward F. Dunne, characterized by a biographer as "the mayor who cleaned up Chicago." His German Republican successor, Fred "fat Freddie" Busse, a Catholic saloonkeeper, better fits the machine stereotype often applied to the Irish. Moreover, his ethnicity figured strongly in his election, helping swing many otherwise Democratic German Catholics.

Irish mayors typically came from the heart of their ethnic community, whereas Germans often came from the fringes. Fewer than half of the German mayors definitely had spouses of the same ethnicity, whereas at least one-quarter of them took Anglo-American wives. But nowhere is the high degree of assimilation of German big-city mayors more clearly reflected than in religious confession. For about one-fifth of these mayors, no confession was indicated, perhaps reflecting a transplanted freethinking tradition characteristic of many educated Germans, especially the politically active. More than one-third of the German mayors adhered to Anglo-American confessions, many simply characterized as Protestant. Fewer than half belonged to transplanted confessions with roots in the Fatherland. Catholics and Lutherans ran neck and neck, and there were also three German Jews. One might question to what extent the latter shared a German ethnic identity, particularly in the case of immigrant Adolph Sutro, Populist mayor of San Francisco in the 1890s. But in the case of second-generation Julius Fleischmann in Cincinnati, his Turnverein membership and his affiliation with the Republican Cox machine indicates considerable support from German Americans. This was even more apparent with another Jewish mayor in the Queen City, German-born Frederick Spiegel, who had edited the *Freie Presse* newspaper, chaired the Public School Committee on the German language, and presided over a number of Vereins.

This leaning toward the Republican Party was characteristic of German mayors as a whole, though the tendency was not overwhelming. Republicans outnumbered Democrats by nearly two to one. Whereas Irish candidates counted on an overwhelming ethnic solidarity, German contenders, especially in the Republican Party, pursued a rather different strategy, trying to bridge the gap between Anglo-American and ethnic constituencies with candidates who were acceptable to both. Hence the small number of Catholic German mayors and the large number who belonged to Anglo-Protestant denominations. In fact, there was only one Catholic among the dozen first-generation German mayors in the cities examined here, and one of the two Catholics in the second generation was Robert Wagner Jr., who was neither very German nor very Catholic. The other, Martin Behrmann of New Orleans, had attended a German-language school, but based his political support on a multiethnic Catholic coalition. By the third generation, however, Catholics were the leading confession among German mayors, but this was more a manifestation of the triple melting pot, with these candidates running essentially not as Germans but as Catholics—as was the case with their Irish counterparts.

Also interesting is the pattern of the outliers, cities where Germans did better or worse than one would expect on the basis of their ethnic makeup. On his travels across the nation, Friedrich Gerstaecker perceptively observed in 1867 that Germans were nowhere more dominant than in St. Louis, not even in Cincinnati where they were proportionally more numerous. He related the anecdote of a German city controller who said he would have to put a sign outside his door, "English is also spoken here," because Americans were afraid to come in among so many Germans. In less than ten years, this same controller, immigrant Henry Overstolz, would take over the mayor's office, the first of a number of German Republicans. St. Louis elected more German mayors relative to its population makeup than any other city, followed closely by Buffalo. Both spent more years under German mayors than Milwaukee, the German capital of the nation, though the German share of their populations was only two-thirds as large.

Still, the routes to electoral success varied in the leading German cities. Including the third generation, St. Louis elected six German Republican mayors through 1948; there was just one German Democrat during the New Deal and another in 1848 before there was a Republican Party. In Cincinnati, the close association between the Germans and the Republican Cox machine was also apparent. In Buffalo, however, two German Republicans, one of them Catholic, gave way to a string of five German Democrats interrupted by only one Republican in 1930. Milwaukee presents yet another pattern, with the tendency switching from Republicans to socialists around 1910, and persisting all the way to 1960, when Frank Zeidler, the last Socialist mayor of a major U. S. city, finally left office. So the route to German electoral success could lead through various political parties.

What kind of payoffs did the political strategies of Germans bring for their ethnic groups? What goods did the mayor's office deliver, besides the psychic reward of having a fellow ethnic presiding over city hall? There were two areas of urban policy where German Americans largely got their way, regardless of whether they personally headed city tickets: in imposing their value system with regard to alcohol regulations, and in placing their mother tongue on the public elementary curriculum in most major cities (treated in greater detail in another chapter). The German association with the alcoholic beverage industry, and beer in particular, is an ethnic stereotype with more than just a (barley) grain of truth. Germans were also heavily involved in the wholesaling and retailing of alcohol, but they appear to have excelled more as producers than as consumers of alcohol. At least their claims of drinking *"mäßig, aber regelmäßig"* ("moderately but regularly") is supported by statistics on alcohol-related disease and arrests. It was as businessmen rather than customers that Germans ran the greatest risk of conflict with alcohol laws.

In the first recorded portrayal of policemen as pigs, cartoonist Thomas Nast in 1874 took aim at Cincinnati police who "do not enforce the laws against the liquor traffic . . . distinguished themselves . . . by arresting forty-three women, who went on the streets to sing and pray." The prominence of the Schwein Kopf Lager Bier Hall in the cartoon left no doubt that Nast's main target was his fellow German Americans, with whom he apparently identified less than with the Anglo-Protestant elite circles into which he married. The Cincinnati incident is symptomatic of broader patterns of cultural clash between German ethnics and the dominant Anglo-American culture involving attitudes toward alcohol and leisure. This was reflected in the diary of New York patrician George Templeton Strong, reacting to Democratic gains in 1867: "There is joy among the canaille [riff-raff] of Manhattan tonight. Its 'Dutch' lager bier saloons and Celtic whiskey mills lift up their heads, for their Republican 'Puritan' excise law and Sunday law enemies are smitten."

Among American big cities, Chicago was the one where Germans came off worst in relation to their numbers in competing for the mayor's office—one-term winner Fred Busse stands alone. Instead, the scene was dominated by three representatives of the Anglo-Protestant elite:

Carter Harrison I and II and William "Big Bill" Thompson. Harrison father and son each won five mayoral elections, while Thompson won three four-year terms. Although on opposite sides of the partisan divide, a common characteristic of the Harrisons and Thompson is that all were decidedly "wet." There were other aspects to their appeals to Chicago's largest ethnic group. The elder Harrison had lent his support to German instruction in Chicago's public schools early in the 1880s. His son had studied three years at a German gymnasium and spoke the language fluently. "Kaiser Bill" Thompson showed outspoken sympathy for neutrality during World War I. Democrats tried in vain to undermine his ethnic appeal by running a Catholic named Robert Sweitzer as his opponent in two elections. But most Chicago German voters were less concerned about ethnic presence at the head of the ticket than with seeing their ethnic values upheld at city hall.

Granted, the German position on alcohol gained widespread de facto—if not always legal—recognition in Chicago and other cities because it also received strong support from the Irish and other Catholic ethnics. However, German stakes in the industry were higher, and German beer generally came off better than Irish whiskey as far as alcohol regulation was concerned. On the issue of German language in the public schools, there is no such ambiguity—the Irish were often its most bitter opponents. Of fourteen major U. S. cities, all offered German instruction in public elementary schools for at least part of the era between the Civil War and World War I except for Boston, New Orleans, Philadelphia, and Pittsburgh, all places where the Irish outnumbered Germans. In cities with larger German populations, even the Irish could not always afford to turn a deaf ear. It was under Irish-born Mayor James Barry that St. Louis in 1849 arranged to have all city ordinances translated into German. This only goes to show the advantages of not putting all one's eggs in one partisan basket. Despite the reputation of nativism among Republicans, it was their party that instituted or maintained German instruction in a number of city systems—St. Louis, Cincinnati, and Indianapolis, for example. In Buffalo, however, Republican resistance to German in the schools was apparently a factor in the switch of German allegiance to the Democrats. In terms of policy outputs, particularly in the realm of cultural issues such as education, language, and alcohol, German Americans were able to wield a considerable amount of influence in urban politics, at least in the era up to World War I. In short, German ethnic candidacies for the office of mayor, like much of American ethnic politics past and present, represented a combination of symbolism and substance.

The importance of cultural politics, and the fluctuating political loyalties of the German vote, held true at the state and national level as well. In a letter from 1868, a German Catholic veteran of the Union Navy sketched the contrasts between the Republicans and Democrats from his home in Illinois: "The former the party of progress, of equal rights for each and all without distinction of status or color—the latter if no longer exactly reactionary still very conservative, that is they would like to leave everything the old way as it was before the [Civil] War." He goes on to characterize the Republican supporters: "in general all the educated property holders, all bigots and religious fanatics, and the major share of the Germans, for the other party all the dumb farmers and less educated laborers, the bigoted Irish of Catholic religion and nearly the whole South. How it comes about that the Catholic element always goes hand in hand with Conservatism, also here in America, I don't know." Note that this writer was ambiguous with regard to German Catholics, though his own sympathies were clearly with the Republicans at this point, but by 1876, he appears to have switched parties.

German Americans were the largest bloc of swing voters in the Midwest during this era, if indeed they can be considered a voting bloc at all. An 1876 survey of voters of Genesco County in northwest Illinois found that their loyalties varied greatly by religious denomination. Like Anglo-Protestants, six of seven German Methodists favored the Republicans, as did two-thirds of the sixty Lutherans surveyed. Those who expressed no religious affiliation split almost evenly between the two parties, whereas three-quarters of the German Catholics identified as Democrats. But even these small Republican inroads set them apart from other Catholics, especially the Irish—all fifty-two polled in Genesco County claimed to be Democrats.

Rather than racial attitudes, it was primarily cultural issues that affected voting patterns in the Midwest. When German Catholics and Protestants managed to unite politically, it was usually against a common enemy, especially when their language or beer-drinking culture was attacked. The *Atlantic Monthly* observed in 1873, "Such being the light in which we appear to those of our German population . . . , it is not much to be wondered at that they do not wish to be Americanized any faster than they can help it." Instead, it appears they were imposing their culture on Anglo-Americans: "Wherever they have settled in any numbers, they hold—or may hold if they so choose—the balance of power, and it would be almost impossible to pass a Maine Liquor Law, or a Sunday Law, or if passed, to enforce it. The principle that Christianity is part of the common law is fast disappearing wherever they settle."

Most Germans, not just the secular "club Germans" but the religiously affiliated "church Germans" as well, would have questioned what Christianity had to do with alcohol prohibition: the pious with reference to Jesus turning water into wine at the wedding of Cana; the freethinkers with reference to the First Amendment's prohibition of the establishment of religion. German Catholic periodicals railed against "Puritan fanatics" as vehemently as any freethinking secularists, and Lutherans, too, often served beer at their church picnics (and still do). "Beer and wine the German looks upon as good gifts of God, to be enjoyed in moderation for lightening the cares of life and adding to its pleasures; and Sunday afternoon is devoted . . . to recreation," observed the Philadelphia literary magazine *Lippincott's* in 1883.

As the magazine portrayed it, the two cultures remained at loggerheads: "Two things [the Germans] insist upon as a class which are contrary to the dominant opinion among the native American element, the right to drink beer and wine in public places at all times, and the right to amuse themselves on Sunday in the ways they were accustomed to in their own country. Most of the hostile feeling which has arisen between them and the native population has grown out of the differences on these two points." If these conflicts are no longer present today, it is because most Anglo-Protestants have adopted the ethnic outlook toward both Sunday amusements and alcohol. Or better said, Anglo-Protestants won the battle in imposing nationwide prohibition, but lost the war when it proved to be a fiasco.

Alcohol and Sabbatarianism were potent issues in the 1880s, even if Germans were politically divided: "No party supporting a Prohibitory Liquor Law or a severe Sunday law can get the German vote. These two points aside, the Germans differ about as much on questions of State and national politics as do their fellow-citizens. . . . [About] two-thirds of the

Germans west of the Alleghenies are Republicans, and two-thirds of those in the East Democrats."

Even the solidly bourgeois *Lippincott's Magazine* showed sympathy for the German outlook on life: "The austere Presbyterian, Methodist, or Congregationalist condemned the levity of 'the Dutch,' but his children looked with less prejudice upon their picnics, shooting-festivals, singing-societies, and other social gatherings. . . . Except in isolated rural localities where the Teutonic immigration has not penetrated, there is no longer any such feeling about dancing, social games, and dramatic performances as was almost universal among respectable people thirty years ago." But alcohol still remained a bone of contention for the rest of the century and beyond.

When Republicans were persuaded by Puritanical crusaders to restrict alcohol, revenge on the part of German voters was quick to follow. Chicago passed a Sunday closing law in 1873, causing Catholics such as the prominent Herting-Dieden family, who, as Republicans, claimed a three-term city alderman and even a state legislator, to go over to the Democrats, along with many other Germans. Republicans lost the Iowa governorship for the first time in thirty years when they passed a prohibition measure in 1889; the winner had switched to the Democratic Party over the prohibition issue. That same year, Republicans lost in Indianapolis for the first time in a dozen years when they more than doubled the saloon license fees. In Ohio, a Sunday saloon closing law led to Republican defeat in 1884; losses were small outstate, but huge in Cincinnati, which was the most German city in the nation besides Milwaukee. As one historian put it, "The Republicans had played with firewater, and were burned." Republicans lost Wisconsin only twice between the Civil War and the end of the century, both times because of cultural issues. The first was a saloon licensing law of 1873, but it was quickly repealed. The second, involving school laws, inflicted broader damage on the GOP.

In fact, the most dramatic cultural clashes of this era were the Bennett Law and Edwards Law controversies in Wisconsin and Illinois respectively, involving school language. In 1888, these two states passed identical laws tightening attendance rules and imposing language regulations on parochial as well as public elementary schools. The stumbling stone was the following provision: "No school shall be regarded as a school . . . unless is taught therein . . . reading, writing, arithmetic, and American history in the English language." Republicans saw this as a reasonable attempt by the state to ensure that all pupils, even those in parochial schools, were adequately equipped for the modern world. The Republican governor of Wisconsin was dismayed to learn that there were 129 Lutheran schools in his state with no English instruction whatsoever. Democrats, however, saw this as an arrogant overreach on the part of the government, sticking its nose into areas where it had no business and encroaching upon parental authority. These laws united German Catholics and Protestants against a common enemy.

Republicans were swept from power in both states. Wisconsin's congressional delegation flipped from a seven-to-two Republican majority to an eight-to-one Democratic advantage, and Democrats took the governorship and a two-thirds majority in the state legislature. Illinois saw the election of its first Democratic governor since the Civil War, and the first immigrant and first Chicagoan ever: German John Peter Altgeld. Ironically, it was discovered shortly before the election that Altgeld had actually supported the school law, as might be expected of a modernizing freethinker, but this did nothing to stop him. Needless to say, the school laws were quickly rescinded in both states. These school law controversies undoubtedly had political repercussions beyond the two states where they occurred. From Hermann, Missouri, the *Volksblatt* editorialized: "The Protestants of Wisconsin are joining their Catholic fellow-citizens to fight the vile Bennett Law. . . . If the church stands up for justice and freedom, even the unbeliever will applaud her." As far away as Texas, a German editor celebrated the revocation of the "infamous" Edwards Law, calling it a "glorious victory" and predicting that "no political party will so lightly dare to attempt to suppress instruction in the German language."

However, the German swing toward the Democratic Party proved to be short-lived. Democrats had the misfortune to occupy the White House when the Panic of 1893 triggered the worst depression the nation had experienced to date. As the economic woes lingered on, Democrats nominated as their 1896 presidential candidate William Jennings Bryan, who seemed tailor-made to repel German voters. He vaulted to the nomination on the strength of his "Cross of Gold" speech and adopted an inflationary program of free coinage of silver. Germans had always supported "sound money"; cartoonist Thomas Nast had demonized the "rag baby" of inflation during the Greenback era two decades earlier. Carl Schurz considered Bryan to be a dangerous radical behind whom the Democratic Party had "thrown itself into the arms of the silver fraud" and a candidate who was "clearly seeking to incite the have-nots against the haves." But there were other factors that probably drove rank and file German voters away from Bryan, who lost ground in German areas across the Midwest and even in Texas. Cultural issues that had recently hurt Republicans now cut in the opposite direction. Germans and urbanites were especially repelled by Bryan. He was the prototypical Protestant crusader with the oratorical style of a revival preacher, a "cold water fanatic" who later as secretary of state achieved notoriety for serving grape juice instead of liquor at official receptions. Republicans saw a net gain of over four hundred thousand votes in the eight leading cities of New York, Chicago, Philadelphia, St. Louis, Brooklyn, Baltimore, Boston, and Minneapolis, all of which they carried, in contrast to 1892, when only St. Louis and Philadelphia had gone for the GOP.

German Americans continued to lean Republican for the next generation, often favoring the progressive wing of the party. For Carl Schurz, however, the rapprochement with the Republican Party did not last long. With the Spanish-American War and the annexation of the Philippines, Schurz broke with the McKinley administration and became one of the founders of the Anti-Imperialist League. This was a matter of principle with Schurz, who saw the resistance to empire as one of the founding principles of the American republic. But it was perhaps tinged with the fear that U. S. imperialism might put the nation on a collision course with the colonial ambitions of an increasingly assertive German empire.

Loyalty to the United States always came first for Schurz, but he had long been an advocate for what later came to be called cultural pluralism. He enunciated his position in an 1897 address on the German language: "I have always been in favor of sensible Americanization, but this need not mean a complete abandonment of all that is German. It means that we should adopt the best traits of American character and join them to the best traits of German character. By so doing we shall make the most valuable contribution to the American nation, to American civilization." At Schurz's death in 1906, this German-American symbiosis was still possible, but a decade later, his compatriots would find it increasingly challenging to uphold his pluralistic ideal.

10

The Radical Side of German America

SINCE ITS FOUNDING, THE UNITED STATES has been a refuge for political dissidents, which in the early nineteenth century included an increasing number of Germans. A generation of young idealists had fought and helped to defeat Napoleon in the years from 1812 to 1814 in the hope of achieving German national unification under a constitutional government that would ensure personal and political liberty for all its citizens. When these hopes were dashed, university students formed the core of a nationwide movement. At the three-hundredth anniversary of the Protestant Reformation in 1817, some five hundred students rallied for German unity and against reactionary politics at the Wartburg Castle where Martin Luther had taken refuge, and in the aftermath made a bonfire of conservative writings. One of its prominent organizers, although he did not personally attend, was Karl (Charles) Follen, a radical agitator who one historian dubbed a "German Robespierre." When one of Follen's deranged admirers, Karl Ludwig Sand, assassinated the reactionary playwright and spy August von Kotzebue in 1819, Follen was suspected in what was probably a lone deed. He took refuge in France, then Switzerland, and ultimately in the United States in 1824. He found a position teaching German language and literature at Harvard University, although he lost it in 1835 because of his abolitionist activities. His influence was cut short when he died in a shipwreck in 1840.

Meanwhile back in Germany, Kotzebue's assassination gave the reactionary Austrian Prince Metternich the pretext to railroad through the German Confederacy the Karlsbad Decrees, intensifying the political repression and censorship across Germany, particularly in the universities. The most prominent radical who was driven into exile by the decrees was Franz (Francis) Lieber, whose career exhibited several parallels to Follen's. A native of Berlin, Lieber also fought against Napoleon, and later for Greek independence. He aroused the hostility of Prussian authorities for his views and was twice imprisoned before seeking refuge in London in 1826, going from there to America the following year. A follower of the Turner movement that saw gymnastic discipline as a means to a unified, republican Germany, Lieber took over the Boston *Turnverein* that Follen had founded. His contacts with New England intellectual circles led to his editing of the *Encyclopedia Americana*, appointments to college professorships, and the authorship of the Army's "Lieber Code" of military justice during the Civil War.

Despite the German repression, political dissent continued to simmer beneath the surface and occasionally boiled over. In 1832, university students took the lead in organizing a political festival at the Hambach Castle in the Palatinate that attracted some twenty-five thousand to thirty thousand participants from all ranks of society across Germany and beyond. In four days of festivities, various orators condemned the German "league of princes" and supported a republican "united free states of Germany." This brought political repression upon the organizers, thirteen of whom were tried for sedition. Against the backdrop of Hambach, some of the more radical student participants decided that the time was ripe for a general revolution. They launched a quixotic attempt to seize the police guard house in Frankfurt on April 3, 1833, which failed miserably, leaving two attackers, six soldiers, and one bystander dead in its wake. Fleeing for their lives, many of the would-be revolutionaries made their way to America, including at least seven who formed the core of the "Latin Farmer" settlement in Belleville, Illinois. Several of them went on to distinguished political and military careers, among them Gustave Koerner.

Rather than triggering a German revolution, the "Frankfurt Putsch" provoked a wave of "*Demagogenverfolgung*": the prosecution (or persecution) of demagogues, real and imagined. More than two thousand persons were listed in its "Black Book" and subjected to judicial proceedings for political offenses before it was lifted in 1842. A number of its victims took refuge in America; so many, in fact, that Koerner devoted an entire book to profiling prominent Germans who had arrived before 1848, many of them political refugees. Not all became prominent, however.

Gert Goebel describes one university student who settled in the Missouri backwoods after his "revolutionary agitation" earned him a three-month sentence: "There was nothing left for him to do except to emigrate, for . . . because of his confinement in the fortress, as well as his most offensive free-thinking views and his sometimes very inopportune frankness, establishing any career would have been blocked for him." Paul Follenius, (despite his Latinized name, the brother of Charles Follen), came under suspicion as an accessory to the Frankfurt attack. In 1834, together with his fellow student and brother-in-law Friedrich Muench, he founded the Giessen Emigration Society and settled in Missouri, where Follenius died young and Muench went on to become the state's most respected German statesman. Koerner and Muench were among the most influential of the so-called *Dreissiger* (political exiles of the 1830s) who became first rivals and then allies of the next wave of refugees in the wake of the 1848 revolution.

The revolution that broke out in March of 1848 in Germany, and in a number of other countries across Europe, brought a springtime of hope for democratization, national unification, and greater international recognition. Prince Metternich, the symbol of reaction for a generation, fled Vienna, and Prussia saw the prospect of a constitutional monarchy. On May 18, 1848, an elected national assembly met at the Paulskirche in Frankfurt, attempting to lay the foundation for a new Germany based on liberty, democracy, and national unity. It took the delegates until December to draft a "Declaration of the Rights of the German People" inspired in part by the U. S. Declaration of Independence. But in the months that the assembly deliberated, the forces of reaction regained their momentum. In April of 1849, the King of Prussia rejected the constitutional monarchy proposed in the Paulskirche, spurning a crown "picked up from the gutter." Two months later, the Frankfurt Parliament was forced to disperse by Prussian troops.

The revolutionary movement was most radical in the German southwest near the French border. In April of 1848, radical democratic forces led by Frederick Hecker were defeated in their attempt to turn Baden into a republic. That September, a second uprising in Baden was foiled with the imprisonment of its leader, Gustav Struve. Struve was freed in May 1849 during a third uprising in Baden, which despite temporary success was put down by Prussian troops, with the last revolutionary forces taking refuge in Switzerland or surrendering in July 1849. Other uprisings in Dresden, the Palatinate, and elsewhere met a similar fate.

Hecker, Struve, and several thousand other supporters of the revolution made their way to the United States in the next couple of years. Among these Forty-Eighters, the one destined to achieve the greatest future prominence was Carl Schurz, a nineteen-year-old student at the University of Bonn when the revolution broke out. For a while, he assisted his revered professor Gottfried Kinkel in publishing a democratic newspaper in Bonn. Schurz joined the military struggle in Baden when the Prussian army put down the revolution. When the besieged fortress of Rastatt was forced to surrender, Schurz, in danger of execution, managed to escape by hiding in a sewer and took refuge across the Rhine in France. But he returned to Germany in disguise and managed to free his friend Kinkel from a lifelong prison sentence in Berlin Spandau and spirit him away to England. From there Schurz immigrated to the United States in 1852 and launched his political career in Wisconsin.

Most of the political refugees of 1848 and before had been bourgeois radicals, many with roots in university student movements. As student radicals tend to do, they became more moderate over time, and more integrated into the American political system, particularly through the rise of the Republican Party and their Civil War experiences, which many saw as a continuation of their struggles in Germany. Lincoln recognized their political support with several appointments to European consulates, although some of them proved to be less than diplomatic, Carl Schurz as a case in point.

Many former radicals also gradually reconciled with the land of their birth, especially after the amnesty of 1862. When Chancellor Otto von Bismarck managed to unite the German Reich, "not by speeches and majority resolutions" as he stated in his notorious 1862 speech, but "by blood and iron," many one-time radical refugees in America were swept up in nationalistic euphoria, like the National Liberal politicians back home who proved to be more national than liberal. Frederick Hecker was one of the few among leading Forty-Eighters who stuck to his republican principles after 1871. Carl Schurz had accepted an audience with Bismarck in 1868, although the two did engage in some verbal sparring.

A few of the Forty-Eighters did maintain their radical stance throughout their lives, foremost among them journalist Karl Heinzen, but they had little in common with the next phase of German radicalism. One exception was Wilhelm Weitling, a self-educated son of the proletariat, who had made a name for himself in Europe as a promoter of utopian communism, which he saw as harmonizing fully with Christianity. He took refuge in the United States before 1848, but like Heinzen, returned in support of the revolution. Soon back in America, he organized a Workingman's League and for five years published a radical monthly, *Die Republik der Arbeiter* (Laborer). But after its demise in 1855, he withdrew from public life until his death in 1871. Swimming "against the current" in his own words, Heinzen promoted a number of radical causes and criticized many aspects of American government in his weekly *Pionier*, which he managed to keep afloat from 1853 until his death in 1879, but he was no Marxist, denouncing "Communist hell-hounds" who deprecated him as a "bourgeois democrat."

Increasingly after the Civil War, another form of German radicalism came to the fore, anarchist and socialist movements involving industrial laborers. Already in the 1840s and 1850s, immigrant workers often drew upon European traditions and experiences to deal with the challenges of industrialization and skill erosion. But while a small communist movement did spring up, as one authority on the subject relates, "the handful of Marxists were overwhelmingly outnumbered by adherents of . . . radical democratic 'red republicanism'—an ideology owing more to Thomas Paine than to Marx." But internal divisions, vestiges of guild loyalties, and ambivalence toward the wage system limited the successes of both strikes and cooperative ventures by antebellum German workers.

Karl Marx himself commented on the Civil War from afar, and upon Lincoln's reelection in 1864 delivered congratulations in the name of the First International Workingmen's Association: "The workingmen of Europe feel sure that, as the American War of Independence initiated a new era of ascendancy for the middle class, so the American Antislavery War will do for the working classes. They consider it an earnest of the epoch to come that it fell to the lot of Abraham Lincoln, the single-minded son of the working class, to lead his country through the matchless struggle for the rescue of an enchained race and the reconstruction of a social world."

Lincoln responded with gratitude, characterizing the Union cause in the conflict with what he called the slavery-maintaining insurgence as the cause of humanity in general, and deriving "new encouragements to persevere from the testimony of the workingmen of Europe that the national attitude is favored with their enlightened approval and earnest sympathies."

Despite their temporary alliance in opposition to slavery, in the long run, the Republicans had little to offer urban workers besides the Homestead Act, which proved to be an unrealistic alternative for most of them. With the increasing scale of the American workplace, relations of laborers with management became more impersonal, and labor conflicts more bitter and more ethnic. By 1880, only one-quarter of the industrial labor force nationwide consisted of native whites of native parentage; the great majority were immigrants or their children. Many were German, especially in the urban Midwest. In Detroit, 14 percent of workers in 1880 were native whites of native parentage, but over half were first- or second-generation Germans. By 1890 in Chicago, only one-third of all workers were American born, and of those, the majority were of foreign parentage. Only one-eighth of Chicago workers were "old stock" whites, but 23 percent were German born. Drawing upon European traditions, Germans were more inclined to unionize than others, and also more attracted to radical socialist and anarchist movements. Almost 60 percent of German metalworkers were unionized; with masons it was 80 percent, with bakers 84 percent, with brickmakers almost 99 percent. Although comprising only 23 percent of Chicago laborers, Germans made up 31 percent of the city's organized labor. They also formed the core of the city's anarchist movement. Most active socialists in late nineteenth-century Detroit were German. Yet ironically, most readers of Robert Reitzel's polemical Detroit weekly, *Der arme Teufel* were not "Poor Devils" but decidedly middle class, unless they read it in saloons; only about one-sixth of the subscribers were blue-collar workers. But as late as the 1920s, socialism in St. Louis had a predominantly German character. More than half of the Socialist ward chairmen, more than three-fourths of the candidates in the 1922 election, and some nine-tenths of campaign donors were German.

In Germany, Otto von Bismarck's antisocialist laws were in effect from 1878 to the end of his chancellorship in 1890. They initially suppressed the Social Democrats' vote, and drove a number of socialist activists to foreign exile in Switzerland, Britain, and the United States. At least sixteen editors and journalists of German-American radical papers had left Germany during these twelve years. But this was only a small fraction of the more than 150 activists in the German radical press in the years between the Civil War and World War I. One of those who fled oppression in Prussia, Berlin native Paul Grottkau, helped found the *Arbeiter Zeitung* in Chicago, and later continued his organizing and publishing in Milwaukee. Most prominent among them was Johann Most, who published the New York *Freiheit* (Freedom) from 1879 until his death in 1906, and a notorious pamphlet whose title translates to "Revolutionary Warfare Science," offering instruction in the production and usage of dynamite, nitroglycerin, and poisons. He found an anonymous disciple in Chicago.

The incident that most indelibly stamped German immigrants with a radical reputation was the Chicago Haymarket Affair of 1886. It grew out of the movement for an eight-hour workday, which culminated in a strike and lockout at the McCormick reaper plant. When a brawl broke out between strikers and strikebreakers, police fired into the crowd, killing two and wounding several others. In response, a meeting was called for the next evening at Haymarket Square to protest this police brutality.

The meeting proceeded peacefully; turnout was light because of a drizzle, and Chicago Mayor Carter Harrison observed most of the proceedings. As more rain threatened and things were winding down, 176 Chicago policemen marched on platform and commanded the meeting to disperse. At this point, someone threw a bomb, which exploded in their midst. Mass confusion ensued; seven policemen were killed, and sixty-seven wounded, some from the bomb but many from indiscriminate friendly fire. Four civilians were also killed and many more wounded.

Conservative forces seized the opportunity to strike a blow against the entire anarchist movement. Several dozen were indicted, but ultimately eight men were tried on trumped-up conspiracy charges. The most prominent among them, Albert Parsons, was a Mayflower descendant and Confederate veteran who took a very different path after the war. Another, Samuel Fielden, was an English-born Methodist lay minister. But the other six were all Germans closely associated with the anarchist daily *Arbeiter-Zeitung*.

In essence, the anarchists were tried not for their deeds but for the radical views they espoused, in what a leading textbook calls "one of the great miscarriages of American justice." Mayor Harrison was asked at the trial whether he recalled "any suggestion made by either of the speakers looking toward calling for the immediate use of force or violence towards any person?" He replied, "There was not." But the presiding judge was highly prejudicial, both with jury selection and in conducting the trial, and predictably all of the defendants were found guilty. Seven were sentenced to death; the eighth received fifteen years. The prosecution alleged that a bombing conspiracy was hatched at a meeting the day before, but circumstantial evidence undermines that charge. Only two of the defendants had attended the meeting. Parsons had just arrived back in town from a speaking tour, and was accompanied by his wife and two young children to Haymarket. Editor August Spies had refused to speak unless a line was deleted from the bilingual handbill with the appeal, "Workingmen arm yourselves and appear in full force." One defendant, Louis Lingg, had actually been involved in another bombing, but had not been within two miles of Haymarket, nor at the meeting where the alleged conspiracy had been formed.

Two of the defendants appealed to the governor for clemency and had their sentences commuted to life in prison, but the other five refused on principle to appeal for mercy. Four of them, Parsons, Spies, Adolph Fischer and George Engel, were hanged on November 11, 1887. The one genuine bomber, Louis Lingg, cheated the hangman by exploding a blasting cap in his mouth while in jail awaiting execution. After thoroughly reviewing the case and concluding "that the judge conducted the case with malicious ferocity," Governor John Peter Altgeld issued an "absolute pardon" to the three surviving Haymarket anarchists in June 1893, and in the process was expelled, as the *Chicago Tribune* wrote, "into the outermost political darkness."

The identity of the bomb thrower remains uncertain to this day, although it was almost certainly not one of the defendants, but rather someone from the anarchist scene acting on his own. In 1985, the leading authority on Haymarket was contacted by an eighty-year-old psychologist who made a plausible claim that her grandfather George Meng was the bomb thrower. A Bavarian immigrant, Meng belonged to the most militant wing of the anarchist movement, but there are no indications that he was part of a larger conspiracy as alleged.

The immigrant community was bitterly divided over the Haymarket Affair. It was a German-speaking Catholic from Luxembourg, police captain Michael Schaack, who assembled much of the evidence and wrote a book about it. There are grounds for skepticism in the fact that he was discharged from the force in 1889 for accepting bribes and trafficking in stolen goods, although he was reinstated two years later. Outside the working class, there were few Germans who defended the anarchists, and many who deplored the damage done to the German image in general. The *Illinois Staats-Zeitung* editorialized in September 1886, "Nothing has hurt the Germans more in the United States in the eyes of its other population elements than the shocking agitation of the anarchists. . . . It is a deplorable fact that most of them bear German names, many talk no other language but German, and the most abominable anarchistic propaganda is printed in German." It went on to deplore "that even enlightened American elements are holding the German nationality responsible for the fantastic and criminal activity of a few fanatics."

Haymarket made waves far beyond Chicago or Illinois. A German Catholic paper in Louisville reacted in the immediate aftermath with a headline in English, "Damned Dutchmen!": "The scandalous and bloody deeds of laborers seduced by the Socialists and Anarchists will bear bitter fruits, above all for the Germans. . . . 'It's all owing to those damned Dutchmen!' And can we brand these speakers and papers as liars and pillory them as Know-Nothings and German haters? No, . . . German agitators and instigators have in their papers and public speeches sown the dragon's seed, which has now sprouted all across the land. . . . It's high time that the Germans of this country take a common stand against these German Socialists and Anarchists."

The country's leading German newspaper, the *New Yorker Staats-Zeitung*, attempted to deflect the blame: "In the conspiracy men like Spies, Schwab and their consorts by no means played such a significant, leading role as the full-blooded Yankee Parsons. . . . Parsons' correspondents, who demanded flyers and murder weapons and called for red revolution . . . are by no means 'Foreigners,' rather they turn out to be mostly Knights of Labor who speak English as their mother tongue and are Parsons' fellow countrymen." Despite such efforts, in the words of the leading authority on the affair, Haymarket "stamped forever the image of the anarchists as wild-eyed, shaggy-haired, foreign-born, bomb-throwing maniacs."

The Haymarket Affair dealt a serious blow to the eight-hour workday movement, and the Knights of Labor were discredited by it even though they were uninvolved, and their leader, Terence Powderly, distanced himself from the cause of the condemned. In Detroit, union membership reached its peak in 1886 at more than 20 percent of the work force; the next year it barely surpassed 8 percent. Thereafter, the most successful labor organizations were pragmatic craft unions of skilled workers (many of them German) under the umbrella of the American Federation of Labor (AFL).

Just as the Germans held their own with the Irish at the mayoral level but elected far fewer members of Congress, Germans played leadership roles mostly at the local level of labor organizations rather than at the national level. A study of late-nineteenth-century labor leaders found only five out of seventy-eight who were German, and only seven German Americans plus one immigrant compatriot out of 150 leaders in the early twentieth century. But there were two outstanding national leaders with German connections, Eugene Victor Debs and Walter Reuther. In the case of Debs, these connections are not immediately apparent. He was born in Indiana the son of Alsatian immigrants. Although named after two progressive French novelists, Debs was also brought up in the German radical tradition, and he spoke both languages. He came up through the Brotherhood of Locomotive Firemen, but rather than concentrate on the aristocracy of labor like the AFL, he went on to organize workers of various skills into the American Railway Union, an industry-wide association numbering 150,000. It was only while serving a jail sentence for his role in the 1894 Pullman Strike that he read *Das Kapital*. He went on to found the Socialist Party of America and ran for president five times, once from prison when sentenced for his opposition to World War I.

Another German-American labor leader nurtured in the Debsian brand of socialism was Walter Reuther, president of the United Auto Workers from 1946 until his death in 1970. He was born in Wheeling, West Virginia, in 1907, nine years after his parents had emigrated from Germany. He was brought up in the parental traditions of Lutheranism and socialism; at age eleven, his father had taken him along on a visit to Eugene Debs in prison. Walter was fired from a job at Ford Motors for supporting Socialist presidential candidate Norman Thomas in 1932. After seeing the New Deal in action, he became a liberal Democrat. Once, in response to accusations of a General Motors official, Reuther retorted, "If fighting for a more equal and equitable distribution of the wealth of this country is socialistic, I stand guilty of being a Socialist." In his first successful strike negotiations in 1936, Reuther also won equal pay for equal work by women. He was a lifelong supporter of civil rights, participating in several marches with Martin Luther King Jr. and helping to organize the rally at the Washington Monument where King delivered his "I Have a Dream" speech.

American developments were so different from those in Europe that in 1906 the German social scientist Werner Sombart posed the question, "Why is there no Socialism in the United States?" His metaphorical answer was, "On the reefs of roast beef and apple pie, socialist utopias of all kinds have foundered." In other words, the American standard of living provided the answer, although Sombart also explored other features of the political system. What he was really asking was why there was no Marxist-influenced labor party in the United States. But he spoke a bit too soon and posed his question a bit too absolutely. What little American socialism there was often involved Germans, especially in Wisconsin where the movement achieved its greatest success.

Among some fifty Socialist mayors elected in U. S. cities, nine were of German origins, most of them second generation, but including two who were immigrants. Like other Socialists, most were elected before World War I in small cities (Sheboygan and Manitowoc, Wisconsin) or industrial suburbs (Murray, Utah; Edgewater, Colorado; Adamston, West Virginia). But Pasadena, California, also elected a German Socialist in 1911. In 1920, voters in Davenport, Iowa, rejecting the Democratic war record and Republican suppression of foreign languages and support for prohibition, elected a Socialist mayor. This was part of a larger pattern. Where Republicans at the state level were as intolerant of Germans as the Wilson administration at the national level, even conservative Catholics and Lutherans sometimes voted for leftist third parties like Wisconsin Socialists and the Minnesota Farmer-Labor Party. Wisconsin's antiwar Senator Robert La Follette attracted considerable German support in his 1924 Progressive Party presidential campaign, even as far away as Texas.

New Braunfels and the surrounding county weighed in at 74 percent for La Follette, higher than any county in his native Wisconsin.

Texas even had a Socialist movement that polled a respectable twenty-five thousand votes in the 1912 presidential election, nearly tied for second place with the Republican and Progressive tickets. In the 1912 and 1914 gubernatorial races, Socialists even outpolled Republicans. With the Populist roots of Texas Socialism, most of its supporters were probably Anglos. But the descendants of Silesian Forty-Eighter Otto Meitzen upheld his radical tradition for the next two generations. His son, E. O. Meitzen, published the Hallettsville socialist weekly, *The Rebel*, from 1911 on, supplemented two years later by a German paper, *Habt Acht* (Take Heed!). By 1917, when *The Rebel* was shut down by government order, it had achieved a statewide circulation of some twenty-three thousand. His grandson E. R. Meitzen was the Socialist candidate for governor in 1914, finishing in second place with nearly 12 percent of the vote. But World War I dealt a blow to the movement.

One major city stood out in its support of socialism and remained undaunted by the war: Milwaukee. Two years before Sombart posed his famous question, nine Socialists were elected as aldermen, and in 1910, one of them, Emil Seidel, was elected mayor, the first Socialist to preside over a major U. S. city. Although native born, Seidel had worked for six years in Berlin and was exposed to the socialist movement there. Socialists also won several other citywide races along with twenty-one of thirty-five seats on the Milwaukee city council and sent immigrant Victor Berger to his first of six terms in Congress. Seidel was defeated two years later when the two major parties joined forces against him, but he was the vice-presidential nominee on the Socialist ticket of Eugene Debs in 1912, which attracted over nine hundred thousand popular votes, 6 percent of the total, the party's best showing ever. Ironically, Socialists in German Milwaukee achieved their greatest success under an Irish-Canadian standard bearer, Daniel Webster Hoan, who was elected a total of seven times and served for twenty-four years beginning in 1916. Tellingly, he claimed German ancestry on his mother's side, a convenient fiction for which there is no evidence in the census. But he delivered what German Milwaukee desired.

This urban socialism was evolutionary rather than revolutionary, concentrating on services to working-class constituents, a pragmatic approach that its more ideological critics derided as "sewer socialism." Its program was summed up by Socialist editor and Congressman Victor Berger, who warned his readers "not to be caught by the current drivel about 'business methods' and 'business principles.' A government is not a personal contrivance like a business. It should not be administered from the point of view of economy as businessmen understand the term. It should bring about the greatest good to all regardless of expense, as long as there is a way to make ends meet." These pragmatic, utilitarian Socialists emphasized services to their working-class constituency—matters such as public health, factory safety, housing inspection, parks and recreation, and regulation or municipal ownership of public utilities. A book on public health reform in Milwaukee during this era bears the title, *The Healthiest City*. While Socialists continued to hold the mayoralty, they lost their majority on the city council by 1920 and were down to six of twenty-five seats by 1928. But even Hoan's defeat in 1940 was not the end of Milwaukee socialism.

Serving three terms from 1948 to 1960, Frank P. Zeidler was the last Socialist mayor of Milwaukee, and during his last term, the sole Socialist officeholder in the United States, although he ran as the Socialist Party's candidate for president in 1976. Following in the city's Socialist tradition, he promoted urban renewal and public housing, improved public services, and fought to preserve public transportation. A vocal supporter of civil rights, Zeidler was attacked in his last election campaign with false charges that he was recruiting in the South for new Black residents. A third-generation ethnic from a working-class German Lutheran family, Zeidler remained active in the church and was a member of the Milwaukee Turners and two German singing societies. A student of history, he traced the roots of Wisconsin liberalism to the heritage of the Forty-Eighters. When he left office for health reasons at the end of his term in 1960, Sombart's assertion of "no socialism in the United States" finally, after more than half a century, became literally (if temporarily) true, but Zeidler remained a beloved public intellectual until his death in 2006.

11

The German-American Experience
in World War I

THE LYNCHING OF GERMAN IMMIGRANT Robert Prager in Collinsville, Illinois, looms large in the image of the World War I experience of German Americans. It was unquestionably a flagrant injustice, even by the standards of "unwritten law," which the defense claimed when the lynchers were unsuccessfully prosecuted. This hapless coal miner, who was strung up by a drunken mob after having been forced to kiss the flag, had actually attempted to enlist in the U. S. Navy but was rejected because of a glass eye. In accordance with his last request, he was buried with an American flag. However, it would be a mistake to see this case as purely a matter of *ethnic* victimization. As much as Prager's ethnicity, his socialist sympathies had made him a target. But it was not until the twenty-first century that anyone remarked upon the obvious German ethnicity of the lynch mob's ringleader Joseph Riegel, and as many as a dozen of his followers. A native of the Pennsylvania coal country, Riegel could read and understand German well enough to "partly translate" Prager's farewell note to his parents. So rather than a tidy case of victimization, we are confronted here with a messy case of opportunism and scapegoating among mob members, and indifference on the part of various officials and authorities in the heavily German town of Collinsville. "Da waren Deutsche auch dabei" ("here too Germans were involved": the title of a celebratory poem) takes on an entirely new meaning in the light of this information.

More typical of the German-American experience in this era than Prager's fate was the silent injustice suffered by Albert H. Pohlman and

George F. Riebling, both from the Nebraska hamlet then known as Germantown. When the United States entered the Great War, local leaders decided their town needed to replace this "unpatriotic" name. And what could be more patriotic than to rename it after the first local boy who gave his life for his country? Pohlman was wounded in battle on July 26, 1918, and died of his wounds on August 4. Riebling suffered a similar fate the next month. But because of their German names and ancestry, their sacrifice went unrecognized. Instead, the town was renamed after a hapless doughboy who caught typhoid fever on the ship over and died in an army hospital on August 18, 1918, never having laid eyes on the enemy, much less come under fire. What set him apart from the others was his Anglo surname, Raymond Garland. Ironically, his mother was a German immigrant, but that was not apparent from his name.

Pohlman and Riebling are symptomatic of the unappreciated loyalty of most German Americans during World War I. But even the fates of various "Germantowns" around the United States are indicative of a wide range of ethnic experiences. Texas followed the same principle as Nebraska but actually applied it fairly, bringing little "improvement." The town was renamed after Paul Schroeder, a second-generation German who paid the ultimate sacrifice. Two Germantowns did receive new names with clearly anti-German overtones. The California hamlet was transformed into Artois, (reportedly after the old name nearly caused a riot when a troop train stopped there), commemorating a French region on the Western Front. The German Catholic community in Kansas was renamed Mercier after the Belgian cardinal who led resistance to German occupation. But across the country, in Pennsylvania, Maryland, Indiana, Tennessee, Wisconsin, and ironically in Illinois just thirty miles east of where Prager was lynched, other Germantowns survived the war unscathed.

This chapter offers an overview of both the attitudes and actions of German Americans in the Great War and the effects of the war on this ethnic group and its language and culture. It is evident that German Americans were misunderstood both by their former countrymen back in the Fatherland and by their fellow Americans. Germans often assumed that because German Americans (comprising less than 11 percent of the 1900 U. S. population, even including the second generation), were unable to prevent Woodrow Wilson's reelection or American entry into World War I, it meant they had quickly shed their ethnicity and immersed themselves in the melting pot, abandoning the German language and culture. Anglo-Americans, on the other hand, often confused these cultural loyalties or mere language preservation with political loyalty to the fatherland. In fact, as a Missouri "German Preacher" touted for "Show[ing] up Kaiserism" remarked, "With by far the most Americans of German origin the language has no political significance."

This is nicely illustrated by an incident related to me by my grandfather, the grandchild of German immigrants on all sides of his family. A subscription agent for the *Westliche Post*, the German-language paper of St. Louis, making his rounds in the rural hinterlands of St. Charles County, declared, "Wenn es Gerechtigkeit gibt, gewinnen die Deutschen": If there is any justice, the Germans will win. Grandpa shot back: "Wenn es Gerechtigkeit gibt, gewinnen die Amerikaner," which should need no translation. Married at the time with his wife expecting, he waited until he was drafted to join the army, and was mustered in on his first wedding anniversary in April 1918. He never made it to France, although a couple of Grandma's letters did. Upon news of the armistice, the troop ship he was supposed to be on turned around midocean; Grandpa himself had been taken off the troop train and hospitalized in Chattanooga with a dangerous case of influenza. But he was just as proud of his service as if he had been in the front line of trenches.

His army experience also illustrates the innocence with which some German Americans approached the language issue. When he went off for his basic training in Texas, his Missouri-born mother wrote him her first letter in German! Of course, he quickly advised her to switch languages.

His caution may have been unnecessary. Some U. S. soldiers not only received letters in German, but also wrote home from the army in that language. The *Seguiner Zeitung* of August 15, 1918, published German letters from two local boys serving in France, both of them third-generation Texans, and there is evidence of German letters written by doughboys from four other states. In May 1918, the bilingual parish newsletter of a St. Charles, Missouri, Lutheran church included excerpts from letters of members who were serving in the military, and one of the fifteen letters was *auf Deutsch*, apparently written from training camp. The Jefferson City *Missouri Volksfreund* published an entire letter that a soldier from nearby Westphalia sent home from France. He writes in typical immigrant German, including a few English nouns like farmer, parlor, or town, and quotes a bit of soldier doggerel, "First we ride, then we float, and then we get—the Kaiser's goat," showing his command of English. Since his name and that of his parents are listed, it was possible to identify him in the census. Not only had he been born in Missouri, so had both of his parents, and his grandparents had all immigrated as children, indicative of a remarkable degree of language persistence among rural Catholic Germans. But language and loyalty were obviously unrelated. At the nearby German Catholic parish of Taos, not ten miles from the Missouri state capitol, a monument in its cemetery consecrates the ultimate sacrifice of three local boys with the words, "Herr gib Ihnen die ewige Ruhe": ("Lord grant them eternal rest"). Similar gravestones, some of them entirely in German, commemorate ethnic soldiers from Texas to Wisconsin who died in World War I.

So perhaps my grandpa was overly cautious, and Great Grandma's naiveté can be excused. Hers was in any case surpassed by that of the Germans in the Texas town of Fayetteville. In February 1918, patriotic Americans were shocked and outraged to see what appeared to be a smoking gun of disloyalty: a German flag flying in front of the Germania lodge's hall. Surprisingly, no one torched the building, but eleven members, including the town mayor, were arrested. But it turned out that there was a rather innocent explanation: the lodge had traditionally flown the German flag on any day that an event was planned at the hall, serving notice in this era before radio and television. The event they were announcing that day was not just harmless but patriotic: an American Red Cross rally. The club did agree, however, to use the Stars and Stripes rather than the German flag in announcing future events.

The premier German-American statesman of the Civil War era, Carl Schurz, had always maintained that an immigrant's love for his native and adopted countries were no more incompatible than the love for mother and wife: "Those who would meanly and coldly forget their old mother could not be expected to be faithful to their young bride." The *Omaha Bee* put it even more succinctly: "Germania our Mother, Columbia our Bride." But as many a rueful husband can relate, this holds true only so long as the two women remain on speaking terms. Schurz, who died in 1906, was mercifully spared having to witness the falling out between the two loves of his life; some 2.5 million other German immigrants were not so fortunate. Given a choice, most German Americans would no doubt have preferred to see America remain neutral in the Great War. Many were critical of American munitions exports that went almost exclusively to the Allies. In a bitter parody of Matthew's Christmas Gospel, the *Lutherbote für Texas* in August 1915 prophesied "but thou Bethlehem, Pennsylvania . . . though thou be little among the cities in America, yet out of thee shall come forth the tools of destruction, through which thousands in Europe will be condemned to death." But when forced to choose between the old homeland and the new, the great bulk of them would have agreed with the *Cincinnati Freie Presse*: "We stand and fall with the land of our choice."

Granted, in surviving immigrant letters it is very rare to find anyone writing back to the Old Country in the early years of the war with criticisms of Germany. Once the United States entered the conflict, very few letters were exchanged because communications with Germany were virtually cut off. But among a dozen people writing back to the Rhineland when they reestablished communications in 1919 or the early 1920s, only one took the position that "the Kaiser now has what he really deserved, managed to become enemies with everyone, couldn't get along with anyone." Most writers were sympathetic with Germany and above all the economic plight of its people. Several correspondents expressed mistrust of the English-language press. With one exception, all who commented on the subject were resentful of Prohibition, and several remarked on the suppression and decline of the German language. After the war, several writers had contributed to charity drives for German relief efforts. There were frequent references to the military service of family members in America, including a few who had visited relatives or ancestral homes in the occupied Rhineland. However, the crucial difference is not between people writing letters sympathetic to Germany as opposed to those writing critically; it's the difference between people still writing to relatives, and those who no longer maintained ties with the Old Country. One striking feature of this correspondence is that it rarely continued into the second, American-born generation. A study of transatlantic correspondence of the war era, drawing upon the largest German immigrant letter collection extant, analyzed 274 letters from seventy-nine different writers, only six of whom, writing a total of twelve letters, were of the second generation. In a typical collection, there is only a single letter from one of the children, announcing the death of the parent who had often been writing home for decades. By the war's outbreak, the second generation outnumbered actual immigrants by more than two to one, so one of the big questions is how much of their parents' language and culture had been passed on to them.

It is sometimes pointed out that the commanding general of the American Expeditionary Force, John Pershing, was of Germanic extraction. However, with respect to language and culture, that was inconsequential, especially compared to someone like General Dwight Eisenhower, whose grandfather had preached in German, not to mention Admiral Chester Nimitz, who was brought up bilingually and probably had German as his first language. Black Jack's Pfoerschin ancestors had emigrated from Alsace in 1724, and he had no association with the German language nor with any transplanted denomination. His mother had southern Anglo roots, and in his later life he was Episcopalian. But there were German Americans from the heart of the ethnic community who distinguished themselves at lower levels of the U. S. Army.

The first Texas officer killed in World War I was a Fredericksburger of German heritage, Louis Jordan. Having grown up on a ranch, he taught school briefly before winning a scholarship to the University of Texas, where he was the captain of the football team and its first All-American. Among the first to volunteer at war's outset, Jordan was commissioned a 1st Lieutenant in August 1917, arrived in France in early October, and was the first man in his regiment killed in action on March 5, 1918. His grandparents were all German immigrants, and like almost everyone in Fredericksburg back then, he was no doubt bilingual. A football story mentions him spurring his teammates on "with a few cuss words in German and some in English." One sports writer remarked, "it is ironic that a young man so proud of his German heritage" would die from a German shell. Fredericksburg, too, was proud of its son; it named its American Legion post after him, and when a new football stadium was built at Austin in 1924, citizens erected a flagpole there in his honor.

Similarly from Quincy and surrounding Adams County, Illinois, the first men to give their lives for their country were of German background. Oscar Vollrath was the son of a prosperous farmer in rural Adams County and a graduate of a German Methodist college, Central Wesleyan, in Warrenton, Missouri. He enlisted in the National Guard in March 1917 even before the U. S. declaration of war, then switched to the Marines, where he became a corporal and squad leader. He died in an artillery bombardment at Chateau Thierry on June 9, 1918. That same week, the first native of Quincy had made the ultimate sacrifice, another Marine named Fred Schulte. He enlisted from Detroit at the outbreak of war, but had grown up and spent most of his life in Quincy. Almost one-third of this heavily German town, ten thousand of some thirty-five thousand, turned out at a demonstration the next month to support the war and commemorate the two men, much as Fredericksburg, Texas, would do for Jordan after the war.

Characteristic of the impersonal, industrial nature of the Great War, all three of these men, Jordan, Vollrath, and Schulte, died from artillery fire in the trenches, not in any dramatic no-man's-land heroics. Another commonality of the three is that all were of unmixed German ancestry and probably bilingual, but all were of the third generation in America, the grandchildren of immigrants. Each had been employed in a white-collar occupation, a further indication of their entry into the American mainstream. Before attempting to generalize from these three cases, one needs to take a more systematic look at military participation rates of German Americans, particularly of the second generation who might have closer ties to the Old Country, especially if their parents were still alive.

The 1930 Census provided a direct measure of military service, and a representative nationwide 1:100 public use sample allows one to analyze ethnic influences on service rates. Looking at men born in the years 1887 through 1900 to immigrant parents (immigrants themselves were exempted from the duty to fight their former homeland), it is evident that second-generation Germans hardly stood out from their fellow Americans in their rate of military service. Despite the Czechoslovakian and Polish nationalist causes, the subject nationalities of the Central Powers served at rates only slightly higher than Germans. Old Stock Americans whose fathers were native born served at only average rates. Whatever their feelings about the Irish nationalist cause or their resentment of British domination, the sons of Erin flocked in unrivaled numbers to the American banner. Although Italy abandoned its neutrality and joined the Allied coalition before the United States, Italian Americans had the lowest service rate of any major ethnic groups in World War I.

There are a number of background factors that influenced a man's likelihood of service regardless of ethnicity. After peace had returned, an Illinois German immigrant reported back to the home folks: "My boys didn't have to go to war, because they were farmers, and each one had a family." As it turns out, he hit upon two of the most influential factors affecting military service. Men who were single in 1917 served at rates thirty points higher than men who were married. Those living on farms had service rates not even two-thirds that of urban dwellers (since agricultural employment was one of the main grounds for draft deferment). The heavy presence of Germans in the farm population, especially compared to a group such as the Poles, makes their overall service rate (more than 90 percent of the national average) all the more impressive.

The 1980 census with its ancestry question allows one more look at military participation, also going beyond the second generation, at least for the World War I veterans who survived to age eighty or beyond. Once again, people of German origins are in the middle of the pack; their overall service rate is almost exactly at the American average, and just 1.2 points below that for whites only. As in the earlier data, Irish had the highest service rates, and men of English and French ancestry also surpassed Germans. But Germans were well ahead of the two other ancestry groups that are separately tallied. Italians had the lowest rates, and men of Polish background also ranked well behind German Americans despite any nationalist motives Poles may have had for serving, or Germans for slacking. So regardless of one's definition of ethnicity, the service rates of German Americans in World War I were only slightly lower than the national average.

There are other measures of war support that one can examine, also in the civilian population. One is the purchase of Liberty Bonds. My native county of St. Charles in the heart of the German belt was second in all Missouri in per-capita subscriptions for the Third Liberty Loan campaign, earning it a place on a propaganda flyer that was dropped behind enemy lines. The banner town in Missouri was Treloar in a heavily German part of neighboring Warren County, where subscribers pledged nearly $200 each. Another German-American record setter was Pioneer Flour Company of San Antonio, then in the second generation of the Guenther family, which bought $50,000 worth of Liberty Bonds, the most of anyone citywide. However, it is difficult to discern how much of such support was voluntary or coerced. In Guenthers' case, support for the cause was probably heartfelt. By the eve of World War I, one of Pioneer's best customers was the U. S. Army at nearby Ft. Sam Houston, which bought a half-million pounds of their flour. But in some instances, it appears that German Americans felt they were paying protection money by purchasing Liberty Bonds.

Beyond the pressure to support the war financially, there were clearly other forms of intimidation and injustice present in both American civilian and military policy. The military draft made few provisions for conscientious objection, and the right of dissent was severely curtailed by the Espionage Act of 1917 and the Sedition Act of 1918. The two groups of German Americans who suffered most were at the opposite ends of the ideological spectrum: on the one hand, members of separatist sects such as the Amish, Mennonites, and Hutterites who practiced a religiously based pacifism; on the other hand, socialists and other leftists, such as members of the radical Industrial Workers of the World, who supported U. S. neutrality in the belief that war benefitted only the capitalist class. Among those charged under the Espionage Act was Victor Berger, an Austrian Jewish immigrant from Milwaukee with a large German constituency who became the first Socialist elected to Congress in 1910, but was twice denied his seat during and after the war until his antiwar conviction was overturned by the courts. Four Hutterite conscientious objectors were subjected to imprisonment and abuse in Alcatraz (torture would hardly be too strong a word), which led to the death of two of them. Many of their brethren, along with more than 1,500 Mennonites, took refuge in Canada, which granted full military exemptions on religious grounds despite having borne the brunt of military service from the war's outset.

There were some 6,300 "enemy aliens," the bulk of them Germans, interned by U. S. authorities on the basis of the 1798 Alien Enemy Act, primarily at Fort Oglethorpe, Georgia, and Fort Douglas, Utah. The majority, however, were not immigrants, but crews of German naval and merchant ships that were stranded in American territory when they took refuge from the British navy in American harbors. Only some 2,300 genuine immigrants or sojourners were interned as "security risks," about one percent of the quarter-million male German citizens above the age of fourteen residing in the United States at the time (the great majority of whom had been present the requisite five years to qualify for naturalization if they had so chosen). The U. S. policy toward enemy aliens was extremely mild compared to the practice of Germany, France, Britain, or even a country equally distant from the theaters of war, Australia, which interned naturalized Germans and even some of the second generation. Although American authorities undertook internment only on the basis of individual hearings rather than collective guilt, there is ample evidence of their overzealousness in the simple fact that, despite the aspersions cast upon them, only about half of those interned agreed to be repatriated to Germany—many of them reluctantly, simply to be released from internment.

However, many ethnic enthusiasts, and some academics as well, have taken this persecution narrative too far. Even academics can be very good at detecting German names among the victims of persecution, but rather myopic in spotting them among the perpetrators. Among those most often cited for inciting the anti-German hysteria during these years was one Gustavus Ohlinger, who authored a book warning of *The German Conspiracy in American Education*. Although his name suggests Scandinavian or German roots, it turns out the author was born in China, the son of Methodist missionaries Franklin Ohlinger and Bertha nee Schweinfurth. The 1910 census, when they resided together, reveals that his mother was born in Michigan of two German immigrant parents; his father, although old stock, had Pennsylvania roots that were almost certainly German. In fact, there is good evidence that Gustavus still knew the language. And he was just one of many German Americans who enthusiastically supported the war.

The experiences of German Americans during the conflict also varied considerably from state to state. Where there were only a scattered few, they were often overlooked; if they were numerous enough, it was politically dangerous to trifle with them. In fact, there was one rare instance, in a tiny, heavily German community of Scheding in the Nebraska Sandhills, where a government sympathizer was stripped and literally shellacked by a pro-German mob. But states that fell into the mid-range of German concentration saw the most serious repression. Missouri may represent a best-case scenario. It had a sizeable German community, but rather few recent immigrants. The state's Germans identified with their adopted country, and remembering their Civil War record, often considered themselves better Americans than the Anglo-Americans who were whistling Dixie when Germans acted decisively to keep the state within the Union. Moreover, with Germans divided in their political loyalties, neither of the two major parties could risk alienating them. Finally, the legislature was out of session throughout the war, reducing the temptation for demagoguery on the part of the state's politicians.

Two recent studies of the German experience in Missouri and Texas during World War I both moderate the charges of wholesale German harassment. The Missouri study concludes that "contrary to the experience of German-speakers in Nebraska, South Dakota or Minnesota, few German-Americans in Missouri encountered the violent aspects of what [Fred] Luebke called the 'fierce hatred of everything German' during World War I." And in both cases, among the denunciators of alleged German sympathizers one finds names that are unmistakably German, an ancestry which the census confirms. For example, when one Erwin Walz was forced to kiss the flag in Osage County, Missouri, among his antagonists were men bearing the names Oidtman and Steinmann. Walz's father, an Evangelical pastor, had editorialized in the *Westliche Post* in 1915 that "whoever has a German tongue and a German heart, who embraces German attitudes and custom, is a true patriot."

In January of 1918, the Patriotic Speakers' Bureau of the Missouri Council on Defense even launched a branch known as the German Speakers' Bureau, to crusade for the war effort in the German language. If any other state attempted this, it has remained a well-kept secret, although Missouri's effort was abandoned after six months because of increasing hysteria about the language issue. Reportedly, sixteen German speakers were recruited (among some two hundred Patriotic Speakers statewide), most of them born abroad to the extent they can be identified. Heading up the effort was Max F. Meyer, a University of Missouri psychology professor who had immigrated in his early twenties. St. Louis clothing manufacturer Rudolph Schmitz, who had arrived at age eighteen, was solicited for a speech in Osage County. Music teacher Victor Lichtenstein, born in St. Louis of Hungarian Jewish parents, had no doubt sharpened his language skills studying in Europe, but he begged off the quixotic task that a clueless Barton County official was proposing: to persuade an Amish congregation to switch to English. At least two of Meyer's crew were Lutheran ministers, Budapest-born Joseph

Frenz, who immigrated in 1900 at age nine, and Hermann Wallner, who had arrived from Germany in 1872 as a small child. Although not part of this official effort, two sons of "founding fathers" of Missouri German Protestantism weighed in on war and language issues. Rev. Ferdinand G. Walther reported to his county defense chairman that his Brunswick Lutheran congregation had been using English every other week for over six years, though he added in slightly accented English, "I hope not that I have to give up German preaching entirely." Higginsville Evangelical pastor N. P. Rieger had his entire sermon published locally and reprinted by the Kansas City *Star Journal* under the headline, "German Preacher Shows up Kaiserism," an address he had also given the previous week in German.

Whether part of the German Speakers campaign or not, a young Jefferson City woman named Mathilde Dallmeyer earned the nickname of "Joan of Arc of Missouri" for her support of the war effort. As both her names suggest, she was of German heritage. Her father had immigrated at age fourteen in 1871 and become a prominent capital city merchant; her mother was born in Missouri to a pioneer German family. Matilda's rousing speech in April 1918 at Hermann, the most German town in Missouri, raised over $6,000 in War Saving Stamp sales and nearly double that in pledges. It is evident from her biography that she moved well beyond ethnic circles. Active in many civic organizations, she was an ardent suffragette, something often frowned upon by German Americans, and attended the first Republican National Convention to which women were admitted in 1919. She subsequently married Frank Shelden, a prominent Kansas City dentist, tennis star, and city council member. Although brought up in the German Evangelical Church where her father was the congregation president during the war, in her married life she was a Presbyterian.

In Texas, one finds similar examples of divisions within the ethnic community, and as in Dallmeyer's case, social class came into play. Brenham was the seat of a county with more Germans than anywhere in the state besides San Antonio and Houston. In June 1918, its German weekly *Texas Volksbote* published a list of eighty-three persons, representing the cream of the town's business community, who publicly distanced themselves from the antiwar American Party. Soon thereafter the statement was carried by the English paper as well, and a few days later the German paper ceased publication. Voting returns show much stronger support for the American Party in the rural parts of the county than in Brenham.

In states such as Iowa, Montana, and Minnesota, conditions were much harsher, but here too, Germans were not the only ones subjected to pressure, nor were they all on the same side of the war issue. The Iowa governor's 1918 "Babel Proclamation" banned not only German but all foreign languages from schools and public places, and Chicago took similar measures. Nearly one thousand complaints against Germans were made to the Minnesota Commission of Public Safety during the war, but this was only 56 percent of the total. Moreover, some of these complaints were raised by fellow Germans. A Carver County Lutheran pastor was forced to resign after berating his parishioners for failing to learn English after thirty or forty years in America. A Le Sueur County jeweler wrote to the Commission, "I am a German born, like the German people[,] but hate the German government." New Ulm, Minnesota, founded as a German colony, was the site of what has been described as the only draft riot in World War I. In fact, it was a peaceful rally of some five to ten thousand people, supporting, among other things, a national referendum on the war, but it led to the suspension of three town officials by the Commission.

Montana was among the most intolerant of any of the states; in 2006, its governor saw cause to issue an official posthumous apology to seventy-eight people fined or imprisoned on allegations of sedition during the war. All except three had been charged merely on the basis of alleged verbal statements, often made while drunk. But here too, not only Germans were singled out; of forty-one people imprisoned, only nine were from Germany and another five from Austria, but there were eight other nationalities among the incarcerated, along with eighteen U. S. natives, few of them with German names. Association with the radical labor organization Industrial Workers of the World was more of a common characteristic of those prosecuted.

A glaring absurdity often cited in the campaign against the German language was the attempt to replace the word "sauerkraut" with "liberty cabbage." However, it appears that this was an initiative by the food industry to combat falling sales due to consumer avoidance. Reportedly, the price had fallen from $45 to $50 per barrel to a mere $14 because of lagging demand. But one seldom encounters the new name in any primary sources, so it seems unlikely that it ever caught on any more than "freedom fries" did recently. A full-text search of the St. Louis *Post Dispatch* for 1918 produces only eight hits for "liberty cabbage," some of them derisive, but thirty-one for "sauerkraut." Although Chicago stands out in its hostility to things German, there too, the *Chicago Tribune* contains thirty-one mentions of sauerkraut during the last year of the Great War, but only three of liberty cabbage. In fact, a nationwide search of digitized English-language newspapers in the Library of Congress "Chronicling America" database reveals only eighty-one uses of the word "liberty cabbage," but nearly six hundred for "sauerkraut" and more than three hundred with the spelling "sauer kraut," giving the traditional Germanic name an eleven-to-one advantage. So while there may have been a temporary aversion to the food, the name was never endangered.

Another issue that is often exaggerated is the renaming of streets with German names. Any time one encounters a Pershing Road or Avenue in the Midwest, it is a good bet that it once had a German name. The one in St. Louis, for example, used to be called Berlin Avenue. However, a recent study looked into this issue more broadly, and found that its prevalence varied widely. Chicago stood out for its hostility to things German, renaming eighty-two of 115 streets with German names, while Cincinnati replaced only a dozen, and Milwaukee and St. Louis even fewer. The difference is explained by the preponderance of Slavic immigrants, subjects of the Dual Monarchy, in Chicago. They also figured prominently in the crusade to end German instruction in the schools of the Windy City. So German street names, like German town names across the country, experienced widely varying fates. In St. Louis, they were even a laughing matter. A letter to the *St. Louis Times*, (an offshoot of the German-language *Westliche Post*), made light of the campaign to abolish German street names, at the same time highlighting the prominence of Germans in city offices: "In place of the objectionable Allemania, Berlin, Carlsbad, Germania, Hamburg, Hannover, Hertling and Unter den Linden, we could have Niederlucke, Otto, Tamme, Fette, Baur, Stockhausen, Rice, Bergman, Schwartz, Kralemann, Udell, Eilers and Schranz"; all, incidentally, drawn from the Board of Aldermen under Mayor Henry Kiel, who was reelected in 1917 by a record margin, the first St. Louis mayor to serve three four-year terms.

The most apparent impact of World War I on private German-American cultural institutions was on the ethnic press. Until their loyalty was certified by the postmaster general, newspapers had to submit translations of all their war-related content to a censor before they received second-class mailing privileges. Permit number one was issued to *Das Wochenblatt*, published out of Austin by William Trenckmann, born in Texas to immigrant parents in 1859. It was his good fortune that Postmaster General Burleson had been his college classmate at Texas A&M. His daughter Clara enlisted in the navy and "fought Germany with her trusty Underwood on Capitol Hill" as she put it. Her father advised her that if she was stricken with influenza and needed help, she should get in touch with Burleson or the local Congressman James Buchanan, "for I can expect of both that they would do something for my daughter." Most were not so lucky or well connected; Socialist editor Victor Berger was not allowed to distribute his *Milwaukee Leader* (successor to his German-language *Vorwärts*) even as first-class mail, though it was in English. A German Socialist daily in Philadelphia suffered the same fate. The Catholic *Nordstern* in St. Cloud, Minnesota, adapted by switching its front-page war news to English on November 1, 1917, but it countered with an image of an American flag and a defiant yet unassailable quote from Carl Schurz: "My country right or wrong: if right to be kept right; if wrong, to be set right." It ran just below the editorial information in every issue until peace was signed in mid-1919. German papers often used the term "fatherland" for the United States, as did the *Warrenton Volksfreund* in its farewell message of April 26, 1918.

Even in the demise of papers such as this Missouri weekly, the war's effect on the ethnic press was not a reversal of fortunes, but merely an acceleration of a decline that had already been underway for two decades. The number of German-language papers in the country had peaked just short of eight hundred in the early 1890s, but the Panic of 1893 and the ensuing depression set off an inexorable downhill slide, with a net loss of some 250 papers before the war even began. America's entry into the Great War plunged the German-American newspaper count to just half its 1914 figure by 1920. At the beginning of the century, total circulation had held up somewhat better than the number of papers might suggest, as subscription lists were often consolidated when a paper bought out its competitor. But during the war, faced with the pressure of public opinion, censorship, translation requirements, postal restrictions, and the loss of advertising revenue, German-American papers lost three-quarters of their prewar subscribers.

The war's impact on language use in German-American churches was considerably less dramatic, as they were less sensitive to public pressure than newspapers, and at least in the short run less driven by profit and loss. Here too, the war merely accelerated a decline that had its beginnings at least a decade before the war's outbreak. Besides the information available from denominational records, the 1906 and 1916 U.S. Census special reports on religious bodies provide a more systematic view of the trends over the decade preceding the U. S. declaration of war. In the first few years of the twentieth century, about half of all church parishes using the German language used it exclusively; by 1916, before the United States had even entered the war, this proportion had fallen below 20 percent. Ten years later in 1926, foreign-language use had declined so much that the census did not bother to tally it. Not surprisingly, there were contrasts among the varying denominations in their German-language loyalty. One Catholic immigrant complained to the home folks in 1920: "The bishops are mostly Irishmen. They are mostly all against German and were also very hostile during the war against us Germans." His experience is reflected in the global figures. The multiethnic nature of the Catholic Church, the prominence of the Irish in its hierarchy, and their frequent indifference or hostility to foreign languages made for a lower level and a sharper drop in German exclusivity than was the case with Protestant denominations that were essentially transplanted from Germany, as the Lutheran and Evangelical synods were. With the two largest denominations transplanted primarily from Germany, Evangelicals were much more liberal than Lutherans theologically, but their language practices were quite similar. By America's entry into the Great War, only about a quarter of their congregations used German exclusively. The small impact of the war on these two denominations becomes even clearer if one looks at annual figures on language use within these two church bodies. Although still high, the use of German had been declining in the Evangelical Church since the beginning of the twentieth century. The only discernible effect of the war was a slight steepening of the downturn between 1917 and 1919. Although comparable figures for Lutherans only begin in 1919, the close parallel of the two lines of decline suggests that their experience, also during the war years, was quite similar to that of the Evangelicals.

The crusade against the German language and culture was most thorough and effective in the educational realm, an area of public life that was clearly subject to government regulation and financing. Largely forgotten in present-day controversies over bilingual education is the degree of public support and funding for German instruction in the half-century before World War I. A 1901 survey found about half a million elementary students receiving German instruction, including nearly a quarter million in public schools. Three rural public grade schools in my native St. Charles County, Missouri, continued to teach German right up to the American entry into World War I. The same held true for the town of Morrison, just a little upstream from Hermann, the most German town in the most German county of Missouri. In fact, the book they were using had a 1915 copyright. In some places German was merely taught as a subject, but in others, including the cities of Cincinnati, Cleveland, Baltimore, and Indianapolis, there were truly bilingual programs, offering what today is called two-way immersion, lasting right down to World War I. In May 1917, writer Booth Tarkington headed up a crusade against German instruction in Indianapolis, considering it to be totally unpatriotic. He was particularly incensed at the singing of the "Star Spangled Banner" *auf Deutsch*. Within a year or two of American entry into the Great War, the German language was practically eliminated from public schools, also at the high school level. On the eve of the war, German was the most important foreign language in the high school curriculum, attracting one of every four students; by 1922, it was down to 0.6 percent, and to the present, it has seldom exceeded 3 percent. Missouri does stand apart in that it did not pass a language law banning German from schools like more than half of all U. S. states, though this may be explained by the simple fact that the legislature was out of session from April 1917 through January 1919 when intolerance was at its peak.

A few more observations from Missouri demonstrate that the language transition proceeded largely independent of the influence of the Great War. It may have been due to the war that the Lutherans in the St. Louis suburb of Black Jack held their first English confirmation class in 1917, though they still had a German class the following week. It had been the custom in the parish for the women to clean the church the week before confirmation, but as the parish history relates, that year they waited a week and cleaned before the German class because "they were not sure the Lord knew English." The war may not have been the only factor promoting the English confirmation; it was held on March 25, two weeks before the United States declared war. Other German congregations had taken similar steps earlier; St. Paul's Evangelical in Creve Coeur introduced a monthly English service in 1906, and by 1923 was alternating English and German every other Sunday. This was rather typical for that denomination. Of sixteen German Evangelical congregations in St. Louis for which information is available, with one or two possible exceptions all had introduced some English by 1914. However, in eight cases where complete transition to English is noted, it took place only after 1930. With the Catholic Church, too, there is evidence of disagreement between the laity and the heavily Irish hierarchy. In 1915, John Cardinal Glennon had banned German sermons and announcements in the churches of his St. Louis Archdiocese, but a benevolent association of laity called the Missouri Catholic Union, meeting at nearby St. Peters in 1920, voted down a resolution to conduct its business exclusively in English, continuing on a bilingual basis as before.

The 1940 census data on mother tongue provides further evidence of language persistence. Less than 30 percent of second-generation Germans nationwide claimed English as their mother tongue. In big cities it was higher, some 37 percent, but among the farm population, all but 16 percent claimed that they grew up with German as their first language. The German language persisted longest in rural Protestant areas. World War I apparently came and went without leaving a trace on language use in the Lutheran congregation of New Melle, Missouri, where my father grew up. He was still confirmed in German in 1927, and when the family moved to the county seat of St. Charles, he was even able to take German in the public high school. The German-language minutes of the nearby Lutheran congregation in Augusta where I grew up showed no indication that the Great War was even going on. There was, however, an amusing incident in 1918 growing out of a bitter dispute between two parishioners over the rerouting of a county road. When a congregational meeting attempted to mediate between the two, one parishioner quoted a county official and apparently continued on in English, only to be called to order by the interjection: "Deutsch!" But language was one thing, patriotism quite another; in 1921, Augusta Lutherans postponed a congregational meeting because many members wanted to attend the funeral of local doughboy Harry Haferkamp at the Evangelical church in town. Finally, in 1935, the Lutherans started keeping the minutes bilingually, but only stopped translating them a few months before Pearl Harbor. At the Lutheran church in Concordia, sixty miles east of Kansas City, English confirmation was not even an option until 1925, and the last pupils were confirmed in German in 1939. Monthly German church services were still being offered there until 1977. So to paraphrase a famous Missourian, rumors of the German language's death from World War I were exaggerated.

The effect of German Americans on the war effort, and the effect of the Great War on German Americans, can be briefly summarized thus: although most would probably have preferred that the United States remain neutral, German Americans served in the U. S. military at rates only slightly lower than the national average, and at higher rates than some ethnic groups that were presumed beneficiaries of a defeat of the Central Powers. And while the war certainly had an impact on the survival of the German language and culture in the United States, this impact was far from universal, and it merely accelerated trends that were already underway well before the fateful shots were fired in Sarajevo or the deadly torpedoes launched against the *Lusitania*.

12

Into the Twilight of Ethnicity

German Americans since World War I

THE INTOLERANCE AND XENOPHOBIA stirred up by World War I persisted to some degree throughout the 1920s, although German Americans were not its only target. Immigration was restricted first by a literacy test in 1917, and then by nationality quota laws enacted in 1921 and 1924. The emotional excesses of the "100 percent Americanism" movement and attacks on "hyphenism" during the war were directed above all at German Americans, but ironically, the immigration quotas of the 1920s left Germans relatively unscathed. It was the "New Immigration" from southern and eastern Europe that was severely restricted. The yearly German quota for most of the decade was 51,227, whereas emigration from Germany had averaged less than thirty-five thousand annually in the first decade of the twentieth century. Nonetheless, it is literally true but misleading to say that the German quota was never filled during the 1920s. There were several years where all visa slots were allocated, although some went unused.

Prohibition was a different story with stronger anti-German overtones. German Americans were almost unanimous in their opposition to Prohibition and managed to fend off the "drys" for a couple of decades. But World War I changed that. Fueled by resentment of German-American brewers, nationwide prohibition was first enacted as a war measure to save grain until the Eighteenth Amendment was ratified in January 1919. Whether Catholic, Lutheran, Evangelical, or freethinking, Germans had absolutely no use for what they called temperance fanatics, and even some German Methodists in Texas enjoyed their homemade wine. German Catholics in Carroll County, Iowa, used three boxcars of sugar a month cooking bootleg whiskey, protected by local authorities. Several Protestant kinfolks of the author were similarly defiant of the Eighteenth Amendment. In one freethinking Latin Farmer stronghold in Texas, the Cat Spring Agricultural Society recorded its beer orders in their minutes right through the 1920s. Of course, they could get by with it because the county sheriff, a welcome guest at their festivities, was himself a Texas German who was reelected every two years through the whole decade. The Agricultural Society was further protected by the fact that it still kept its minutes in German down to 1942.

Apropos language, the "100 percent American" and Ku Klux Klan crusades of the World War I era virtually eliminated German instruction in *public* schools (and that of most other languages as collateral damage), and also brought a new wave of legislative interference with *parochial* schools. A Nebraska law of 1919, and similar measures in Iowa, Ohio, and several other states, forbad instruction in any school, parochial included, in any language except English. And a 1922 Oregon law, passed by referendum with Ku Klux Klan support, in effect outlawed parochial schools entirely by requiring public school attendance for all children aged eight to fifteen. Germans fought back in the courts, and, surprisingly, Lutherans and Catholics managed to cooperate, as they had in the 1890s in defense of their language and parochial schools, and in defeating a 1920 Michigan referendum and another in 1924 to mandate public school attendance. The Nebraska language law was challenged when Robert Meyer, the teacher of a one-room Lutheran grade school, was fined $25 for teaching religion class in the German language—his pupil was reading the story of Jacob's Ladder from a German Bible. Supported by Lutheran officials and an Irish Catholic lawyer, he took his case all the way to the Supreme Court, where the law was overturned along with similar ones in Iowa and Ohio in the 1923 case *Meyer v. Nebraska*. The Oregon law was challenged by Catholics, with Lutheran support, leading to victory in the high court in the 1925 case, *Pierce v. Society of Sisters*, which drew upon the *Meyer* precedent. However, by then most of the damage to foreign-language instruction, driven as it was by multiple factors, was irreversible.

Political means were not the only methods the Klan used to promote its English-only agenda after 1920. In Brenham and rural Washington

County, Texas, Klansmen used anonymous threats, beatings, and tar-and-feathering in an attempt to force churches and other institutions to abandon their use of German. A notice posted on the door of a Lutheran church in Berlin, Texas, just outside Brenham, warned, "The eyes of the unknown hath seen and doth constantly observe those whose hearts are not right. . . . Be 100 per cent American. Speak the English language or move out of this city and county." The loyalty of Texas Germans was vouched for by none other than Colonel Mayfield, the publisher of a Klan weekly in Houston: "The Records show that our soldiers of German descent fought as valiantly overseas as those of families of longer resident [sic] in America. . . . Still, this is America, all America and nothing but America. . . . The people who do not care to speak our native tongue . . . should be driven from it." It demanded in bold headlines to PREACH IN ENGLISH. One of the Brenham Klan's demands was that soldiers' funerals not be conducted in German; it seems that Klansmen could not bear this prima facie evidence that language use and loyalty were unrelated. In neighboring Austin County, a dispute over the use of German at a political rally put on by the Cat Spring Agricultural Society escalated several months later into a shootout on the streets of Sealy, Texas, between Klansmen and Germans that left four people dead (two on each side), one German hospitalized with severe stab wounds, and a Klansman convicted of murder. But even such violence and intimidation could not stamp out the German language. As late as the 1970 census, more than one-third of the whites in Washington County, and more than one-quarter in Austin County, claimed German as their mother tongue.

But local context is important. Ironically, while Texas Germans were being targeted by the Klan, in the northeast, where the presence of the "New Immigration" from eastern and southern Europe was much more pronounced, Protestant German Americans, especially the more prosperous ones, were increasingly identifying themselves as "Old Stock" in order to distance themselves from such newcomers, and were quite at home in nativist circles. In Philadelphia, the rolls of the nativist Patriotic Order of the Sons of America were "peppered with German surnames." Setting themselves up as "real Americans," they argued that if their parents were immigrants, "They are the kind of immigrants we want . . . and in just one generation, all assimilated," whereas "God save us from what we are getting now—close the gates." On the membership rolls of one Klan chapter in Buffalo, a third or more of the names were German, and their presence was especially pronounced in the East Side neighborhoods where Poles were gaining ground in what had previously been a heavily German quarter of the city, which nativists of an earlier era had denounced as being "as little American as the duchy of Hesse Cassel." However, Buffalo Germans were split along confessional lines. Mayor Frank Xavier Schwab, a name that screams German-American Catholicism, accused the KKK of "conducting guerilla warfare against the Catholic church." Waging a bitter campaign against the Klan, he succeeded in reducing it to the point of "utter insignificance" on the way to his landslide reelection in 1925 against a "strong prohibition advocate."

The 1928 presidential race raised the question of whether German Protestants hated Prohibition more than Catholics when the Democrats nominated Al Smith, an Irish New Yorker pledged to repeal the Eighteenth Amendment. Many Anglo Protestants abandoned the Democrats, who lost five Southern states for the first time since Reconstruction. Despite these losses, Smith gained considerable ground in German communities, obviously among German Catholics, who were doubly mobilized on the grounds of both religion and alcohol. But as widespread as Smith's gains were, one suspects that many German Protestants overcame their aversion to Catholicism if they thought it would get them their beer back. This trend was most pronounced in the Upper Midwest, but the German areas of Texas and Missouri, even the two Texas counties where Lutherans outnumbered Catholics or Baptists, also showed gains for Smith as large as in the Cajun parishes of Louisiana.

Although domestic politics continued to dominate in the Depression era, the rise of Hitler also caught the attention of many German Americans. It is revealing to see the reactions to Nazism in two German denominations' religious periodicals, the *Lutheran Witness* of the conservative Missouri Synod and the *Messenger* of the newly consolidated and more liberal Evangelical and Reformed denomination. The Lutheran organ openly praised the Nazi regime in a 1933 article titled "Germany Teaches Us a Lesson," and ran a three-part series on "The New Germany" in 1936. Ironically, the *Lutheran Witness* cast doubt on American reports of antisemitic repression despite the fact that the Berlin Bureau Chief of the Associated Press was himself the son and brother of Missouri Synod pastors, and joked that he had grown up in Milwaukee with English as a second language. Until Pearl Harbor, Missouri Synod publications followed a strict isolationist line. The Evangelical *Messenger* took a strikingly different tone. It even reported on the closing of all Catholic schools in Germany. Following closely the struggles of the Confessing Church and the plight of Pastor Martin Niemoeller, it branded as "patently absurd" the claims of the so-called German Christians that Jesus was an anti-Semite. On this point, at least, there was some agreement: the Lutherans dubbed the German Christians "German Heathen." The stronger Evangelical reaction to Nazism is explained in part by their closer relationship to members of the Confessing Church. While in America, Dietrich Bonhoeffer became friends with Reinhold Niebuhr and remained in contact after his return to Germany, explaining to Niebuhr, who would have arranged for him to stay here, "I have to live through the difficult period of our national history with the Christians in Germany." One suspects, however, that the laity of German Evangelicals was more conservative than its leading clergy, whereas the Missouri Synod laity was more liberal than its clergy, as it had been in the Civil War era.

There was certainly a broad spectrum of opinion on the Catholic side as well. One of the most notorious anti-Semites of the 1930s was the Detroit priest Charles Coughlin, dubbed the "Father of Hate Radio" by one of his biographers. It appears, however, that fellow Irish Americans were among his most devoted followers. He was "sternly rebuked" (as the *Chicago Tribune* put it) by Chicago Cardinal George Mundelein even though his authority did not extend to Detroit. This prominent German American, albeit of the third generation, had made headlines a year earlier in 1937 with a speech ridiculing Hitler as "an alien, an Austrian paperhanger, and a poor one at that I am told."

A systematic study of reactions to the rise of Hitler in the secular German-language press is still lacking, but scattered evidence indicates widespread skepticism. One of the last surviving German papers in Iowa, The *Sioux City Volksfreund*, warned against "The Road to Dictatorship" as early as November 1932, and within two weeks of Hitler's seizure of power in 1933, reported critically on his limits on the press and civil rights. At that time, there were still a half-dozen German newspapers in Texas that weighed in on the subject. Five of the six were rather critical, although they also noted that the United States itself was not immune to antisemitism. Most outspoken among them was W. A. Trenckmann, who had taken a decisive stand in his *Wochenblatt* against German anti-semitism as early as May 1932, and the following January upon Hitler's assumption of power wrote, "The boundary beyond which the consti-tutional government in Germany totally ceases, is thus crossed. The Wochenblattmann will spare himself saying more about this today; it is too painful for him and many others."

However, one of the six Texas papers, the *Taylor Herold*, was quite sympathetic to the Third Reich. But it turns out that its editor, Hans Ackermann, had only arrived in the country in 1924, and in 1943 had his citizenship revoked for swearing a false oath of loyalty. He had invited G. Wilhelm Kunze, a high official and future Bundsführer of the fascist German-American Bund for three visits to Texas to promote the orga-nization, although he managed to attract only eight or nine people to a meeting he called. One was immigrant Fritz Bleidiessel, who (by then a U.S. Army sergeant) testified against Ackermann at the denaturalization hearing.

This incident raises the general issue of the degree of German-American support for the Bund or sympathies for Hitler's Germany. It appears that Ackermann was the kind of person most susceptible to recruitment by the Bund, one-quarter of whose members were immi-grants who were still German citizens. Its strength in the urban north-east, especially the greater New York area, also points in that direction. A Bund rally at Madison Square Garden in February 1939 drew a crowd of more than twenty thousand. One of the main speakers was Kunze, who was born in New Jersey of parents who had immigrated after 1900; his wife was a German immigrant. But according to the Bund's founder, Fritz Kuhn, 40 percent of the Bund activists were not even of German background. American fascists drew support from various ethnic groups including Anglos. One such example was William Dudley Pelley, who formed the Silver Legion, patterned after the Nazi S. A. Brownshirts. He claimed that Lutherans would join his "Silver Shirts" in droves, but *Lutheran Witness* editor Theodore Graebner vigorously refuted him in a January 1934 issue: "This is written to let Mr. Pelley and the public know that Lutheranism thoroughly disowns him and all that he repre-sents." Only a small proportion of German Americans supported U.S. fascists. A German with a son in Hitler's S. A. Brownshirts urged that his immigrant brother "as a true-born German, should promote German culture" in America. But after fifty-three years there, the brother wrote from St. Louis, "I am proud of my German heritage, but American from head to toe."

It does appear that many German Americans tended toward isolationism. Artist Thomas Hart Benton wrote, "Old fashioned isolationist sentiment . . . was rising and particularly in the middle west. So also was a peculiar brand of acquiescence in the rise of Nazi power. As early as 1936 I had seen evidence of this while going around the farm country of Missouri. Old native-born American farmers, of German stock, were by no means shocked by Nazi racialism, nor were a lot of other people without natural German sympathies, in more well-to-do circles." The isolationist strength in the upper Midwest was no doubt due in part to the heavy German presence, but given its prominence in the Dakotas, perhaps even more to Germans from Russia, whose grievances with the Soviet Union were understandable. Nor were Scandinavian Americans immune, Charles Lindbergh being a case in point. But isolationism and antisemitism were passionately and polemically combatted by one German American who is seldom even recognized as such: cartoonist Theodore Geisel, the future Dr. Seuss.

Also prominent in the fight against antisemitism was an influential Catholic who had emigrated from Germany as a six-year-old, New York Senator Robert Wagner. He stood apart from an array of indifferent or hostile political leaders by cosponsoring a 1939 bill that would have bypassed quotas to admit twenty thousand mostly Jewish refugee children from Germany, even if his efforts were in vain. He was not alone; in 1942, a "Christmas Declaration" appeared as a full-page ad in ten major dailies including the *New York Times*, stating that "we Americans of German descent raise our voices in denunciation of the Hitler policy of cold-blooded extermination of the Jews of Europe and against the barbarities committed by the Nazis against all other innocent peoples under their sway." Theologian Reinhold Niebuhr, who had grown up in the German Evangelical Synod was one of the signers, as was Elmer Arndt, the president of the Synod's Eden Seminary. Immigrant Ernest Brennecke, pastor of the prestigious Trinity Lutheran Church in Manhattan, and his Columbia University professor son and namesake, both lent their support. Three members of the Catholic Ritter family of newspaper publishers also signed. But the most prominent, or at least the best known among its fifty signatories was a Catholic named George Hermann Ruth, who included his nickname "Babe" for clarity. The fourth generation of Ruths in America, Babe still spoke German "surprisingly well."

Even loyal German immigrants sometimes encountered suspicion. A former student related her grandfather's experience as a naturalized German immigrant during World War II. He was working at the U.S. Naval Yard in Philadelphia but was dismissed on security grounds when the war broke out. Although he was immediately hired by a civilian contractor and put back to work at his old job for higher pay, he was outraged at the disparagement of his loyalty. He challenged his dismissal in court and (within a year or less) received an apology, reinstatement, and back pay. So much for loyal German Americans. There is considerable evidence that disloyal German Americans were not treated any worse than loyal Japanese Americans with whom they are often compared.

Fewer than eleven thousand of the more than three hundred thousand German citizens living in America at the time were interned. Although American authorities were perhaps overzealous in their internment policies, it was not done indiscriminately, but based on individual hearings. In contrast to the Japanese immigrants who were barred from naturalization on the basis of their race, most German immigrants had the option of naturalization but chose not to exercise it, whether from negligence, preoccupation, or divided loyalties. Two-thirds of interned Japanese were Nisei of American birth and citizenship, whereas no U.S. citizens of German ancestry were interned unless they voluntarily accompanied interned alien parents or spouses. Most egregious was the U.S. policy of pressuring Latin America countries to deport some four thousand of their German residents—even some Jewish refugees from Nazism—for internment in U.S. camps. When one such deportee from Ecuador arrived in Crystal City, Texas, in 1944, an internee warned him: "In this camp we're all Nazis and anyone who doesn't agree, we'll break his skull." As late as January 1944, internees there commemorated the eleventh anniversary of Hitler's seizure of power in their mimeographed camp newspaper, *Die Lager*, and in April of that year celebrated the Fuhrer's birthday with marches and songs. Most parents sent their children to the German school in the camp rather than the American one. But there was probably a generation gap in many of the interned families, and a much greater American loyalty among children than with their parents.

In the author's family, with his grandparents already of the third generation and several Union Army veterans among the first two, there was no trace of ambivalence during World War I or II. The anti-Hitler ditty "Der Fuhrer's Face" was passed down on both sides of the family, on a seventy-eight phonograph record on the paternal side and in sheet music on the maternal side. A more distant cousin-in-law, still fluent in German in the fourth generation, served in army intelligence in the aftermath of the war, using his language skills to conduct interrogations and combat black marketing. Another fourth-generation German speaker from a Catholic community in central Missouri had the unenviable task of informing families they had to vacate their homes to billet U.S. occupation troops. Four decades after arriving in America, one immigrant mother in the Lutheran community of Freistatt, Missouri, still wrote in German to her GI son serving in France, only to learn that he was killed in action the first day he crossed the German border. Of the Texas veterans from Fayette County interviewed in 2015, the majority of those with German names remarked that they had grown up with the language—some of them just noting it in passing, others in greater detail. One claimed to be Polish after being called a "damn Nazi" in training camp, but knowledge of German helped him evade capture in the Battle of the Bulge, and "probably" saved the life of another interviewee. The first American soldier to set foot on German territory was Sgt. Warner Holzinger, who had emigrated from Wurttemberg with his family at age five, selected for a reconnaissance patrol because of his language facility. The real-life GI who inspired the 1998 film "Saving Private Ryan" was actually named "Fritz" Niland, one of four brothers who volunteered in World War II. Their mother was the daughter of German immigrants; her grandson characterized her as a "tough old German lady."

In general, there is little evidence that German Americans had any reluctance to serve in World War II. According to the 1980 census figures, almost two-thirds of the men of German ancestry born between 1906 and 1925 had served. They participated at a rate 97 percent as high as men of English ancestry, and even closer to service rates of Polish Americans. Some of the difference is probably explained by draft exemptions for the farming population, where German Americans were more heavily concentrated than almost any other ethnicity. Also, these figures do not exclude people of the immigrant generation, who could not have been U. S. soldiers if they arrived after the war. Those who arrived before the war are another story entirely.

A highly motivated group of German Americans who contributed more than their share to U.S. military victory were refugees from Nazi Germany, the majority of them Jewish. Some 2,200 of them were "Ritchie Boys," a secret unit trained at Camp Ritchie, Maryland, who proved to be particularly valuable because of their knowledge of the German language and mentality. Especially after D-Day, their interrogation of prisoners and deserters yielded priceless information and tools to spread disinformation and undermine enemy morale.

One of the Ritchie Boys, Lt. Hans Trefousse, put his knowledge of German culture to work at Leipzig in the final days of the war, negotiating for eleven hours with a die-hard German colonel ensconced in the massive Battle of Nations monument with three hundred troops and seventeen American captives, bent on following the Fuhrer's orders never to surrender. As conversant in German literature and culture as his adversary, Trefousse cited Heinrich von Kleist's romantic drama "The Prince of Homburg," in which the hero wins a battle by disobeying orders. He managed to negotiate a surrender, saving hundreds of American and German lives.

Studying on the GI Bill, Trefousse became a history professor combatting another "master race" by restoring the reputation of Radical Republicans, "Lincoln's Vanguard for Racial Justice" as he characterized them in a book title. But he also served as a bridge between U.S. and German academia, helping to strengthen its nascent democracy. He called attention to earlier democratic traditions in Germany, authoring a biography of Forty-Eighter Carl Schurz and organizing an international symposium to commemorate his 150th birthday. Trefousse was just one of many of this refugee generation who played a similar role in re-establishing and promoting intellectual ties between American academia and the democratic elements in Germany.

Just as the negative images of Nazi Germany rubbed off to some extent on German Americans, the reemergence of a democratic West Germany as a Cold War ally tended to reflect positively on the ethnic group in America. The experiences of U.S. soldiers in Germany further contributed to this image and humanized the former enemy. Some fifteen million Americans lived in Germany from 1945 to the end of the century, the great majority of them with military ties. From 1953 to 1991, U.S. troop strength in Germany never fell below two hundred thousand and usually hovered around a quarter million, exposing more than one generation of American men to Germany and its people, sometimes on a very intimate basis. As the result of a campaign in the 1952 Christmas season, 175,000 GIs were invited into German homes. Despite the army's best efforts to discourage fraternization, by 1950 more than fourteen thousand German brides of American soldiers had come to America, numbers that would continue to climb. A few of these courtships involved soldiers who still spoke the German language. More than five thousand such marriages took place each year during the 1950s, despite serious bureaucratic hurdles these couples still faced. The breadth of this exposure is reflected in the 1957 hit song, "Fraulein, Fraulein." It topped the country charts for a month and stayed in the country top forty for an entire year, crossing over into the pop charts as well. That song was of the "girl I left behind" genre, but the German brides who were not left behind functioned for decades as unofficial ambassadors and mediators between the two countries.

Even a quirky little car helped to redefine a German image previously dominated by tanks and terror rockets, the VW Beetle. "Owning a VW is Like Being in Love," *Popular Mechanics* gushed in 1956, when sales were a mere 28,907. By the sixties, they had climbed to hundreds of thousands, and the "Love Bug" even starred in a Disney movie in 1968, a time when annual sales surpassed half a million. If ever there was a symbol of pacifist postwar Germany, it was this modest, unthreatening vehicle favored by the antiwar hippie counterculture.

With some German Americans, the suffering in postwar Germany induced them to reconnect with their heritage and language, and sometimes even with distant relatives. Obviously, postwar relief efforts and the sending of CARE packages mobilized many Americans regardless of ethnic background, but people of German ethnicity tended to be especially responsive, as they had been in the aftermath of World War I. One refugee from Nazi Germany who settled among German Lutherans in Missouri wrote, "Conniving Germans . . . searched maps of America for German place-names, and then sent letters to them begging for aid. In the German town on the Mississippi, such letters were given to the local pastors to deal with, and to the best of my knowledge no supplicant was ever ignored." Some Germans could still turn to distant relatives. An appeal by German Kamphoefners, now migrated from small-town Melle to the industrial Ruhr district, reached my father's Uncle Hermann, the last Kamphoefner in New Melle, and led to numerous care packages and exchanges of letters, before the contact faded again as the German economic miracle gained traction. The family of my mother's aunt and godmother had a similarly extended, cordial exchange with an unrelated German family they had become acquainted with through an address in a CARE package. And in both instances, these families reconnected in the next generation against the background of heritage tourism.

In many rural communities, there were still people with enough command of the German language to carry on a conversation, or even a correspondence. Although the New Melle Lutherans had suspended German services during World War II, they resumed them after the war until 1950. Their daughter congregation in nearby Augusta continued German worship just as long; in fact, the author must have attended some of these monthly services when he was a toddler, but too young to remember. Rev. Robert Kamphoefner, Uncle Hermann's son, dutifully tallied attendance. When he started his pastorate in 1945, German attendance was a respectable ninety-four per service, close behind the 117 for English services. But while the latter held steady and climbed slightly to 123 by 1948, German attendance had declined to a mere forty-four. His departure in 1950 brought an end to German worship.

As transatlantic travel became more affordable in the 1980s, heritage tourism, town partnerships, and school exchanges both profited from and reinforced German-American ethnic consciousness. German women who had immigrated as soldiers' brides often played facilitating roles. One example among many, a German high school exchange with St. Lucas, Iowa, was initiated by a local soldier's wife who reached out to friends who were teaching in Germany. In its thirty-sixth year as of 2018, the exchange program has survived well beyond its founder's lifetime.

Into the 1980s and 1990s, there were still people, especially in rural communities, who although born in America had grown up with the German language. When town partnerships were established between mother and daughter communities, the German visitors were often pleasantly surprised to discover that not only the German language, but even the local dialect, had survived in America. But by the twenty-first century, the ranks of these American-born bilinguals have become increasingly thinned. "When we're gone, it will be," commented two eighty-three-year-old speakers of the Saxon German dialect from the Lutheran settlement in Perry County, Missouri, in 2018. Despite their cultural conservatism, Mennonites in Hutchinson, Kansas, fared no better: in 2017 they announced the "60th & Last Low German Supper & Auction."

Texas is the state where the German language survived longest without being reinforced by separatist religion as with Amish or Mennonites. Only in Texas did the 1940 census find more people with German mother tongue in the third generation and beyond than in the second generation. In that census, there were a mere five German natives in Lee County born in the twentieth century, yet one Lutheran congregation there only introduced regular English services in 1960, and continued with weekly German church services until 1985, when they were reduced to once a month. These monthly German communion services continued until 2007.

Since 2001, the Texas German Dialect Project at the University of Texas has been interviewing and recording native Texans, some of them in the fifth or sixth generation, who grew up with German as their first language. Thus far they have interviewed some 750 people, the majority born before World War II, but including a few from the Baby Boom era, in one instance as late as 1953. But if their descendants have learned German at all, it is the formal language taught in school rather than the Texas German dialect. At the two hundredth anniversary of German settlement of Texas in 2032, there may still be a handful of Texas German speakers left to celebrate. Project linguists estimate that the dialect will be extinct by 2040. Nevertheless, counting from Philadelphia in 1683, the persistence of German language and culture over 350 years in America has been impressive indeed.

A Note on Sources

GENERAL OVERVIEWS

The last person to attempt this daunting task of synthesis was a professor of German who published mostly in history, LaVern J. Rippley, *The German-Americans* (Boston: Twayne Publishers, 1976). A helpful template was furnished by Kathleen Neils Conzen, "Germans," in *Harvard Encyclopedia of American Ethnic Groups*, eds. Stephan Thernstrom, Ann Orlov, and Oscar Handlin (Cambridge, MA: Harvard University Press, 1980). My monograph, *The Westfalians: From Germany to Missouri* (Princeton, NJ: Princeton University Press, 1987), although a transatlantic regional study, includes many side glances at other regions of Germany and the United States. Many of the immigrant letters cited here were published in Walter D. Kamphoefner, Wolfgang Helbich, and Ulrike Sommer, eds., *News From the Land of Freedom: German Immigrants Write Home* (Ithaca, NY: Cornell University Press, 1991). A number of chapters in the anthology edited by Wolfgang Helbich and Walter D. Kamphoefner, *German-American Immigration and Ethnicity in Comparative Perspective* (Madison, WI: Max Kade Institute, 2004), were drawn upon in various chapters. Two eyewitness memoirs quoted frequently in this work were coedited with colleagues of mine: Gert Goebel, *Longer than a Man's Lifetime in Missouri*, ed., with Adolf E. Schroeder, (Columbia: State Historical Society of Missouri, [1877] 2013); and *Preserving German Texan Identity: Reminiscences of William A. Trenckmann, 1859–1935*, ed., with Walter L. Buenger (College Station: Texas A&M University Press, 2019). Also referenced in multiple chapters are Adolf E. Schroeder, ed. and trans., *Hold Dear, as Always: Jette, A German Immigrant Life in Letters* (Columbia: University of Missouri Press, 1988); and Hans L. Trefousse, *Carl Schurz, a Biography* (Knoxville: University of Tennessee Press, 1982). The cartoons cited here were reprinted in Thomas Nast St. Hill, *Thomas Nast: Cartoons and Illustrations* (New York: Dover Pulications, Inc., 1974).

Many of the newspaper citations here were derived from two online databases with full-text search capacity: the WPA translations in the Chicago Foreign Language Press Survey digitized by the Newberry Library, https://flps.newberry.org/; and the Texas Digital Newspaper Collection, which is part of the Portal to Texas History created at the University of North Texas: https://texashistory.unt.edu/explore/collections/TDNP/.

An important resource, not only for manuscript census information on the ancestry and generation of individuals, but also (besides published census returns) for many of the city and county population figures cited here, is Ancestry.com. It is a well-kept secret that searches on Ancestry do not require a name, but can be conducted for exact matches of other characteristics—for example, American-born persons with one Irish and one German parent nationwide. Searches can be further restricted to a specific geographic area—for example, female domestics living in St. Louis who were born in Illinois with a German father.

CHAPTER 1: BEFORE THE GREAT FLOOD:
GERMANS IN COLONIAL AND REVOLUTIONARY AMERICA

This chapter relies heavily on Aaron Fogelman, *Hopeful Journeys: German Immigration, Settlement, and Political Culture in Colonial America, 1717–1775* (Philadelphia: University of Pennsylvania Press, 1996), and the parallel work of Marcus Häberlein, *The Practice of Pluralism: Congregational Life and Religious Diversity in Lancaster, Pennsylvania, 1730–1820* (University Park: Pennsylvania State University Press, 2009). On the beginnings, see Stephanie Grauman Wolf, *Urban Village: Population, Community, and Family Structure in Germantown, Pennsylvania, 1683–1800* (Princeton, NJ: Princeton University Press, 1977). On the language issue, see Hermann Wellenreuther, *Citizens in a Strange Land: A Study of German-American Broadsides and their Meanings for Germans in North America, 1730–1830* (University Park: Pennsylvania State University Press, 2015); and Friederike Baer, *The Trial of Frederick Eberle: Language, Patriotism, and Citizenship in Philadelphia's German Community, 1790 to 1830* (New York: New York University Press, 2008).

A NOTE ON SOURCES

CHAPTER 2: SOURCES AND CAUSES OF
NINETEENTH-CENTURY EMIGRATION

Two important works on the German background are Mack Walker, *Germany and the Emigration, 1816–1885* (Cambridge, MA: Harvard University Press, 1964); and Wolfgang Köllmann and Peter Marschalck, "German Emigration to the United States," *Perspectives in American History* 7 (1973): 499–554. More recent work includes my chapter, "German Migration Research, North, South, and East: Findings, Methods, and Open Questions" and two other chapters drawn from published dissertations available only in German: Axel Lubinski, "Overseas Emigration from Mecklenburg-Strelitz: The Geographic and Social Contexts"; and Uwe Reich, "Emigration from Regierungsbezirk Frankfurt/Oder, 1815–1893," all in Dirk Hoerder and Jörg Nagler, eds., *People in Transit: German Migrations in Comparative Perspective* (Cambridge, MA: Cambridge University Press, 1995): 19–33, 57–78, 79–100. For an analysis of migration selectivity, see Timothy G. Anderson, "On the Pre-Migration Social and Economic Experience of Nineteenth-Century German Immigrants," *Yearbook of German-American Studies* 36 (2001): 91–108. On the effects of inheritance patterns, see Simone A. Wegge, "To Part or Not to Part: Emigration and Inheritance Institutions in Nineteenth-Century Hesse-Cassel," *Explorations in Economic History* 36 (1999): 30–55. For the latest on shipping, see Raymond L. Cohn and Simone A. Wegge, "Overseas Passenger Fares and Emigration from Germany in the Mid-Nineteenth Century," *Social Science History* 41 (2017): 393–413; and Raymond L. Cohn, *Mass Migration under Sail: European Immigration to the Antebellum United States* (New York: Cambridge University Press, 2009).

CHAPTER 3: GERMAN SETTLEMENT PATTERNS
IN NINETEENTH-CENTURY AMERICA

This chapter leans heavily on my article, "Immigrant Epistolary and Epistemology: On the Motivators and Mentality of Nineteenth-Century German Immigrants," *Journal of American Ethnic History* 28 (2009): 34–54; supplemented by "Uprooted or Transplanted? Reflections on Patterns of German Immigration to Missouri," *Missouri Historical Review*

103 (2009): 71–89. It also draws upon my chapter, "Paths of Urbanization: St. Louis in 1860," and others in the anthology by Eberhard Reich-
mann, LaVern J. Rippley, and Jörg Nagler, eds., *Emigration and Settlement Patterns of German Communities in North America* (Indianapolis,
IN: Max Kade German-American Center, 1995): 258–72. For contrasting views on the chain migration paradigm, see Robert W. Frizzell,
"Migration Chains to Illinois: The Evidence from German-American
Church Records," *Journal of American Ethnic History* 7 (1987): 59–73; and
Jochen Krebber, "Creed, Class, and Skills: Three Structural Limitations
of Chain Migration," in *European Mobility: Internal, International, and
Transatlantic Moves in the 19th and Early 20th Centuries*, eds. Annemarie
Steidl, Josef Ehmer, et al., (Göttingen, Germany: V&R Unipress, 2009):
69–77, presenting results from a larger work available only in German.
For a quantitative analysis of other immigrant destinations, see my arti-
cle, "Who Went South? The German Ethnic Niche in the Northern and
Southern Hemispheres," *Social Science History* 41 (2017): 363–92. Three
of the best urban case studies are Kathleen Neils Conzen, *Immigrant
Milwaukee, 1836–1860: Accommodation and Community in a Frontier City*
(Cambridge, MA: Harvard University Press, 1976); Stanley Nadel, *Little
Germany: Ethnicity, Religion, and Class in New York City, 1845–1880* (Chicago: University of Illinois Press, 1990); David A. Gerber, *The Making of
an American Pluralism: Buffalo, New York, 1825–1860* (Chicago: University of Illinois Press, 1989). For the rural counterpart, see Terry G. Jor-
dan, *German Seed in Texas Soil: Immigrant Farmers in Nineteenth-Century
Texas* (Austin: University of Texas Press, 1966); Kathleen Neils Conzen,
The Germans of Minnesota (St. Paul: Minnesota Historical Society Press,
2003); Russel L. Gerlach, *Immigrants in the Ozarks: A Study in Ethnic
Geography* (Columbia: University of Missouri Press, 1976).

CHAPTER 4: RELIGION, EDUCATION, AND
INTERETHNIC RELATIONS

This chapter draws heavily from my essay, "German Americans: Still
Divided by the Reformation 500 Years Later?" *Yearbook of German-
American Studies* 52 (2017): 1–19. The standard works on several denom-
inations are still valuable resources: Carl E. Schneider, *The German*

Church on the American Frontier (St. Louis, MO: Eden Seminary Press, 1939); Walter O. Forster, *Zion on the Mississippi: The Settlement of the Saxon Lutherans in Missouri, 1839–1841* (St. Louis, MO: Concordia Publishing House, 1953); Emmet H. Rothan, *The German Catholic Immigrant in the United States (1830–1860)* (Washington, DC: Catholic University of America Press, 1946). Other essential readings include Kathleen Neils Conzen, *Making Their Own America: Assimilation Theory and the German Peasant Pioneer* (New York: Berg, 1990); Kathleen Neils Conzen, "Immigrant Religion and the Public Sphere: The German Catholic Milieu in America," in *German-American Immigration and Ethnicity*, eds. Wolfgang Helbich and Walter D. Kamphoefner, 69–114. Heinz Kloss, *The American Bilingual Tradition* (Rowley, MA: Newbury House, 1977), remains an essential if ethnocentric resource on education and language. See also Paul Fessler, "The Political and Pedagogical in Bilingual Education: Yesterday and Today," in *German-American Immigration and Ethnicity*, eds. Helbich and Kamphoefner, 273–91. Other relevant case studies include Selwyn K. Troen, *The Public and the Schools: Shaping the St. Louis School System, 1838–1920* (Columbia: University of Missouri Press, 1975); Carlos Kevin Blanton, *The Strange Career of Bilingual Education in Texas, 1836–1981* (College Station: Texas A&M University Press, 2004); and Lloyd P. Jorgenson, *The State and the Non-Public School, 1825–1925* (Columbia: University of Missouri Press, 1987).

CHAPTER 5: THE GERMAN-LANGUAGE PRESS AND GERMAN CULTURE IN AMERICA

The standard work on the subject remains Carl Wittke, *The German-Language Press in America* (Lexington: University of Kentucky Press, 1957). A monumental resource on individual publications and their personnel is Carl J. R. Arndt and May E. Olson, eds., *German-American Newspapers and Periodicals, 1732–1955, History and Bibliography*, second revised edition (New York: Johnson Reprint Co., 1965). Also helpful on such matters was the Library of Congress "Chronicling America" database. The seminal work on German-American culture, high and low, is Peter Conolly-Smith, *Translating America: An Immigrant Press Visualizes American Popular Culture, 1895–1918* (Washington, DC: Smithsonian Books, 2004). See also, John Koegel, *Music in German Immigrant Theater: New York City 1840–1940* (Rochester, NY: University of Rochester Press, 2009).

CHAPTER 6: GERMAN NICHES IN THE AMERICAN ECONOMY

Analyses of agricultural patterns are indebted to the pioneering work of Jordan, *German Seed in Texas Soil*, which inspired several studies of other states, my own included. Among them is the work of Helmut Schmahl, "Truthful Letters and Irresistible Wanderlust: 19th-Century Immigrants from Hessen-Darmstadt in Wisconsin," in *Wisconsin German Land and Life*, eds. Heike Bungert, Cora Lee Kluge and Joseph Salmons (Madison, WI: Max Kade Institute, 2006), 145–62, drawn from a larger work available only in German. The rest of the chapter is based on my web article, "The German Component to American Industrialization," in *Immigrant Entrepreneurship: German-American Business Biographies, 1720 to the Present*, vol. 2, ed. William J. Hausman (German Historical Institute, 2014): http://www.immigrantentrepreneurship.org/entry.php?rec=189. For an industrial case study, see Robert Paul McCaffery, *Islands of Deutschtum: German-Americans in Manchester, New Hampshire and Lawrence, Massachusetts, 1870–1942* (New York: Peter Lang, 1996). The relative concentration of Germans in various occupations and industries is derived from E. P. Hutchinson, *Immigrants and their Children, 1850–1950* (New York: John Wiley and Son, 1956), and from my calculations based on a full-count 1880 census dataset made available through the North Atlantic Population Project: https://www.nappdata.org/napp/.

CHAPTER 7: WOMEN'S ROLES AND
WOMEN'S WORK: PAID AND UNPAID

On the rural and urban sides of women's experience, see Linda S. Pickle, *Contented among Strangers: Rural German-Speaking Women and Their Families in the Nineteenth-Century Midwest* (Urbana: University of Illinois Press, 1996); and Christiane Harzig, "Creating a Community, German-American Women in Chicago," in *Peasant Maids, City Women: From the European Countryside to Urban America*, ed. Christiane Harzig (Ithaca,

NY: Cornell University Press, 1997), 185–222. An excellent case study by Carol K. Coburn, *Life at Four Corners: Religion, Gender, and Education in a German-Lutheran Community, 1868–1945* (Lawrence: University Press of Kansas, 1992), provided many insights on domestic service. Sex roles are explored in Jon Gjerde, "Prescriptions and Perceptions of Labor and Family among Ethnic Groups in the Nineteenth-Century America Middle West," in *German-American Immigration and Ethnicity*, eds. Wolfgang Helbich and Walter D. Kamphoefner, 117–37. On rural German cultural patterns that have persisted throughout the twentieth century, see Sonya Salamon, *Prairie Patrimony: Family, Farming, and Community in the Midwest* (Chapel Hill: University of North Carolina Press, 1992).

CHAPTER 8: GERMAN POLITICAL AND MILITARY ROLES IN THE CIVIL WAR ERA

Modern approaches to Civil War ethnic politics date from Frederick C. Luebke, ed., *Ethnic Voters and the Election of Lincoln* (Lincoln: University of Nebraska Press, 1971). I weighed in with another case study, "St. Louis Germans and the Republican Party, 1848–1860," *Mid-America* 57 (1975), 69–88. I attempted to synthesize the literature on the 1860 election in "German-Americans and Civil War Politics: A Reconsideration of the Ethnocultural Thesis," *Civil War History* 37 (1991), 226–40, and turned my attention south with "New Perspectives on Texas Germans and the Confederacy," *Southwestern Historical Quarterly* 102 (1999): 441–55. Both articles fed into the introduction to an anthology of letters coedited by me and Wolfgang Helbich, *Germans in the Civil War: The Letters They Wrote Home*, trans. Susan Carter Vogel, (Chapel Hill: University of North Carolina Press, 2006), the source of most of the soldiers quoted here. Among several anthologies of soldiers' letters translated and edited by Joseph R. Reinhart, the most utilized was *Yankee Dutchmen Under Fire: Civil War Letters from the 82nd Illinois Infantry* (Kent, OH: Kent State University Press, 2013). I have also drawn upon my case studies, "Missouri Germans and the Cause of Union and Freedom," *Missouri Historical Review* 106 (2012), 115–36; and "New Americans or New Southerners? Unionist German Texans," in *Lone Star Unionism, Dissent, and Resistance: Other Sides of Civil-War Texas*, ed. J. F. de la Teja (Norman: University of

Oklahoma Press, 2016), 101–22. On Turners, see Annette R. Hofmann, *The American Turner Movement: A History from its Beginnings to 2000* (Indianapolis: Max Kade German-American Center, 2010). An insightful study of ethnic cooperation and its limits is Mischa Honeck, *We Are the Revolutionists: German-Speaking Immigrants and American Abolitionists after 1848* (Athens: University of Georgia Press, 2011). Although I disagree with some of her conclusions, the most detailed examination of Germans in the three largest cities of the Confederacy is provided by Andrea Mehr-länder, *The Germans of Charleston, Richmond and New Orleans during the Civil War Period, 1850–1870: A Study and Research Compendium* (Berlin: De Gruyter, 2011). A more balanced assessment of one of these cities is offered by Jeff Strickland, *Unequal Freedoms: Ethnicity, Race, and White Supremacy in Civil War-era Charleston* (Gainesville: University Press of Florida, 2015).

CHAPTER 9: RACE, CULTURE, AND POLITICS IN
THE LATE NINETEENTH CENTURY

Besides the material cited in the previous chapter, the most insightful recent work on Germans and race is Alison Clark Efford, *German Immigrants, Race, and Citizenship in the Civil War Era* (Cambridge, UK: Cambridge University Press, 2013). See also the anthology, Randall M. Miller, ed., *States of Progress: Germans and Blacks in America over 300 Years* (Philadelphia: German Society of Pennsylvania, 1989); and the special issue, "Forum: German Americans and Their Relations with African Americans during the Mid-Nineteenth Century," *Journal of American Ethnic History* 28 (2008): 10–76. An essential study of Gilded Age politics from the "ethnocultural school" is Richard Jensen, *The Winning of the Midwest: Social and Political Conflict, 1888–1896* (Chicago: University of Chicago Press, 1971). The authoritative work in the genre is Jon Gjerde, *The Minds of the West: Ethnocultural Evolution in the Rural Middle West, 1830–1917* (Chapel Hill: University of North Carolina Press, 1997). Here and in the previous chapter, I have drawn upon my article, "Liberal Catholicism, Up to a Point: The Social and Political Outlook of the Louisville *Katholische Glaubensbote*, 1866–1886," *Yearbook of German-American Studies* 31 (1996): 13–23. On mayors and congressmen, see my chapter,

"German and Irish Big City Mayors: Comparative Perspective on Ethnic Politics," and that of Willi Paul Adams, "Ethnic Politicians in Congress: German-American Congressmen between Ethnic Group and National Government circa 1800," both in *German-American Immigration and Ethnicity in Comparative Perspective*, ed. Wolfgang Helbich and Walter D. Kamphoefner (Madison, WI: Max Kade Institute, 2004), 221–42, 243–72.

CHAPTER 10: THE RADICAL SIDE OF GERMAN AMERICA

Two standard works on the Forty-Eighters date from the time of the revolution's centennial: A. E. Zucker, ed., *The Forty-Eighters: Political Refugees of the German Revolution of 1848* (New York: Columbia University Press, 1950); and Carl Wittke, *Refugees of Revolution: The German Forty-Eighters in America* (Philadelphia: University of Pennsylvania Press, 1952). On labor radicals, see Ray Ginger, *Altgeld's America: The Lincoln Ideal versus Changing Realities* (New York: Funk & Wagnalls Co., 1958); and Hartmut Keil and John B. Jentz, eds., *German Workers in Chicago: A Documentary History of Working-Class Culture from 1850 to World War I* (Urbana: University of Illinois Press, 1988). Another anthology that goes beyond what its title implies is Elliott Shore, Ken Fones-Wolf, and James P. Danky, eds., *The German-American Radical Press: The Shaping of a Left Political Culture, 1850–1940* (Urbana: University of Illinois Press, 1992).

CHAPTER 11: THE GERMAN-AMERICAN EXPERIENCE IN WORLD WAR I

The standard work on the World War I experience remains Frederick C. Luebke, *Bonds of Loyalty: German Americans and World War I* (De Kalb: Northern Illinois University Press, 1974). Two excellent state studies add nuance: Petra DeWitt, *Degrees of Allegiance: Harassment and Loyalty in Missouri's German-American Community during World War I* (Athens: Ohio University Press, 2012); and Matthew D. Tippens, *Turning Germans into Texans: World War I and the Assimilation and Survival of German Culture in Texas, 1900–1930* (Austin: Kleingarten Press, 2010). This chapter is largely based on my article, "The German-American

Experience in World War I: A Centennial Assessment," *Yearbook of German-American Studies* 49 (2014): 3–30; see also my "Doughboys *auf Deutsch*: U.S. Soldiers Writing Home in German from France," *Yearbook of German-American Studies* 54 (2019): 114–34. The latest and most accurate work on the Paul Prager lynching is Pete Stehman, *Patriotic Murder: A World War I Hate Crime for Uncle Sam* (Lincoln: University of Nebraska Press [Potomac Press], 2018).

CHAPTER 12: INTO THE TWILIGHT OF ETHNICITY:
GERMAN AMERICANS SINCE WORLD WAR I

An excellent work on the trajectory of German assimilation is Russell A. Kazal, *Becoming Old Stock: The Paradox of German American Identity* (Princeton, NJ: Princeton University Press, 2004). The aftermath of World War I in Texas is covered in my article, "The Handwriting on the Wall: The Klan, Language Issues, and Prohibition in the German Settlements of Eastern Texas," *Southwestern Historical Quarterly* 111 (2008): 52–66. See also, Shawn Lay, *Hooded Knights on the Niagara: The Ku Klux Klan in Buffalo, New York* (New York: New York University Press, 1995). On reactions to the rise of Hitler, see Dwayne E. May, "Changing Attitudes of the German-Americans in Texas towards *Deutschtum* and the Fatherland," (M.A. thesis, Sam Houston State University, 1973); and Kenneth Barnes, "The Missouri Synod and Hitler's Germany," *Yearbook of German-American Studies* 24 (1989): 131–47. On the language transition and recent linguistic trends, see my "German-American Bilingualism: *Cui Malo?* Mother Tongue and Socioeconomic Status among the 2nd Generation in 1940," *International Migration Review* 28 (1994): 846–64; and "German Texans: In the Mainstream or Backwaters of Lone Star Society?" *Yearbook of German-American Studies* 38 (2003): 119–38.

Index

About the Author

Walter D. Kamphoefner is descended from five or six generations of Missouri Germans on all sides of his ancestry. He grew up on a family farm near Defiance, Missouri, and put up hay bales in Daniel Boone's back yard as a teenager. He received his first eight years of education in a one-room Lutheran grade school. Originally on the path to the ministry, he instead earned a PhD in history at the University of Missouri-Columbia in 1978. His dissertation, financed by a DAAD fellowship, involved some of the first transatlantic tracing of German immigrants, among them a half-dozen of his great-great grandparents. The resulting book, *The Westfalians: From Germany to Missouri* (1987), appeared in one English and two German editions. Since then, Kamphoefner has published widely in the field of immigration and ethnicity, with articles appearing in four languages and nine more authored or coedited books, among them two immigrant letter anthologies in both German and English versions. From 2015 to 2017, he served a term as President of the Society of German American Studies.

Kamphoefner has spent his entire teaching career in immigration hotbeds: first Southern California (Caltech), then University of Miami, Florida, and since 1988, at Texas A&M University—punctuated by three yearlong guest professorships at the German universities of Bremen, Bochum, and most recently in Osnabrück near his ancestral home. On the side, he helped to initiate several town partnerships between mother and daughter communities on opposite sides of the Atlantic. Kamphoefner also pens the occasional op-ed on historical and contemporary issues for the local daily *Eagle* and other papers such as the *Houston Chronicle*, the *Austin American-Statesman*, and the *Washington Post*, and has been interviewed on National Public Radio and Deutschlandfunk on matters of immigration and ethnicity.